The Ordinary Parent's Guide to
TEACHING READING

By Jessie Wise and Sara Buffington

WELL-TRAINED MIND PRESS

CHARLES CITY, VIRGINIA

ALSO BY JESSIE WISE
First Language Lessons for the Well-Trained Mind, Level 1
(WELL-TRAINED MIND PRESS, 2003, 2010)
First Language Lessons for the Well-Trained Mind, Level 2
(WELL-TRAINED MIND PRESS, 2003, 2010)

WITH SARA BUFFINGTON
First Language Lessons for the Well-Trained Mind, Level 3
(WELL-TRAINED MIND PRESS, 2007)
First Language Lessons for the Well-Trained Mind, Level 4
(WELL-TRAINED MIND PRESS, 2008)

WITH SUSAN WISE BAUER
The Well-Trained Mind: A Guide to Classical Education at Home
(W. W. NORTON, 1999, 2004, 2009, 2016)
www.welltrainedmind.com

Copyright © 2005 by Jessie Wise and Sara Buffington

Manufactured by Corley Printing Company.
Cover design by Andrew J. Buffington

Publisher's Cataloging-in-Publication
(Provided by Quality Books, Inc.)

Wise, Jessie.
 The ordinary parent's guide to teaching reading / by
Jessie Wise and Sara Buffington.
 p. cm.
 Includes index.
 LCCN 2003111093
 ISBN 0-9728603-1-2

 1. Reading--Parent participation--Handbooks, manuals,
etc. 2. Children--Books and reading--Handbooks,
manuals, etc. I. Buffington, Sara II. Title

LB1050.2.W57 2004   372.41
               QBI33-2002

Well-Trained Mind Press, Inc., 18021 The Glebe Lane, Charles City, VA 23030
www.welltrainedmind.com
info@welltrainedmind.com

The Ordinary Parent's Guide to
TEACHING READING

By Jessie Wise and Sara Buffington

WELL-TRAINED MIND PRESS

CHARLES CITY, VIRGINIA

Table of Contents

Preface

When I was in elementary school, a kid told me, "You can read good because you're so smart." I know now I did well in school, not because I was smart, but because *I could read well.*

A child who reads well possesses a tool to make academic success possible. Reading is a lifetime skill that allows the child to fulfill professional dreams and function in a world of educated people. It can give pleasure and access to worlds beyond his reach both in space and in time.

I advocate teaching reading to the very young when possible. Children can recognize and name hundreds of things. They understand thousands of words. They are excited about learning new grown-up skills. If you can teach your child to read before school-age, he will be ahead in reading for the rest of his education.

But if you have a school-age child who is struggling with reading, don't waste time. The longer a child struggles, the more discouraged he becomes, and this discouragement will affect his overall academic performance.

If you have been told your child has a learning disability, teach him yourself before you give up on him. I have taught many children who had been given a disability label. They all learned to read. I believe that in each case there was a *teaching* disability in the child's educational history—usually a faulty method of teaching reading. I believe that all children who are not suffering from severe mental retardation or severe emotional upset can learn to read. And anyone who can read can teach another to read if provided with a systematic method that is used frequently, patiently, and consistently.

You can begin with Lesson 1 right away, or, if you'd like additional guidance on reading readiness, pre-reading, the reading process, managing the reading lesson, remedial reading, or other issues, go to page 346.

Introduction
How I Came to the Conclusion That Ordinary Parents Need to Teach Reading

I've been working on this book for most of my life. When I was in second grade, I wrote a simple phonics reading book for a fellow classmate. His name was Elmore, and he couldn't read. I wrote the reading book in pencil, in a tiny notebook with "Royster Fertilizer Company" printed on the front.

Throughout my school years, I felt sorry for classmates who struggled with reading. I didn't understand why they didn't just sound out the letters. But these children had been taught with the "new method" of the time: memorizing whole words. I had been taught phonics at home.

I was adopted by an elderly couple who had been educated in an isolated, rural one-room schoolhouse. By her eighth and final year of school, Meme had studied algebra, Latin, and the literature excerpts in the old McGuffey's readers. Uncle Luther had stopped school after sixth grade, but he had an aptitude for mathematics and taught himself carpentry and draftsmanship. They lived on a small subsistence farm in Tidewater Virginia.

Meme and Uncle Luther had been taught reading and spelling by sounding out letters, and they began to teach me the same way, forming words with alphabet blocks. Later they taught me to write on a small blackboard—I'm sure their own school experience had included a slate!

The first-grade teacher in the local public school heard that Meme and Uncle Luther were teaching me to read at home using old-fashioned methods. The teacher made a special visit to our home to tell them to stop teaching me. "Reading is not taught this way anymore," she warned. "There are new methods. You will ruin her education if you persist in doing things the old-fashioned way."

Meme and Uncle Luther went right on teaching me as before.

The high-school boy who helped Meme with chores brought us books from the local public school. Soon I was reading the old Elson-Grey readers and other books from the school library—Raggedy Ann, fairy tales, Aesop's fables, and easy history books.

My education wasn't ruined by my early reading lessons; I was placed directly into second grade when I started school. I consistently remained at the top of my class throughout school. I was also the only girl in that small, rural class to graduate from college. I think the foundation that I was given in reading and the encouragement to do well academically were keys to that success.

When I went to college, I knew that I wanted to be a teacher. One of the required courses for teacher certification was "Teaching Reading in the Elementary School." It was a hodge-podge of lists of sight words, boring readers, and curricula planned around the child's interest rather than his academic skills.

When I was face-to-face with my own sixth-grade class that included two boys who had not yet learned to read, I knew I couldn't use the ineffective methods I had been taught in college. I had to rely on the memory of how I had been taught to read. The next year when I taught a second-grade class of thirty-eight children (fifteen of whom didn't yet know their alphabet), I made up phonics cards, again from my memory. I wrote the letter sounds on construction paper and posted them on the walls of my classroom. We drilled these sounds each morning. By the end of the year, every child except one was reading on or above grade level.

Having observed so many children in school who could not read, I remember thinking, "If I ever have a child, he will know how to read *before* he goes to school."

So when my oldest child turned four, I said to him one day, "Bob, would you rather take a nap, or would you like to learn how to read?" He chose reading! I started him on the old-fashioned phonics I'd been taught when I was a child. I'd lie down with him on his little bed after lunch and work on letter sounds. (Since I also had a two-year-old and a thirteen-month-old, I was always glad to lie down.) That year we practiced vowels and consonants and sounded out new words. We called it "doing kindergarten."

The next year, my middle child was three, and she wanted to be included. "My do kindergarten, too," she said. I held her in my lap and taught her the letter sounds. She learned to read that year!

When I had the children tested by a psychologist two years later, Bob, a second-grader, was reading on a seventh-grade level. Susan, a kindergartner, was reading on a fifth-grade level. The psychologist suggested that I teach the children at home because they were so advanced. In 1973, I had never heard of modern homeschooling, but I began that academic journey. I believe early reading instruction played a major role in the academic success of my three children.

I have also taught my three oldest grandchildren to read. I started their formal reading instruction when they were each four years old. By second grade, they were all reading books on or above a fourth-grade level. All three children are exuberant about their accomplishments, love to read, and are happy, playful children.

I began by telling you about Meme and Uncle Luther (the elderly couple who adopted me). Except for driving me to college, they never went more than fifty miles from their subsistence farm. Yet, because of their diligence in my early education, their influence is reaching a *third* generation in my family.

I am sure they would find it unbelievable that through travel, writing, and the internet, their sphere of influence has spread to parts of the world quite distant from their little Virginia farm. So as you work with your child, you cannot know what effect your work will have on the life of your child and on generations to come!

PART 1

THE LESSONS

Section 1

SHORT-VOWEL SOUNDS

By now your child knows how to talk, and you have read books to him. It will help his progress if he knows the names of the alphabet letters in sequence (either by saying or singing) and recognizes all of the individual big and little alphabet letters when they are not in **a-z** sequence.

Lessons 1-26 are "hear-see-and-say-after-me" exercises. The child is *not* expected to read words. Spend as many days as necessary repeating Lessons 1-26 until the child has mastered each letter and the sound. In the lessons, the sounds of the letters are written with special notation, such as /ă/. A complete list of the phonetic symbols used in this book is located on page 369.

Some of the lessons require the use of word cards (to learn the letters, sight words, and for use in games). You may make up these cards yourself by writing the words or phrases on 3 x 5 index cards as you go through the lessons, or you may purchase a set of printed cards from Well-Trained Mind Press (www.welltrainedmind.com). The set contains all the cards you will need for this book: over three hundred. If you purchase this set, you will show the appropriate card when the instructions in the book tell you to "write on a card."

You will also need a magnetic board with alphabet tiles. You may purchase this from Dowling Magnets or from a store that sells education products. If you would like to keep the letter-tiles organized, you should consider purchasing another magnetic board (without the tiles). You can use one board to store the letters and the other for the lesson activity.

You will need for the lessons:

a magnetic board with alphabet tiles

3 x 5 index cards (or use the printed word cards you can purchase), scissors, pens, pencils, and drawing supplies

paperclips, yarn, magnets, and a dowel (for one special activity)

Using the Lessons:

Instructor: Words that the instructor will say to the child are written in this format.
If the instructor is to spell letters aloud, they will be written like this: the vowel **a**, the consonant **b**, the ending **ing**.

Notes that the instructor reads to himself are written in this format.

Child: *Suggested wording for the child is written in this format.*

Lesson 1:   The Vowel A a

You will need the following: *a blank index card and a pen. If you purchased the printed cards, use the card marked for Lesson 1. Anytime the lesson materials call for blank index cards, substitute the appropriate printed cards (each card is marked with its lesson number). When the lesson tell you to write a letter or a word on a card, you will just show the already printed card.*

Some children may need to see the letters in three dimensions. You may substitute foam, wooden, or plastic letters for the index cards in Lessons 1-26.

The **a** vowel sound in this lesson is the sound at the beginning of **apple**. It is the short sound of **a** and is marked in the dictionary as **a** with a breve over it: /ă/.

Instructor: Today we are going to learn the letter **a**. **A** is a special kind of letter called a *vowel*. All letters stand for sounds. Your tongue or lips do not block the sounds of the vowel letters when you say them. Watch my mouth as I say the names of the vowels. I will not close my lips or use my tongue to block the sound.

Prolong each vowel name so the child can see that you do not block the sound.

Instructor: **a, e, i, o, u. A** is the first vowel you will learn. This is the big **A**. It is also called the capital or uppercase **A**. We will say big **A** from now on.

Point to the letter below.

A

Instructor: There are two ways to write the little or lowercase **a**. You will need to know them both because different books print the little **a** different ways.

Point to the letters below.

a ɑ

Instructor: The first **a** is the kind you will read in this book. The second **ɑ** is used in handwriting books. I will write the vowel **a** on a card for you. First I will write the big **A** and then I will write both kinds of little **a**'s.

Write **A** and **a** and **ɑ** side-by-side on a card (or show the purchased **A a ɑ** card).

Instructor: When you see the letter **a** at the beginning or in the middle of a short word, you usually say this sound: /ă/ in **apple**. The letter **a** stands for the sound /ă/. The sound /ă/ is called the short-**a** vowel sound. Remember, the little **a** is written two different ways. I will point to the card and say the short-**a** vowel sound five times: /ă/, /ă/, /ă/, /ă/, /ă/. Now we will say the sound together.

Together: /ă/, /ă/, /ă/, /ă/, /ă/.

Instructor: I am going to teach you a poem that will help you remember the sounds of the short vowels. It is called "The Five Vowels." This is the first verse:

A is the first vowel we will say.
/ă/ is the short-vowel sound of **a**.

Instructor: I will say this to you three more times.

Say the verse slowly three times, taking care to emphasize the sound /ă/.

Instructor: Now repeat after me: "**A** is the first vowel we will say."

Child: *A is the first vowel we will say.*

Instructor: /ă/ is the short-vowel sound of **a**.

Child: */ă/ is the short-vowel sound of **a**.*

Instructor: Now let's say both lines together three times.

Together (three times):
  A is the first vowel we will say.
  /ă/ is the short-vowel sound of **a**.

Instructor: What is the short-vowel sound of **a**? The answer is the last part of the verse.

Child: */ă/ is the short-vowel sound of **a**.*

Follow-Up:
Ask the child to repeat the **a** verse from the poem two more times during the day. You may also record yourself or your child saying this verse onto a tape so that he can listen to the poem over and over. As each verse of the poem is added in subsequent lessons, record them onto the same tape. Point out the letter **a** to the child whenever you see it (on signs, on food boxes or cans, and in books you read aloud to him). Ask him to recite the verse from this lesson to you.

Lesson 2:   The Vowel E e

You will need the following: *the **a** card you previously used, one blank index card, and a pen.*

The **e** vowel sound in this lesson is the sound at the beginning of **elephant**. It is the short sound of **e** and is marked in the dictionary as **e** with a breve over it: /ĕ/.

Review

Instructor: Let's begin this lesson by saying the first verse of the poem "The Five Vowels" together three times.

Together (three times):
　　　　　A is the first vowel we will say.
　　　　　/ă/ is the short-vowel sound of **a**.

Instructor: Now I will show you the card from last lesson. Remember there are two ways the little **a** is written.

Point to the **a** card.

Instructor: Now I am going to ask you some questions about the sounds of the short vowels. What is the short-vowel sound of **a**? The answer is the last part of the verse we said together.

Point to the **a** card. If the child can't remember the answer, say the first part of the verse as a reminder.

Child: */ă/ is the short-vowel sound of **a**.*

New

Instructor: Today we are going to learn the letter **e**. **E** is also a vowel. This is the big **E** and little **e**:

Point to the letters below.

E   e

Instructor: I will write the vowel **e** on a card for you. First I will write the big **E** and then I will write the little **e**.

Write **E** and **e** side-by-side on a card (or show the purchased **E e** card).

Instructor: When you see the letter **e** at the beginning or in the middle of a short word, you usually say this sound: /ĕ/ in **elephant**. The letter **e** stands for the sound /ĕ/. The sound /ĕ/ is called the short-**e** vowel sound. I will point to the card and say the short-**e** vowel sound five times: /ĕ/, /ĕ/, /ĕ/, /ĕ/, /ĕ/. Now we will say the sound together.

Together: /ĕ/, /ĕ/, /ĕ/, /ĕ/, /ĕ/.

Instructor: I am going to teach you the next verse of the poem "The Five Vowels." This is the second verse:

　　　　　E is the next vowel, don't you see?
　　　　　/ĕ/ is the short-vowel sound of **e**.

Instructor: I will say this to you three more times.

Say the verse slowly three times, taking care to emphasize the sound /ĕ/.

Instructor: Now repeat after me: "**E** is the next vowel, don't you see?"

Child: *E is the next vowel, don't you see?*

Instructor: /ĕ/ is the short-vowel sound of **e**.

Child: */ĕ/ is the short-vowel sound of* **e.**

Instructor: Now let's say both lines together three times.

Together (three times):
> **E** is the next vowel, don't you see?
> /ĕ/ is the short-vowel sound of **e**.

Instructor: Now let's combine the verse you learned last lesson with the verse you learned today. Let's say this together three times.

Together (three times):
> **A** is the first vowel we will say.
> /ă/ is the short-vowel sound of **a**.
> **E** is the next vowel, don't you see?
> /ĕ/ is the short-vowel sound of **e**.

Instructor: What is the short-vowel sound of **e**?

Child: */ĕ/ is the short-vowel sound of* **e.**

Follow-Up:
Ask the child to repeat the **e** verse from the poem two more times during the day. If you recorded a tape, record the new verse onto the same tape. Point out the letter **e** to the child whenever you see it (on signs, on food boxes or cans, and in books you read aloud to him). Ask him to recite the verse from this lesson to you.

Lesson 3:   The Vowel I i

You will need the following: *the cards you previously used, one blank index card, and a pen.*

The **i** vowel sound in this lesson is the sound at the beginning of *igloo*. It is the short sound of **i** and is marked in the dictionary as **i** with a breve over it: /ĭ/.

Review

Instructor: Let's begin this lesson by saying the first and second verses of the poem "The Five Vowels" together three times.

Together (three times):
> **A** is the first vowel we will say.
> /ă/ is the short-vowel sound of **a**.
> **E** is the next vowel, don't you see?
> /ĕ/ is the short-vowel sound of **e**.

Instructor: Now I will show you the cards from the previous lessons. Together let's point to the **a** card and say the short-**a** vowel sound: /ă/. Now let's point to the **e** card and say the short-**e** vowel sound: /ĕ/.

Instructor: Now I am going to ask you some questions about the sounds of the short vowels. What is the short-vowel sound of **a**?

Point to the **a** card. If the child can't remember the answer, say the first part of each verse as a reminder.

Child: */ă/ is the short-vowel sound of **a**.*

Instructor: What is the short-vowel sound of **e**?

Point to the **e** card.

Child: */ĕ/ is the short-vowel sound of **e**.*

New

Instructor: Today we are going to learn the letter **i**. **I** is also a vowel. There are two ways to write the big **I**. You will need to know them both because different books print the big **I** different ways. The second printed **I** is the kind you will read in this book.

Point to the letters below.

I   I

Instructor: This is the little **i**.

Point to the letter below.

i

Instructor: I will write the vowel **i** on a card for you. First I will write both kinds of big **I**'s and then I will write the little **i**.

Write **I** and **l** and **i** side-by-side on a card (or show the purchased **I I i** card).

Instructor: When you see the letter **i** at the beginning or in the middle of a short word, you usually say this sound: /ĭ/ in ***igloo***. The letter **i** stands for the sound /ĭ/. The sound /ĭ/ is called the short-i vowel sound. Remember, the big **i** is written two different ways. I will point to the card and say the short-i vowel sound five times: /ĭ/, /ĭ/, /ĭ/, /ĭ/, /ĭ/. Now we will say the sound together.

Together: /ĭ/, /ĭ/, /ĭ/, /ĭ/, /ĭ/.

Instructor: I am going to teach you the third verse of the poem "The Five Vowels."

> **I** is the third vowel that goes by.
> /ĭ/ is the short-vowel sound of **i**.

Instructor: I will say this to you three more times.

Say the verse slowly three times, taking care to emphasize the sound /ĭ/.

Instructor: Now repeat after me: "**I** is the third vowel that goes by."

Child: ***I** is the third vowel that goes by.*

Instructor: /ĭ/ is the short-vowel sound of **i**.

Child: */ĭ/ is the short-vowel sound of **i**.*

Instructor: Now let's say both lines together three times.

Together (three times):
> **I** is the third vowel that goes by.
> /ĭ/ is the short-vowel sound of **i**.

Instructor: Let's add today's verse to all the verses you have learned, and say them together three times.

Together (three times):
> **A** is the first vowel we will say.
> /ă/ is the short-vowel sound of **a**.
> **E** is the next vowel, don't you see?
> /ĕ/ is the short-vowel sound of **e**.
> **I** is the third vowel that goes by.
> /ĭ/ is the short-vowel sound of **i**.

Instructor: What is the short-vowel sound of **i**?

Child: */ĭ/ is the short-vowel sound of **i**.*

Follow-Up:
Ask the child to repeat the **i** verse from the poem two more times during the day. If you recorded a tape, record the new verse onto the same tape.

Lesson 4:   The Vowel O o

You will need the following: *the cards you previously used, one blank index card, and a pen.*

The **o** vowel sound in this lesson is the sound at the beginning of ***octopus***. It is the short sound of **o** and is marked in the dictionary as **o** with a breve over it: /ŏ/.

Review

Instructor: Let's begin this lesson by saying the first, second, and third verses of the poem "The Five Vowels" together three times.

Together (three times):
>   **A** is the first vowel we will say.
>   /ă/ is the short-vowel sound of **a**.
>   **E** is the next vowel, don't you see?
>   /ĕ/ is the short-vowel sound of **e**.
>   **I** is the third vowel that goes by.
>   /ĭ/ is the short-vowel sound of **i**.

Instructor: Now I will show you the cards from the previous lessons. Together let's point to the **a** card and say the short-**a** vowel sound: /ă/. Now let's point to the **e** card and say the short-**e** vowel sound: /ĕ/. Now let's point to the **i** card and say the short-**i** vowel sound: /ĭ/.

Instructor: Now I am going to ask you some questions about the sounds of the short vowels. What is the short-vowel sound of **a**?

Point to the **a** card. If the child can't remember the answer, say the first part of each verse as a reminder.

Child: */ă/ is the short-vowel sound of* **a**.

Instructor: What is the short-vowel sound of **e**?

Point to the **e** card.

Child: */ĕ/ is the short-vowel sound of* **e**.

Instructor: What is the short-vowel sound of **i**?

Point to the **i** card.

Child: */ĭ/ is the short-vowel sound of* **i**.

New

Instructor: Today we are going to learn the letter **o**. **O** is also a vowel. This is the big **O** and the little **o**:

Point to the letters below.

Instructor: I will write the vowel **o** on a card for you. I will write the big **O** and the little **o**.

Write **O** and **o** side-by-side on a card (or show the purchased **O o** card).

Instructor: When you see the letter **o** at the beginning or in the middle of a short word, you usually say this sound: /ŏ/ as in *octopus*. The letter **o** stands for the sound /ŏ/. The sound /ŏ/ is called the short-**o** vowel sound. I will point to the card and say the short-**o** vowel sound five times: /ŏ/, /ŏ/, /ŏ/, /ŏ/, /ŏ/. Now we will say the sound together.

Together: /ŏ/, /ŏ/, /ŏ/, /ŏ/, /ŏ/.

Instructor: I am going to teach you the fourth verse of the poem "The Five Vowels."

> **O** is the fourth vowel that I know.
> /ŏ/ is the short-vowel sound of **o**.

Instructor: I will say this to you three more times.

Say the verse slowly three times, taking care to emphasize the sound /ŏ/.

Instructor: Now repeat after me: "**O** is the fourth vowel that I know."

Child: *O is the fourth vowel that I know.*

Instructor: /ŏ/ is the short-vowel sound of **o**.

Child: */ŏ/ is the short-vowel sound of **o**.*

Instructor: Now let's say both lines together three times.

Together (three times):
> **O** is the fourth vowel that I know.
> /ŏ/ is the short-vowel sound of **o**.

Instructor: Let's add today's verse to all the verses you have learned, and say them together three times.

Together (three times):
> **A** is the first vowel we will say.
> /ă/ is the short-vowel sound of **a**.
> **E** is the next vowel, don't you see?
> /ĕ/ is the short-vowel sound of **e**.
> **I** is the third vowel that goes by.
> /ĭ/ is the short-vowel sound of **i**.
> **O** is the fourth vowel that I know.
> /ŏ/ is the short-vowel sound of **o**.

Instructor: What is the short-vowel sound of **o**?

Child: */ŏ/ is the short-vowel sound of **o**.*

Follow-Up:
Ask the child to repeat the **o** verse from the poem two more times during the day. If you recorded a tape, record the new verse onto the same tape. Point out the letter **o** to the child whenever you see it (on signs, on food boxes or cans, and in books you read aloud to him). Ask him to recite the verse from this lesson to you.

Lesson 5:   The Vowel U u

You will need the following: *the cards you previously used, one blank index card, and a pen.*

The **u** vowel sound in this lesson is the sound at the beginning of **umbrella**. It is the short sound of **u** and is marked in the dictionary as **u** with a breve over it: /ŭ/.

Review

Instructor: Let's begin this lesson by saying the first four verses of the poem "The Five Vowels" together three times.

Together (three times):
> **A** is the first vowel we will say.
> /ă/ is the short-vowel sound of **a**.
> **E** is the next vowel, don't you see?
> /ĕ/ is the short-vowel sound of **e**.
> **I** is the third vowel that goes by.
> /ĭ/ is the short-vowel sound of **i**.
> **O** is the fourth vowel that I know.
> /ŏ/ is the short-vowel sound of **o**.

Instructor: Now I will show you the cards from the previous lessons. Together let's point to the **a** card and say the short-**a** vowel sound: /ă/. Now let's point to the **e** card and say the short-**e** vowel sound: /ĕ/. Let's point to the **i** card and say the short-**i** vowel sound: /ĭ/. Let's point to the **o** card and say the short-**o** vowel sound: /ŏ/.

Instructor: Now I am going to ask you some questions about the sounds of the short vowels. What is the short-vowel sound of **a**?

Point to the **a** card. If the child can't remember the answer, say the first part of each verse as a reminder.

Child: */ă/ is the short-vowel sound of **a**.*

Instructor: What is the short-vowel sound of **e**?

Point to the **e** card.

Child: */ĕ/ is the short-vowel sound of **e**.*

Instructor: What is the short-vowel sound of **i**?

Point to the **i** card.

Child: */ĭ/ is the short-vowel sound of **i**.*

Instructor: What is the short-vowel sound of **o**?

Point to the **o** card.

Child: */ŏ/ is the short-vowel sound of **o**.*

New

Instructor: Today we are going to learn the letter **u**. **U** is also a vowel. This is the big **U** and the little **u**.

Point to the letters below.

U u

Instructor: I will write the vowel **u** on a card for you. First I will write the big **U** and then I will write the little **u**.

Write **U** and **u** side-by-side on a card (or show the purchased **U u** card).

Instructor: When you see the letter **u** at the beginning or in the middle of a short word, you usually say this sound: /ŭ/. The letter **u** stands for the sound /ŭ/ in *umbrella*. The sound /ŭ/ is called the short-**u** vowel sound. I will point to the **u** card and say the short-**u** vowel sound five times: /ŭ/, /ŭ/, /ŭ/, /ŭ/, /ŭ/. Now we will say the sound together.

Together: /ŭ/, /ŭ/, /ŭ/, /ŭ/, /ŭ/.

Instructor: I am going to teach you the last verse of the poem "The Five Vowels":

U is the fifth vowel; that is true.
/ŭ/ is the short-vowel sound of **u**.

Instructor: I will say this to you three more times.

Say the verse slowly three times, taking care to emphasize the sound /ŭ/.

Instructor: Now repeat after me: "**U** is the fifth vowel; that is true."

Child: *U is the fifth vowel; that is true.*

Instructor: /ŭ/ is the short-vowel sound of **u**.

Child: */ŭ/ is the short-vowel sound of u.*

Instructor: Now let's say both lines together three times.

Together (three times):
U is the fifth vowel; that is true.
/ŭ/ is the short-vowel sound of **u**.

Instructor: Now let's combine the verses you learned the last four lessons with the verse you learned today. Let's say the entire poem together three times.

Together (three times):

> **A** is the first vowel we will say.
> /ă/ is the short-vowel sound of **a**.
> **E** is the next vowel, don't you see?
> /ĕ/ is the short-vowel sound of **e**.
> **I** is the third vowel that goes by.
> /ĭ/ is the short-vowel sound of **i**.
> **O** is the fourth vowel that I know.
> /ŏ/ is the short-vowel sound of **o**.
> **U** is the fifth vowel; that is true.
> /ŭ/ is the short-vowel sound of **u**.

Instructor: What is the short-vowel sound of **u**?

Child: */ŭ/ is the short-vowel sound of **u**.*

Game: Short Vowel Pick-Up

Put all the vowel cards on the table. Say one of the short-vowel sounds. The child will then pick up the letter card that he thinks represents that sound. If he picks the right card, he gets the card; if he doesn't, you get the card. Once you have gone through all the vowels, have the child practice the vowel sounds on the cards that you are holding. Then shuffle all the cards and begin the game again.

Follow-Up:

Ask the child to repeat the **u** verse from the poem two more times during the day. If you recorded a tape, record the new verse onto the same tape. Point out the letter **u** to the child whenever you see it (on signs, on food boxes or cans, and in books you read aloud to him). Ask him to recite the verse from this lesson to you.

Section 2

CONSONANT SOUNDS

Lesson 6: The Consonant B b

You will need the following: *the cards you used previously, one blank index card, and a pen.*

Review

Instructor: We have learned all of the names of the vowels, **a**, **e**, **i**, **o**, **u,** as well as the short-vowel sounds, /ă/, /ĕ/, /ĭ/, /ŏ/, /ŭ/. Do you remember that a vowel sound is not blocked by your tongue or your lips? I will show you each vowel card, and we will say the sound of that short vowel together.

Go through the cards in order, and say each sound slowly. If the child has trouble, have him repeat the sounds after you. Many children need extra practice hearing and saying the difference between the short-**e** vowel sound and the short-**i** vowel sound.

New

Instructor: The letters that are not vowels are called *consonants*. When you say the sound of a consonant, you do block the sound or the air with your tongue or your lips. Today we are going to learn the consonant **b**. This is the big **B** and the little **b**:

B b

Instructor: I will write the consonant **b** on a card for you. First I will write the big **B** and then I will write the little **b**.

Write the big **B** and the little **b** side-by-side on the index card.

Instructor: The letter **b** usually stands for the sound /b/. Watch my mouth as I say that sound. My lips will block the sound of my voice: /b/. Remember, the sound of a consonant letter is blocked by your tongue or your lips. The sound /b/ is called a *voiced* consonant sound because you use your voice to pronounce the sound. I will point to the letter **b** card and say the consonant sound five times.

Even though the sound /b/ requires using the voice, don't prolong the sound of /b/ so it sounds like /buh/.

Instructor: /b/, /b/, /b/, /b/, /b/. Now we will say the sound together.

Together: /b/, /b/, /b/, /b/, /b/.

Instructor: Listen as I say these words that begin with the sound /b/: ***bat***, ***bad***, ***bed***, ***bet***. Now repeat after me: /b/, /b/, ***bat***.

Child: */b/, /b/, bat.*

17

Instructor:	/b/, /b/, **bed**.
Child:	*/b/, /b/, bed.*

Instructor: Now listen as I read words that end with the sound /b/: **tab**, **fib**, **sob**, **tub**. Listen for the sound of the letter **b** as you repeat these words after me: **tab**.

Child: *tab.*

Instructor: **fib.**

Child: *fib.*

Instructor: Now I am going to teach you a poem that will help you remember the sounds of the consonants. It is called "The Consonant Rhyme." This is the first line:

> **B** stands for /b/ in /b/, /b/, **bat**.

Instructor: I will say this to you three more times.

Say the line slowly three times, taking care to emphasize the sound /b/.

Instructor: Repeat after me: "**B** stands for /b/ in /b/, /b/, **bat**."

Child: ***B*** *stands for /b/ in /b/, /b/, bat.*

Instructor: Let's say that together three times.

Together (three times):
> **B** stands for /b/ in /b/, /b/, **bat**.

Instructor: I am going to ask you a question. Answer me with the line from the poem. For what sound does the letter **b** stand?

Child: ***B*** *stands for /b/ in /b/, /b/, bat.*

Follow-Up:
The child should repeat the **b** line from the poem two more times during the day. You may also wish to record yourself or your child saying this line onto a tape so that the child can listen to the poem over and over. As each line of the poem is added in subsequent lessons, record it onto the same tape.
Point out the letter **b** to the child whenever you see it (on signs, on food boxes or cans, in books you read aloud to him). Ask him to recite the line from this lesson to you.

Lesson 7: The Consonant C c

You will need the following: *the cards you used previously, one blank index card, and a pen.*

Review

Instructor: I will show you each vowel card, and we will say the *sound* of that short vowel together.

Go through the cards in order, and say each sound slowly. If the child has trouble, have him repeat the sounds after you.

Instructor: Let's practice the first line of the poem "The Consonant Rhyme." Let's say it together three times.

Together (three times):
B stands for /b/ in /b/, /b/, **bat**.

Instructor: Now I will show you the card from the previous lesson.

Point to the **b** card and say the sound: /b/. Have the child repeat the sound back to you.

Instructor: Now I am going to ask you a question about the sound of the consonant **b**. Answer me with the line from the poem. For what sound does the letter **b** stand?

Point to the **B b** card.

Child: ***B*** *stands for /b/ in /b/, /b/, bat.*

New

Instructor: Today we are going to learn the consonant **c**. This is the big **C** and the little **c**:

C c

Instructor: I will write the consonant **c** on a card for you. First I will write the big **C** and then I will write the little **c**.

Instructor: The letter **c** often stands for the sound /k/. The sound /k/ is called an *unvoiced* consonant sound because you do not use your voice to pronounce the sound. You just use air. I will point to the letter **c** card and say the consonant sound five times.

Be sure you do not add any voice (do not say /kuh/); you just whisper: /k/. This is the *hard* sound of the letter **c**, which is identical to the sound for which the letter **k** stands: /k/. The soft sound of the letter **c** is /s/ in **cent** and **cell** (see Lesson 77).

Instructor: /k/, /k/, /k/, /k/, /k/. Now we will say the sound together.

Together: /k/, /k/, /k/, /k/, /k/.

Instructor: Listen as I say these words that begin with the sound /k/: **cat, can, cup**. Now repeat after me: /k/, /k/, **cat**.

Child: */k/, /k/, cat.*

Instructor: /k/, /k/, **cup.**

| Child: | /k/, /k/, cup. |

No short common words for young children end with the letter **c**. The /k/ is spelled **ck** at the end of short-vowel words.

| Instructor: | Listen for the unvoiced /k/ at the end of these words: ***tack, peck, sick, lock***. Listen for the sound of the letter **c** as you repeat two words after me: ***tack***. |

| Child: | *tack.* |

| Instructor: | ***peck.*** |

| Child: | *peck.* |

| Instructor: | Now I am going to teach you the next line of the poem "The Consonant Rhyme." This is the second line: |

> **C** stands for /k/ in /k/, /k/, ***cat***.

| Instructor: | I will say this to you three more times. |

Say the line slowly three times, taking care to emphasize the sound /k/.

| Instructor: | Repeat after me: "**C** stands for /k/ in /k/, /k/, ***cat***." |

| Child: | ***C*** *stands for /k/ in /k/, /k/, cat.* |

| Instructor: | Let's say that together three times. |

Together (three times):
> **C** stands for /k/ in /k/, /k/, ***cat***.

| Instructor: | Let's add that line to the line you learned last lesson. Let's say both lines together three times. |

Together (three times):
> **B** stands for /b/ in /b/, /b/, ***bat***.
> **C** stands for /k/ in /k/, /k/, ***cat***.

| Instructor: | Now I am going to ask you a question. Answer me with the line from the poem. For what sound does the letter **c** stand? |

| Child: | ***C*** *stands for /k/ in /k/, /k/, cat.* |

Follow-Up:
The child should repeat the **c** line from the poem two more times during the day. Point out the letter **c** to the child whenever you see it (on signs, on food boxes or cans, in books you read aloud to him). Ask him to recite the line from this lesson to you.

Lesson 8:   The Consonant D d

You will need the following: *the cards you used previously, one blank index card, and a pen.*

Review

Instructor: I will show you each vowel card, and we will say the *sound* of that short vowel together.

Go through the cards in order, and say each sound slowly. If the child has trouble, have him repeat the sounds after you.

Instructor: Let's practice the first two lines of the poem "The Consonant Rhyme." Let's say them together three times.

Together (three times):
B stands for /b/ in /b/, /b/, ***bat***.
C stands for /k/ in /k/, /k/, ***cat***.

Instructor: I will show you the consonant cards from the previous lessons. I will point to each card and say the sound that consonant represents. Then you will repeat that sound back to me.

Instructor: Now I am going to ask you some questions about the sounds of the consonants as I point to each consonant card. You will answer these questions with a line from the poem. For what sound does the letter **b** stand?

Child: ***B*** *stands for /b/ in /b/, /b/, bat.*

Instructor: For what sound does the letter **c** stand?

Child: ***C*** *stands for /k/ in /k/, /k/, cat.*

New

Instructor: Today we are going to learn the consonant **d**. This is the big **D** and the little **d**:

D d

Instructor: I will write the consonant **d** on a card for you. First I will write the big **D** and then I will write the little **d**.

Instructor: The letter **d** usually stands for the sound /d/. The sound /d/ is a voiced consonant sound because you use your voice to pronounce the sound. I will point to the letter **d** card and say the consonant sound five times.

Even though the sound /d/ requires using the voice, don't prolong the sound of /d/ so it sounds like /duh/.

Instructor: /d/, /d/, /d/, /d/, /d/. Now we will say the sound together.

Together: /d/, /d/, /d/, /d/, /d/.

Instructor: Listen as I say these words that begin with the sound /d/: ***dog***, ***dip***, ***dot***. Now repeat after me: /d/, /d/, ***dog***.

Child: */d/, /d/, dog.*

Instructor: /d/, /d/, ***dip.***

Child:	/d/, /d/, dip.

Instructor: Listen for the voiced sound /d/ at the end of these words: **had**, **bed**, **did**. Listen for the sound of the letter **d** as you repeat after me: **had**.

Child:	had.

Instructor: **bed.**

Child:	bed.

Instructor: I am going to teach you the third line of the poem "The Consonant Rhyme."

D stands for /d/ in /d/, /d/, **dog**.

Instructor: I will say this to you three more times.

Instructor: Repeat after me: "**D** stands for /d/ in /d/, /d/, **dog**."

Child: *D stands for /d/ in /d/, /d/, **dog**.*

Instructor: Let's say that together three times.

Together (three times):
    D stands for /d/ in /d/, /d/, **dog**.

Instructor: Let's add that line to the lines you have already learned, and say them together three times.

Together (three times):
    B stands for /b/ in /b/, /b/, **bat**.
    C stands for /k/ in /k/, /k/, **cat**.
    D stands for /d/ in /d/, /d/, **dog**.

Instructor: For what sound does the letter **d** stand?

Child: *D stands for /d/ in /d/, /d/, **dog**.*

Game: Consonant Pick-Up
Place the three consonant cards on the table: **B b**, **C c**, and **D d**. Say the sound that one of the letters represents and ask the child to pick up the correct consonant card. If the child picks the right card, he gets the card; if he doesn't, the instructor gets the card. Once you have gone through all three cards, have the child practice the cards he missed. Then shuffle all the cards and begin the game again. Once the child shows mastery, add the vowel cards and play the game with all of the cards.

Follow-Up:
The child should repeat the **d** line from the poem two more times during the day. Point out the letter **d** to the child whenever you see it (on signs, on food boxes or cans, in books you read aloud to him, etc...). Ask him to recite the line from this lesson to you.

Lesson 9:   The Consonant F f

You will need the following: *the cards you used previously, one blank index card, and a pen.*

Review

Instructor: I will show you each vowel card, and we will say the *sound* of that short vowel together.

Instructor: Let's practice the first three lines of the poem "The Consonant Rhyme." Let's say them together three times.

Together (three times):
> **B** stands for /b/ in /b/, /b/, **bat**.
> **C** stands for /k/ in /k/, /k/, **cat**.
> **D** stands for /d/ in /d/, /d/, **dog**.

Instructor: Now I will show you each consonant card from the previous lessons. I will say the sound that consonant represents, and you will repeat it back to me.

Instructor: Now I am going to ask you some questions about the sounds of the consonants. I want you to answer me with a line from the poem.

Point to each consonant card in order, and ask the child, "For what sound does the letter *(insert consonant)* stand?"

New

Instructor: Today we are going to learn the consonant **f**. This is the big **F** and the little **f**:

F f

Instructor: I will write the big **F** and the little **f** on a card for you.

Instructor: The letter **f** stands for the sound /f/. The sound /f/ is an unvoiced consonant sound because you do not use your voice to pronounce the sound. You just use air. I will point to the letter **f** card and say the consonant sound five times.

Place your top teeth on your bottom lip and blow air (do not use your voice): /f/.

Instructor: /f/, /f/, /f/, /f/, /f/. Now we will say the sound together.

Together: /f/, /f/, /f/, /f/, /f/.

Instructor: Listen as I say these words that begin with the sound /f/: **fat, fan, fed**. Now repeat after me: /f/, /f/, **fat**.

Child: */f/, /f/, fat.*

Instructor: /f/, /f/, **fan.**

Child: */f/, /f/, fan.*

Instructor: Listen for the unvoiced /f/ at the end of these words: **if, off, huff**. Listen for the sound of the letter **f** as you repeat after me: **if**.

Child: *if.*

23

Instructor:	*off.*
Child:	*off.*

Instructor:	Now I am going to teach you the next line of the poem "The Consonant Rhyme." This is the fourth line:

F stands for /f/ in /f/, /f/, *fog*.

Instructor:	I will say this to you three more times.

Instructor:	Repeat after me: "**F** stands for /f/ in /f/, /f/, *fog*."

Child:	***F*** *stands for /f/ in /f/, /f/, fog.*

Instructor:	Let's say that together three times.

Together (three times):
  F stands for /f/ in /f/, /f/, *fog*.

Instructor:	Let's add that line to the lines you have already learned. Let's say these lines together three times.

Together (three times):
  B stands for /b/ in /b/, /b/, ***bat***.
  C stands for /k/ in /k/, /k/, ***cat***.
  D stands for /d/ in /d/, /d/, ***dog***.
  F stands for /f/ in /f/, /f/, ***fog***.

Instructor:	For what sound does the letter **f** stand?

Child:	***F*** *stands for /f/ in /f/, /f/, fog.*

Follow-Up:
The child should repeat the **f** line from the poem two more times during the day. Point out the letter **f** to the child whenever you see it (on signs, on food boxes or cans, in books you read aloud to him, etc...).
Ask him to recite the line from this lesson to you.

Lesson 10: The Consonant G g

You will need the following: *the cards you used previously, two blank index cards, and a pen.*

Review

Instructor: I will show you each vowel card, and we will say the *sound* of that short vowel together.

Instructor: Now let's practice the first four lines of the poem "The Consonant Rhyme." Let's say them together three times.

Together (three times):
        B stands for /b/ in /b/, /b/, ***bat***.
        C stands for /k/ in /k/, /k/, ***cat***.
        D stands for /d/ in /d/, /d/, ***dog***.
        F stands for /f/ in /f/, /f/, ***fog***.

Instructor: Now I will show you each consonant card from the previous lessons. I will say the sound that consonant represents, and you will say the sound back to me.

Instructor: Now I am going to ask you some questions about the sounds of the consonants. You will answer me with a line from the poem.

Point to each consonant card in order, and ask the child, "For what sound does the letter *(insert consonant)* stand?"

New

Instructor: Today we are going to learn the consonant **g**. This is the big **G**:

G

Instructor: The little **g** can be written two different ways. You will need to know them both because books can have either little **g** in them.

g   g

The first little **g** is the kind the child will read in this book.

Instructor: I will write the consonant **g** on two cards for you. On the first card I will write the big **G** and then I will write the first little **g**. On the second card I will write the big **G** and the second kind of little **g**.

Instructor: The letter **g** usually stands for the sound /g/ in ***gum***. The sound /g/ is a voiced consonant sound because you use your voice to pronounce the sound. I will point to each letter **g** card and say the consonant sound five times.

Even though the sound /g/ requires using the voice, don't prolong the sound of /g/ so it sounds like /guh/. This is the hard sound of the letter **g**. The soft sound of **g** (/j/ in ***gel*** and ***gem***) will be discussed in Lesson 78.

Instructor: /g/, /g/, /g/, /g/, /g/. Now we will say the sound together as I point to each card.

Together: /g/, /g/, /g/, /g/, /g/.

Instructor:	Listen as I say these words that begin with the sound /g/: **get**, **got**, **gum**. Now repeat after me: /g/, /g/, **get**.
Child:	*/g/, /g/, get.*
Instructor:	/g/, /g/, **gum.**
Child:	*/g/, /g/, gum.*
Instructor:	Listen for the voiced /g/ at the end of these words: **bag**, **dig, hug**. Repeat after me: **bag**.
Child:	*bag.*
Instructor:	**dig.**
Child:	*dig.*
Instructor:	I am going to teach you the fifth line of the poem "The Consonant Rhyme."
	G stands for /g/ in /g/, /g/, **gum**.
Instructor:	I will say this to you three more times.
Instructor:	Repeat after me: "G stands for /g/ in /g/, /g/, **gum**."
Child:	**G** *stands for /g/ in /g/, /g/, gum.*
Instructor:	Let's say that together three times.

Together (three times):
  G stands for /g/ in /g/, /g/, **gum**.

Instructor:	Let's add that line to the lines you have already learned. Let's say these lines together three times.

Together (three times):
  B stands for /b/ in /b/, /b/, **bat**.
  C stands for /k/ in /k/, /k/, **cat**.
  D stands for /d/ in /d/, /d/, **dog**.
  F stands for /f/ in /f/, /f/, **fog**.
  G stands for /g/ in /g/, /g/, **gum**.

Instructor:	For what sound does the letter **g** stand?
Child:	**G** *stands for /g/ in /g/, /g/, gum.*

Follow-Up:
The child should repeat the **g** line from the poem two more times during the day. Point out the letter **g** to the child whenever you see it (on signs, on food boxes or cans, in books you read aloud to him, etc…).
Ask him to recite the line from this lesson to you.

Lesson 11: The Consonant H h

You will need the following: *the cards you used previously, a blank index card, and a pen.*

Review

Instructor: I will point to each vowel card, and we will say the *name* of each vowel together.

Instructor: Now I will point again to each vowel card, and you will say its short-vowel *sound.*

Instructor: Let's practice the first five lines of the poem "The Consonant Rhyme." Let's say them together three times.

Together (three times):
  B stands for /b/ in /b/, /b/, ***bat.***
  C stands for /k/ in /k/, /k/, ***cat.***
  D stands for /d/ in /d/, /d/, ***dog.***
  F stands for /f/ in /f/, /f/, ***fog.***
  G stands for /g/ in /g/, /g/, ***gum.***

Instructor: Now I will show you the consonant cards from the previous lessons. I will say the sound each consonant represents, and you will repeat that sound after me.

Instructor: Now I am going to ask you some questions about the sounds of the consonants. You will answer me with a line from the poem.

Point to each consonant card in order, and ask the child, "For what sound does the letter *(insert consonant)* stand?"

New

Instructor: Today we are going to learn the consonant **h**. This is the big **H** and the little **h**:

H h

Instructor: I will write the big **H** and the little **h** on a card for you.

Instructor: The letter **h** usually stands for the sound /h/. The sound /h/ is an unvoiced consonant sound because you do not use your voice to pronounce the sound. You just use air. I will point to the letter **h** card and say the consonant sound five times.

Do not use your voice to produce this sound; the only sound will be the rushing of air from your mouth.

Instructor: /h/, /h/, /h/, /h/, /h/. Now we will say the sound together.

Together: /h/, /h/, /h/, /h/, /h/.

Instructor: Listen as I say these words that begin with the sound /h/: ***hat, ham, hog.*** Now repeat after me: /h/, /h/, ***hat.***

Child: */h/, /h/, hat.*

Instructor: /h/, /h/, ***ham.***

Child: */h/, /h/, ham.*

Instructor: You do not hear the sound /h/ at the ends of words. Now I am going to teach you the next line of the poem "The Consonant Rhyme." This is the sixth line:

H stands for /h/ in /h/, /h/, ***hum***.

Instructor: I will say this line to you three more times.

Instructor: Repeat after me: "**H** stands for /h/ in /h/, /h/, ***hum***."

Child: ***H*** *stands for /h/ in /h/, /h/, hum.*

Instructor: Let's say that together three times.

Together (three times):
H stands for /h/ in /h/, /h/, ***hum***.

Instructor: Let's add that line to the lines you have already learned. Let's say these lines together three times.

Together (three times):
B stands for /b/ in /b/, /b/, ***bat***.
C stands for /k/ in /k/, /k/, ***cat***.
D stands for /d/ in /d/, /d/, ***dog***.
F stands for /f/ in /f/, /f/, ***fog***.
G stands for /g/ in /g/, /g/, ***gum***.
H stands for /h/ in /h/, /h/, ***hum***.

Instructor: For what sound does the letter **h** stand?

Child: ***H*** *stands for /h/ in /h/, /h/, hum.*

Game: Consonant Pick-Up
Place the four consonant cards on the table: **F f**, **G g**, **G g**, and **H h**. Say the sound that one of the letters represents and ask the child to pick up the correct consonant card. If the child picks the right card, he gets the card; if he doesn't, the instructor gets the card. Once you have gone through all four cards, have the child practice the cards he missed. Then shuffle all the cards and begin the game again. Once the child shows mastery, add the vowel and previously used consonant cards and play the game with all of the cards.

Follow-Up:
The child should repeat the **h** line from the poem two more times during the day. Point out the letter **h** to the child whenever you see it (on signs, on food boxes or cans, in books you read aloud to him, etc...). Ask him to recite the line from this lesson to you.

Lesson 12: The Consonant J j

You will need the following: *the cards you used previously, a blank index card, and a pen. From this point on, you will only need the **G g** card. Do not use the **G g** card for the review.*

Review

Instructor: I will point to each vowel card, and we will say the *name* of each vowel together.

Instructor: Now I will point again to each vowel card, and you will say its short-vowel *sound*.

Instructor: Let's practice the first six lines of the poem "The Consonant Rhyme." Let's say them together three times.

Together (three times):
> **B** stands for /b/ in /b/, /b/, ***bat***.
> **C** stands for /k/ in /k/, /k/, ***cat***.
> **D** stands for /d/ in /d/, /d/, ***dog***.
> **F** stands for /f/ in /f/, /f/, ***fog***.
> **G** stands for /g/ in /g/, /g/, ***gum***.
> **H** stands for /h/ in /h/, /h/, ***hum***.

Instructor: Now I will show you the consonant cards from the previous lessons. I will say the sound each consonant represents, and you will repeat that sound after me.

Instructor: Now I am going to ask you some questions about the sounds of the consonants. You will answer me with a line from the poem.

Point to each consonant card in order, and ask the child, "For what sound does the letter *(insert consonant)* stand?"

New

Instructor: Today we are going to learn the consonant **j**. This is the big **J** and the little **j**:

J   j

Instructor: I will write the big **J** and the little **j** on a card for you.

Instructor: The letter **j** stands for the sound /j/. The sound /j/ is a voiced consonant sound because you use your voice to pronounce the sound. I will point to the letter **j** card and say the consonant sound five times.

Instructor: /j/, /j/, /j/, /j/, /j/. Now we will say the sound together.

Together: /j/, /j/, /j/, /j/, /j/.

Instructor: Listen as I say these words that begin with the sound /j/: ***jam***, ***jet***, ***Jeep***. Now repeat after me: /j/, /j/, ***jam***.

Child: */j/, /j/, jam.*

Instructor: /j/, /j/, ***Jeep***.

Child: */j/, /j/, Jeep.*

The ending /j/ sound (which is not spelled with a **j**, but with **ge** or **dge**) will be taught in later lessons.

Instructor: Now I am going to teach you the next line of the poem "The Consonant Rhyme." This is the seventh line:

J stands for /j/ in /j/, /j/, ***Jeep***.

Instructor: I will say this to you three more times.

Say the line slowly three times, taking care to emphasize the sound /j/.

Instructor: Now repeat after me: "**J** stands for /j/ in /j/, /j/, ***Jeep***."

Child: *J stands for /j/ in /j/, /j/, Jeep.*

Instructor: Now let's say that together three times.

Together (three times):
J stands for /j/ in /j/, /j/, ***Jeep***.

Instructor: Now let's add that line to the lines you have already learned. Let's say these lines together three times.

Together (three times):
B stands for /b/ in /b/, /b/, ***bat***.
C stands for /k/ in /k/, /k/, ***cat***.
D stands for /d/ in /d/, /d/, ***dog***.
F stands for /f/ in /f/, /f/, ***fog***.
G stands for /g/ in /g/, /g/, ***gum***.
H stands for /h/ in /h/, /h/, ***hum***.
J stands for /j/ in /j/, /j/, ***Jeep***.

Instructor: For what sound does the letter **j** stand?

Child: *J stands for /j/ in /j/, /j/, Jeep.*

Follow-Up:
The child should repeat the **j** line from the poem two more times during the day. Point out the letter **j** to the child whenever you see it (on signs, on food boxes or cans, in books you read aloud to him, etc...). Ask him to recite the line from this lesson to you.

Lesson 13: The Consonant K k

You will need the following: *the cards you used previously as well as a blank index card and a pen.*

Review

Instructor: I will point to each vowel card, and we will say the *name* of each vowel together.

Instructor: Now I will point again to each vowel card, and you will say its short-vowel *sound*.

Instructor: Let's practice the first seven lines of the poem "The Consonant Rhyme." Let's say them together three times.

Together (three times):
> **B** stands for /b/ in /b/, /b/, ***bat***.
> **C** stands for /k/ in /k/, /k/, ***cat***.
> **D** stands for /d/ in /d/, /d/, ***dog***.
> **F** stands for /f/ in /f/, /f/, ***fog***.
> **G** stands for /g/ in /g/, /g/, ***gum***.
> **H** stands for /h/ in /h/, /h/, ***hum***.
> **J** stands for /j/ in /j/, /j/, ***Jeep***.

Instructor: Now I will show you the consonant cards from the previous lessons. I will say the sound each consonant represents, and you will repeat the sound after me.

Instructor: Now I am going to ask you some questions about the sounds of the consonants. You will answer me with a line from the poem.

Point to each consonant card in order, and ask the child, "For what sound does the letter *(insert consonant)* stand?"

New

Instructor: Today we are going to learn the consonant **k**. This is the big **K** and the little **k**:

K k

Instructor: I will write the big **K** and the little **k** on a card for you.

Instructor: Now do you remember for what sound the letter **c** stands?

Child: /k/.

Instructor: The letter **k** usually stands for that same sound: /k/. Remember, the sound /k/ is an unvoiced consonant sound because you do not use your voice to pronounce the sound. You just use air. I will point to the letter **k** below and say the consonant sound five times.

Instructor: /k/, /k/, /k/, /k/, /k/. Now we will say the sound together.

Together: /k/, /k/, /k/, /k/, /k/.

Instructor: Listen as I say these words that begin with the sound /k/ and the letter **k**: ***kid, kit, keep***. Now repeat after me: /k/, /k/, ***kid***.

Child: /k/, /k/, kid.

Instructor: /k/, /k/, **_keep._**

Child: _/k/, /k/, keep._

Words that end with the /k/ sound are spelled with **ck**.

Instructor: Listen as I say these words that end with the sound /k/: **_pack_**, **_sock_**, **_luck_**. Now repeat after me: **_pack_**.

Child: _pack._

Instructor: **_luck._**

Child: _luck._

Instructor: Now I am going to teach you the eighth line of the poem "The Consonant Rhyme."

                K stands for /k/ in /k/, /k/, **_keep._**

Instructor: I will say this to you three more times.

Instructor: Repeat after me: "**K** stands for /k/ in /k/, /k/, **_keep._**"

Child: **_K_** _stands for /k/ in /k/, /k/, keep._

Instructor: Let's say that together three times.

Together (three times):
                K stands for /k/ in /k/, /k/, **_keep._**

Instructor: Let's add that line to the lines you have already learned. Let's say these lines together three times.

Together (three times):
                B stands for /b/ in /b/, /b/, **_bat_**.
                C stands for /k/ in /k/, /k/, **_cat_**.
                D stands for /d/ in /d/, /d/, **_dog_**.
                F stands for /f/ in /f/, /f/, **_fog_**.
                G stands for /g/ in /g/, /g/, **_gum_**.
                H stands for /h/ in /h/, /h/, **_hum_**.
                J stands for /j/ in /j/, /j/, **_Jeep_**.
                K stands for /k/ in /k/, /k/, **_keep_**.

Instructor: For what sound does the letter **k** stand?

Child: **_K_** _stands for /k/ in /k/, /k/, keep._

Follow-Up:
The child should repeat the **k** line from the poem two more times during the day. Point out the letter **k** to the child whenever you see it (on signs, on food boxes or cans, in books you read aloud to him, etc…). Ask him to recite the line from this lesson to you.

Lesson 14: The Consonant L l

You will need the following: *the cards you made previously as well as a blank index card, and a pen.*

Review

Instructor: I will point to each vowel card and you will say the *name* of each vowel by yourself. Then I will point again to each vowel card, and you will say its short-vowel *sound*.

Instructor: Let's practice the first eight lines of the poem "The Consonant Rhyme." Let's say them together three times.

Together (three times):
   B stands for /b/ in /b/, /b/, ***bat***.
   C stands for /k/ in /k/, /k/, ***cat***.
   D stands for /d/ in /d/, /d/, ***dog***.
   F stands for /f/ in /f/, /f/, ***fog***.
   G stands for /g/ in /g/, /g/, ***gum***.
   H stands for /h/ in /h/, /h/, ***hum***.
   J stands for /j/ in /j/, /j/, ***Jeep***.
   K stands for /k/ in /k/, /k/, ***keep***.

Instructor: I will show you the consonant cards from the previous lessons. I will say the sound each consonant represents, and you will repeat that sound after me.

Instructor: Now I am going to ask you some questions about the sounds of the consonants. You will answer me with a line from the poem.

Point to each consonant card, and ask the child, "For what sound does the letter *(insert consonant)* stand?"

New

Instructor: Today we are going to learn the consonant l. This is the big **L** and the little **l**:

L   l

You may notice that the little l (in *letter*) looks like the big I (in *Isaac*). Don't discuss this with the child unless it is causing a problem. Once the child begins reading words, the similarity of print is rarely an issue.

Instructor: I will write the big **L** and the little **l** on a card for you.

Instructor: The letter l usually stands for the sound /l/, a voiced consonant sound. You use your voice to pronounce the sound. I will point to the l card and say the consonant sound five times.

The sound /l/ is particularly hard for some children to master. Place the tip of your tongue on your gums just behind your front teeth while you make a voice sound. Do not release your tongue while sounding the voice or you will make a /la/ sound. If the child has difficulty with this particular sound, pleasantly model it correctly for him, and move on. It often takes young children a year or two to say some sounds perfectly. Do not make the child self-conscious.

Instructor: /l/, /l/, /l/, /l/, /l/. Now we will say the sound together.

Together: /l/, /l/, /l/, /l/, /l/.

Instructor:	Listen as I say words that begin with the sound /l/: **lap**, **lid**, **lot**. Repeat after me: /l/, /l/, **lap**.
Child:	*/l/, /l/, lap.*
Instructor:	/l/, /l/, **lot.**
Child:	*/l/, /l/, lot.*
Instructor:	Listen as I say these words that end with the sound /l/: **pal**, **hill**, **dull**. Now repeat after me: **pal**.
Child:	*pal.*
Instructor:	**hill.**
Child:	*hill.*
Instructor:	I am going to teach you the ninth line of the poem "The Consonant Rhyme."
	L stands for /l/ in /l/, /l/, **lap**.
Instructor:	I will say this to you three more times.
Instructor:	Repeat after me: "**L** stands for /l/ in /l/, /l/, **lap**."
Child:	*L stands for /l/ in /l/, /l/, lap.*
Instructor:	Let's say that together three times.

Together (three times):
    L stands for /l/ in /l/, /l/, **lap**.

Instructor:	Let's add that line to the lines you have already learned, and say them together three times.

Together (three times):
    B stands for /b/ in /b/, /b/, **bat**.
    C stands for /k/ in /k/, /k/, **cat**.
    D stands for /d/ in /d/, /d/, **dog**.
    F stands for /f/ in /f/, /f/, **fog**.
    G stands for /g/ in /g/, /g/, **gum**.
    H stands for /h/ in /h/, /h/, **hum**.
    J stands for /j/ in /j/, /j/, **Jeep**.
    K stands for /k/ in /k/, /k/, **keep**.
    L stands for /l/ in /l/, /l/, **lap**.

Instructor:	For what sound does the letter **l** stand?
Child:	*L stands for /l/ in /l/, /l/, lap.*

Follow-Up:
The child should repeat the **L** line from the poem two more times throughout the day.

34

Lesson 15:   The Consonant M m

You will need the following: *the cards you used previously, a blank index card, and a pen.*

Review

Instructor: I will point to each vowel card and you will say the *name* of each vowel by yourself. Once we have finished going through all five vowels, I will point again to each vowel card, and you will say its short-vowel *sound*.

Instructor: Let's practice the first nine lines of the poem "The Consonant Rhyme." Let's say them together three times.

Together (three times):
B stands for /b/ in /b/, /b/, ***bat***.
C stands for /k/ in /k/, /k/, ***cat***.
D stands for /d/ in /d/, /d/, ***dog***.
F stands for /f/ in /f/, /f/, ***fog***.
G stands for /g/ in /g/, /g/, ***gum***.
H stands for /h/ in /h/, /h/, ***hum***.
J stands for /j/ in /j/, /j/, ***Jeep***.
K stands for /k/ in /k/, /k/, ***keep***.
L stands for /l/ in /l/, /l/, ***lap***.

Instructor: Now I will show you the consonant cards from the previous lessons. I will say the sound each consonant represents, and you will repeat that sound after me.

Instructor: I am going to ask you some questions about the sounds of the consonants. You will answer me with a line from the poem.

Point to each consonant card. Ask the child, "For what sound does the letter *(insert consonant)* stand?"

New

Instructor: Today we are going to learn the consonant **m**. This is the big **M** and the little **m**:

M m

Instructor: I will write the big **M** and the little **m** on a card for you.

Instructor: The letter **m** stands for the sound /m/. This is the sound you make when something tastes really good: Mmm… The sound /m/ doesn't come out of your mouth—your mouth is closed! The sound has to come out of your nose! The sound /m/ is called a *nasal* consonant sound. The word ***nasal*** refers to the nose. I will point to the letter **m** card and say the consonant sound five times.

To correctly pronounce the /m/ sound, do not say /muh/ and do not clench your teeth.

Instructor: /m/, /m/, /m/, /m/, /m/. Now we will say the sound together.

Together: /m/, /m/, /m/, /m/, /m/.

Instructor: These words begin with the sound /m/: ***map***, ***met***, ***mud***. Repeat after me: /m/, /m/, ***map***.

Child: */m/, /m/, map.*

Instructor:	/m/, /m/, **mud.**
Child:	*/m/, /m/, mud.*

Instructor: These words end with the sound /m/: **ham**, **gum**, **hum**. Repeat after me: **ham**.

Child: *ham.*

Instructor: **gum.**

Child: *gum.*

Instructor: Now I am going to teach you the tenth line of the poem "The Consonant Rhyme."

M stands for /m/ in /m/, /m/, **map.**

Instructor: I will say this to you three more times.

Instructor: Repeat after me: "**M** stands for /m/ in /m/, /m/, **map**."

Child: **M** *stands for /m/ in /m/, /m/, map.*

Instructor: Let's say that together three times.

Together (three times):
M stands for /m/ in /m/, /m/, **map.**

Instructor: Let's add that line to the lines you have already learned, and say them together three times.

Together (three times):
B stands for /b/ in /b/, /b/, **bat**.
C stands for /k/ in /k/, /k/, **cat**.
D stands for /d/ in /d/, /d/, **dog**.
F stands for /f/ in /f/, /f/, **fog**.
G stands for /g/ in /g/, /g/, **gum**.
H stands for /h/ in /h/, /h/, **hum**.
J stands for /j/ in /j/, /j/, **Jeep**.
K stands for /k/ in /k/, /k/, **keep**.
L stands for /l/ in /l/, /l/, **lap**.
M stands for /m/ in /m/, /m/, **map**.

Instructor: For what sound does the letter **m** stand?

Child: **M** *stands for /m/ in /m/, /m/, map.*

Follow-Up:
The child should repeat the **m** line from the poem two more times during the day. Point out the letter **m** to the child whenever you see it. Ask him to recite the line from this lesson to you.

Lesson 16: The Consonant N n

You will need the following: *the cards you previously used, a blank index card, and a pen.*

___

Review

Instructor: I am going to teach you a version of the song "Old MacDonald Had a Farm" that uses the names and short sounds of all five vowels. Listen as I sing it to you.

When you get to the part, "And on that farm he had an **a**," pick up the **A a** card when you say the letter **a** and hold the card until the end of the verse.

Instructor: Old MacDonald had a farm—**a, e, i, o, u**.
And on that farm he had an **a**—**a, e, i, o, u**.
With an /ă/, /ă/, here,
And an /ă/, /ă/, there,
Here an /ă/, there an /ă/,
Everywhere an /ă/, /ă/,
Old MacDonald had a farm—**a, e, i, o, u**.

Sing the song four more times, each time substituting the name and short-vowel sound of each of the next vowels: **e, i, o, u.** Pick up the appropriate vowel card when you sing, "And on that farm he had an (vowel)."

Instructor: Now we'll sing the song together. When you think you can sing it by yourself, let me know. Pick up the card when you say the name of the vowel that Old MacDonald had on his farm. I will place the vowel cards in order in front of you.

Instructor: Let's practice the first ten lines of the poem "The Consonant Rhyme." Let's say them together three times.

Together (three times):
B stands for /b/ in /b/, /b/, ***bat***.
C stands for /k/ in /k/, /k/, ***cat***.
D stands for /d/ in /d/, /d/, ***dog***.
F stands for /f/ in /f/, /f/, ***fog***.
G stands for /g/ in /g/, /g/, ***gum***.
H stands for /h/ in /h/, /h/, ***hum***.
J stands for /j/ in /j/, /j/, ***Jeep***.
K stands for /k/ in /k/, /k/, ***keep***.
L stands for /l/ in /l/, /l/, ***lap***.
M stands for /m/ in /m/, /m/, ***map***.

Instructor: I will show you the consonant cards from the previous lessons. I will say the sound each consonant represents, and you will repeat that sound after me.

Instructor: I am going to ask you some questions about the sounds of the consonants. You will answer me with a line from the poem.

Point to each consonant card in order, and ask the child, "For what sound does the letter (insert consonant) stand?"

Instructor: Today we are going to learn the consonant **n**. This is the big **N** and the little **n**:

N n

Instructor: I will write the big **N** and the little **n** on a card for you.

Instructor: The letter **n** stands for the sound /n/. The sound /n/ seems to come out of your nose! Just like the sound /m/, the sound /n/ is called a nasal consonant sound. Remember, the word **nasal** refers to the nose. I will point to the letter **n** card and say the consonant sound five times.

Do not say /nuh/, say /n/.

Instructor: /n/, /n/, /n/, /n/, /n/. Now we will say the sound together.

Together: /n/, /n/, /n/, /n/, /n/.

Instructor: Listen as I say these words that begin with the sound /n/: **net, not, nap**. Now repeat after me: /n/, /n/, **net**

Child: */n/, /n/, net.*

Instructor: /n/, /n/, **nap.**

Child: */n/, /n/, nap.*

Instructor: Listen as I say these words that end with the sound /n/: **tan, win, sun**. Now repeat after me: **tan**.

Child: *tan.*

Instructor: **sun.**

Child: *sun.*

Instructor: Now I am going to teach you the next line of the poem "The Consonant Rhyme." This is the eleventh line:

N stands for /n/ in /n/, /n/, **net**.

Instructor: I will say this to you three more times.

Instructor: Repeat after me: "**N** stands for /n/ in /n/, /n/, **net**."

Child: ***N** stands for /n/ in /n/, /n/, net.*

Instructor: Let's say that together three times.

Together (three times):
N stands for /n/ in /n/, /n/, **net**.

Instructor: Let's add that line to the lines you have already learned. Let's say these lines together three times.

Together (three times):

> **B** stands for /b/ in /b/, /b/, *bat*.
> **C** stands for /k/ in /k/, /k/, *cat*.
> **D** stands for /d/ in /d/, /d/, *dog*.
> **F** stands for /f/ in /f/, /f/, *fog*.
> **G** stands for /g/ in /g/, /g/, *gum*.
> **H** stands for /h/ in /h/, /h/, *hum*.
> **J** stands for /j/ in /j/, /j/, *Jeep*.
> **K** stands for /k/ in /k/, /k/, *keep*.
> **L** stands for /l/ in /l/, /l/, *lap*.
> **M** stands for /m/ in /m/, /m/, *map*.
> **N** stands for /n/ in /n/, /n/, *net*.

Instructor: For what sound does the letter **n** stand?

Child: **N** *stands for /n/ in /n/, /n/, net.*

Follow-Up:
The child should repeat the **n** line from the poem two more times during the day. Point out the letter **n** to the child whenever you see it (on signs, on food boxes or cans, in books you read aloud to him, etc…). Ask him to recite the line from this lesson to you.

Reminder:
I encourage you to spend as many days as necessary on each lesson until you feel the child has mastered the letter and the sound.

Lesson 17:   The Consonant P p

You will need the following: *the cards you used previously, a blank index card, and a pen.*

Review

Lay out the five vowel cards on the table in alphabetical order. Have the child sing "Old MacDonald Had a Farm" as printed in the previous lesson. Remind him to pick up the appropriate vowel card when he gets to the line, "And on that farm he had an (vowel)."

Instructor: Let's practice the first eleven lines of the poem "The Consonant Rhyme." Let's say them together three times.

Together (three times):

        B stands for /b/ in /b/, /b/, *bat*.
        C stands for /k/ in /k/, /k/, *cat*.
        D stands for /d/ in /d/, /d/, *dog*.
        F stands for /f/ in /f/, /f/, *fog*.
        G stands for /g/ in /g/, /g/, *gum*.
        H stands for /h/ in /h/, /h/, *hum*.
        J stands for /j/ in /j/, /j/, *Jeep*.
        K stands for /k/ in /k/, /k/, *keep*.
        L stands for /l/ in /l/, /l/, *lap*.
        M stands for /m/ in /m/, /m/, *map*.
        N stands for /n/ in /n/, /n/, *net*.

Instructor: Now I will show you the consonant cards from the previous lessons. I will say the sound each consonant represents, and you will repeat that sound after me.

Instructor: I am going to ask you some questions about the sounds of the consonants. You will answer me with a line from the poem.

Point to each consonant card in order, and ask the child, "For what sound does the letter *(insert consonant)* stand?"

New

Instructor: Today we are going to learn the consonant **p**. This is the big **P** and the little **p**:

P   p

Instructor: I will write the big **P** and the little **p** on a card for you.

Instructor: The letter **p** usually stands for the sound /p/. The sound /p/ is an unvoiced consonant sound because you do not use your voice to pronounce the sound. You just use air. I will point to the letter **p** card and say the consonant sound five times.

Close your lips. The air escaping from your lips will make a soft, popping sound: /p/. Do not use your voice and say /puh/.

Instructor: /p/, /p/, /p/, /p/, /p/. Now we will say the sound together.

Together: /p/, /p/, /p/, /p/, /p/.

Instructor: Listen as I say these words that begin with the sound /p/: **pet**, **pan**, **pig**. Now repeat after me: /p/, /p/, **pet.**

Child: /p/, /p/, pet.

Instructor: /p/, /p/, **pig.**

Child: /p/, /p/, pig.

Instructor: Listen as I say these words that end with the sound /p/: **sip**, **lap**, **top**. Now repeat after me: **sip**.

Child: sip.

Instructor: **top.**

Child: top.

Instructor: Now I am going to teach you the next line of the poem "The Consonant Rhyme." This is the twelfth line:

P stands for /p/ in /p/, /p/, **pet.**

Instructor: I will say this to you three more times.

Instructor: Now repeat after me: "**P** stands for /p/ in /p/, /p/, **pet.**"

Child: **P** stands for /p/ in /p/, /p/, pet.

Instructor: Now let's say that together three times.

Together (three times):
P stands for /p/ in /p/, /p/, **pet.**

Instructor: Now let's add that line to the lines you have already learned. Let's say these lines together three times.

Together (three times):
B stands for /b/ in /b/, /b/, **bat.**
C stands for /k/ in /k/, /k/, **cat.**
D stands for /d/ in /d/, /d/, **dog.**
F stands for /f/ in /f/, /f/, **fog.**
G stands for /g/ in /g/, /g/, **gum.**
H stands for /h/ in /h/, /h/, **hum.**
J stands for /j/ in /j/, /j/, **Jeep.**
K stands for /k/ in /k/, /k/, **keep.**
L stands for /l/ in /l/, /l/, **lap.**
M stands for /m/ in /m/, /m/, **map.**
N stands for /n/ in /n/, /n/, **net.**
P stands for /p/ in /p/, /p/, **pet.**

Instructor: For what sound does the letter **p** stand?

Child: ***P*** *stands for /p/ in /p/, /p/, pet.*

Game: Consonant Pick-Up

Place the following six consonant cards on the table: **J j**, **K k**, **L l**, **M m**, **N n**, and **P p**. Say the sound that one of the letters represents and ask the child to pick up the correct consonant card. If the child picks the right card, he gets the card; if he doesn't, the instructor gets the card. Once you have gone through all six cards, have the child practice the cards he missed. Then shuffle all the cards and begin the game again. Once the child shows mastery, add the vowel cards and the other consonant cards and play the game with all the cards.

Follow-Up:

The child should repeat the **p** line from the poem two more times during the day. Point out the letter **p** to the child whenever you see it (on signs, on food boxes or cans, in books you read aloud to him, etc…). Ask him to recite the line from this lesson to you.

Lesson 18: The Consonant Q q

You will need the following: *the cards you used previously, a blank index card, and a pen.*

Review

Begin the lesson with the "Old MacDonald Had a Farm" vowel exercise from Lesson 16.

Instructor: Let's practice the first twelve lines of the poem "The Consonant Rhyme." Let's say them together three times.

Together (three times):
        B stands for /b/ in /b/, /b/, ***bat***.
        C stands for /k/ in /k/, /k/, ***cat***.
        D stands for /d/ in /d/, /d/, ***dog***.
        F stands for /f/ in /f/, /f/, ***fog***.
        G stands for /g/ in /g/, /g/, ***gum***.
        H stands for /h/ in /h/, /h/, ***hum***.
        J stands for /j/ in /j/, /j/, ***Jeep***.
        K stands for /k/ in /k/, /k/, ***keep***.
        L stands for /l/ in /l/, /l/, ***lap***.
        M stands for /m/ in /m/, /m/, ***map***.
        N stands for /n/ in /n/, /n/, ***net***.
        P stands for /p/ in /p/, /p/, ***pet***.

Instructor: Now I will show you the consonant cards from the previous lessons. I will say the sound each consonant represents, and you will repeat that sound after me.

Instructor: I am going to ask you some questions about the sounds of the consonants. You will answer me with a line from the poem.

Point to each consonant card in order, and ask the child, "For what sound does the letter *(insert consonant)* stand?"

New

Instructor: Today we are going to learn the consonant **q**. This is the big **Q** and the little **q**:

Q q

Instructor: The letter **q** is unusual because it does not appear without the letter **u**. You could say that the letter **q** is too scared to go anywhere without its buddy, the letter **u**. Here is the big **Q** with the letter **u**.

Qu

Instructor: This is the little **q** with its buddy, the letter **u**.

qu

Instructor: Because the letter **q** is always followed by the letter **u**, I am going to write them as a pair on a card for you. First I will write the big **Q** with a little **u** and then I will write the little **q** with the little **u**.

Instructor: The letters **qu** usually stand for the sound /kw/. The sound is an unvoiced consonant sound because you do not use your voice to pronounce the sound. You just use air. I will point to the **qu** card and say the consonant sound five times.

Say the sounds /k/ and /w/ together very quickly. Do not use your voice; you should say /kw/ and not /kwuh/ when you model the sound.

Instructor: /kw/, /kw/, /kw/, /kw/, /kw/. Now we will say the sound together.

Together: /kw/, /kw/, /kw/, /kw/, /kw/.

Instructor: Listen as I say these words that begin with the sound /kw/: **quack**, **quit**, **quiz**. Now repeat after me: /kw/, /kw/, **quack.**

Child: */kw/, /kw/, quack.*

Instructor: /kw/, /kw/, **quit.**

Child: */kw/, /kw/, quit.*

There are no words that end with the sound /kw/.

Instructor: Now I am going to teach you the next line of the poem "The Consonant Rhyme." This is the thirteenth line:

Qu stands for /kw/ in /kw/, /kw/, **quack.**

Instructor: I will say this to you three more times.

Instructor: Repeat after me: "**Qu** stands for /kw/ in /kw/, /kw/, **quack.**"

Child: ***Qu** stands for /kw/ in /kw/, /kw/, quack.*

Instructor: Let's say that together three times.

Together (three times):
Qu stands for /kw/ in /kw/, /kw/, **quack.**

Instructor: Let's add that line to the lines you have already learned. Let's say these lines together three times.

Together (three times):

> **B** stands for /b/ in /b/, /b/, ***bat***.
> **C** stands for /k/ in /k/, /k/, ***cat***.
> **D** stands for /d/ in /d/, /d/, ***dog***.
> **F** stands for /f/ in /f/, /f/, ***fog***.
> **G** stands for /g/ in /g/, /g/, ***gum***.
> **H** stands for /h/ in /h/, /h/, ***hum***.
> **J** stands for /j/ in /j/, /j/, ***Jeep***.
> **K** stands for /k/ in /k/, /k/, ***keep***.
> **L** stands for /l/ in /l/, /l/, ***lap***.
> **M** stands for /m/ in /m/, /m/, ***map***.
> **N** stands for /n/ in /n/, /n/, ***net***.
> **P** stands for /p/ in /p/, /p/, ***pet***.
> **Qu** stands for /kw/ in /kw/, /kw/, ***quack***.

Instructor: For what sound do the letters **qu** stand?

Child: ***Qu*** *stands for /kw/ in /kw/, /kw/, quack.*

Follow-Up:
The child should repeat the **qu** line from the poem two more times during the day. Point out the letters **qu** to the child whenever you see them (on signs, on food boxes or cans, in books you read aloud to him, etc…). Ask him to recite the line from this lesson to you.

Lesson 19:   The Consonant R r

You will need the following: *the cards you used previously, a blank index card, and a pen.*

Review

Begin the lesson with the "Old MacDonald Had a Farm" vowel exercise from Lesson 16.

Instructor: Let's practice the first thirteen lines of the poem "The Consonant Rhyme." Let's say them together three times.

Together (three times):
   B stands for /b/ in /b/, /b/, **bat**.
   C stands for /k/ in /k/, /k/, **cat**.
   D stands for /d/ in /d/, /d/, **dog**.
   F stands for /f/ in /f/, /f/, **fog**.
   G stands for /g/ in /g/, /g/, **gum**.
   H stands for /h/ in /h/, /h/, **hum**.
   J stands for /j/ in /j/, /j/, **Jeep**.
   K stands for /k/ in /k/, /k/, **keep**.
   L stands for /l/ in /l/, /l/, **lap**.
   M stands for /m/ in /m/, /m/, **map**.
   N stands for /n/ in /n/, /n/, **net**.
   P stands for /p/ in /p/, /p/, **pet**.
   Qu stands for /kw/ in /kw/, /kw/, **quack**.

Instructor: Now I will show you the consonant cards from the previous lessons. I will say the sound each consonant represents, and you will repeat that sound after me.

Instructor: I am going to ask you some questions about the sounds of the consonants. You will answer me with a line from the poem.

Point to each consonant card, and ask the child, "For what sound does the letter *(insert consonant)* stand?"

New

Instructor: Today we are going to learn the consonant **r**. This is the big **R** and the little **r**:

R r

Instructor: I will write the big **R** and the little **r** on a card for you.

Instructor: The letter **r** stands for the sound /r/. The sound /r/ is a voiced consonant sound because you use your voice to pronounce the sound. I will point to the letter **r** card and say the consonant sound five times.

Although you use your voice to produce this sound, do not say /ruh/ or /er/. The sound of **r** is like a growl (grr…) without the **g**: /r/. The sound /r/ is particularly hard for some children to master. If the child has difficulty with this particular sound, pleasantly model it correctly for him, and move on. It often takes young children a year or two to say some sounds perfectly. Do not make the child self-conscious.

Instructor: /r/, /r/, /r/, /r/, /r/. Now we will say the sound together.

Together: /r/, /r/, /r/, /r/, /r/.

Instructor: Listen as I say these words that begin with the sound /r/: ***rack***, ***red***, ***rub***. Now repeat after me: /r/, /r/, ***rack***.

Child: /r/, /r/, rack.

Instructor: /r/, /r/, ***red***.

Child: /r/, /r/, red.

Emphasize a true /r/ sound at the end of the next words.

Instructor: Listen as I say these words that end with the sound /r/: ***far***, ***door***, ***bear***. Now repeat after me: ***far***.

Child: far.

Instructor: ***door***.

Child: door.

Instructor: Now I am going to teach you the next line of the poem "The Consonant Rhyme." This is the fourteenth line:

R stands for /r/ in /r/, /r/, ***rack***.

Instructor: I will say this to you three more times.

Instructor: Repeat after me: "**R** stands for /r/ in /r/, /r/, ***rack***.

Child: **R** *stands for /r/ in /r/, /r/, rack.*

Instructor: Let's say that together three times.

Together (three times):
R stands for /r/ in /r/, /r/, ***rack***.

Instructor: Let's add that line to the lines you have already learned. Let's say these lines together three times.

The poem is printed on the following page.

Together (three times):

        B stands for /b/ in /b/, /b/, ***bat***.
        C stands for /k/ in /k/, /k/, ***cat***.
        D stands for /d/ in /d/, /d/, ***dog***.
        F stands for /f/ in /f/, /f/, ***fog***.
        G stands for /g/ in /g/, /g/, ***gum***.
        H stands for /h/ in /h/, /h/, ***hum***.
        J stands for /j/ in /j/, /j/, ***Jeep***.
        K stands for /k/ in /k/, /k/, ***keep***.
        L stands for /l/ in /l/, /l/, ***lap***.
        M stands for /m/ in /m/, /m/, ***map***.
        N stands for /n/ in /n/, /n/, ***net***.
        P stands for /p/ in /p/, /p/, ***pet***.
        Qu stands for /kw/ in /kw/, /kw/, ***quack***.
        R stands for /r/ in /r/, /r/, ***rack***.

Instructor: For what sound does the letter **r** stand?

Child: ***R*** *stands for /r/ in /r/, /r/, rack.*

Follow-Up:
The child should repeat the **r** line from the poem two more times during the day. Point out the letter **r** to the child whenever you see it (on signs, on food boxes or cans, in books you read aloud to him, etc…). Ask him to recite the line from this lesson to you.

Lesson 20: The Consonant S s

You will need the following: *the cards you used previously, a blank index card, and a pen.*

Review

Begin the lesson with the "Old MacDonald Had a Farm" vowel exercise from Lesson 16.

Instructor: Let's practice the first fourteen lines of the poem. Let's say them together three times.

Together (three times):
>   **B** stands for /b/ in /b/, /b/, ***bat***.
>   **C** stands for /k/ in /k/, /k/, ***cat***.
>   **D** stands for /d/ in /d/, /d/, ***dog***.
>   **F** stands for /f/ in /f/, /f/, ***fog***.
>   **G** stands for /g/ in /g/, /g/, ***gum***.
>   **H** stands for /h/ in /h/, /h/, ***hum***.
>   **J** stands for /j/ in /j/, /j/, ***Jeep***.
>   **K** stands for /k/ in /k/, /k/, ***keep***.
>   **L** stands for /l/ in /l/, /l/, ***lap***.
>   **M** stands for /m/ in /m/, /m/, ***map***.
>   **N** stands for /n/ in /n/, /n/, ***net***.
>   **P** stands for /p/ in /p/, /p/, ***pet***.
>   **Qu** stands for /kw/ in /kw/, /kw/, ***quack***.
>   **R** stands for /r/ in /r/, /r/, ***rack***.

Instructor: Now I will show you the consonant cards from the previous lessons. I will say the sound the consonant represents and you will repeat that sound after me. Then I will ask you questions about the consonant sounds. You will answer me with a line from the poem.

Point to each consonant card, and ask the child, "For what sound does the letter *(insert consonant)* stand?"

New

Instructor: Today we are going to learn the consonant **s**. This is the big **S** and the little **s**:

S   s

Instructor: I will write the big **S** and the little **s** on a card for you.

Instructor: The letter **s** usually stands for the sound /s/. This is the sound that a snake makes: /s/. It is an unvoiced consonant sound because you do not use your voice to pronounce the sound. You just use air. I will point to the letter **s** card and say the consonant sound five times.

Instructor: /s/, /s/, /s/, /s/, /s/. Now we will say the sound together.

Together: /s/, /s/, /s/, /s/, /s/.

Instructor: I will say words that begin with the sound /s/: ***sip***, ***sad***, ***set***. Now repeat after me: /s/, /s/, ***sip***.

Child: */s/, /s/, sip.*

Instructor: /s/, /s/, ***sad***.

| Child: | /s/, /s/, sad. |

Instructor: Now I will say words that end with the sound /s/: **gas**, **bus**, **yes**. Now repeat after me: **bus.**

| Child: | bus. |

| Instructor: | **yes.** |

| Child: | yes. |

Instructor: Now I am going to teach you the fifteenth line of the poem "The Consonant Rhyme."

    S stands for /s/ in /s/, /s/, **sip.**

Instructor: I will say this to you three more times and then you will say the line by yourself.

| Child: | *S stands for /s/ in /s/, /s/, **sip.*** |

Instructor: Now let's say the line together three times.

Together (three times):
    S stands for /s/ in /s/, /s/, **sip.**

Instructor: Let's add that line to the lines you have already learned. Let's say them together three times.

Together (three times):
    B stands for /b/ in /b/, /b/, **bat.**
    C stands for /k/ in /k/, /k/, **cat.**
    D stands for /d/ in /d/, /d/, **dog.**
    F stands for /f/ in /f/, /f/, **fog.**
    G stands for /g/ in /g/, /g/, **gum.**
    H stands for /h/ in /h/, /h/, **hum.**
    J stands for /j/ in /j/, /j/, **Jeep.**
    K stands for /k/ in /k/, /k/, **keep.**
    L stands for /l/ in /l/, /l/, **lap.**
    M stands for /m/ in /m/, /m/, **map.**
    N stands for /n/ in /n/, /n/, **net.**
    P stands for /p/ in /p/, /p/, **pet.**
    Qu stands for /kw/ in /kw/, /kw/, **quack.**
    R stands for /r/ in /r/, /r/, **rack.**
    S stands for /s/ in /s/, /s/, **sip.**

Instructor: For what sound does the letter **s** stand?

| Child: | *S stands for /s/ in /s/, /s/, sip.* |

Follow-Up:
The child should repeat the **s** line from the poem two more times during the day. Point out the letter **s** to the child whenever you see it. Ask him to recite the line from this lesson to you.

Lesson 21: The Consonant T t

You will need the following: *the cards you used previously, a blank index card, and a pen.*

Review

Try this beginning exercise without using the vowel cards. If the child can't remember the names and sounds of the vowels, use the cards and review the poem "The Five Vowels" from Lesson 5.

Instructor: What are the *names* of the five vowels?

Child: ***a, e, i, o, u.***

Instructor: What are the short *sounds* for these five vowels?

Child: */ă/, /ĕ/, /ĭ/, /ŏ/, /ŭ/.*

Instructor: Let's practice the first fifteen lines of the poem "The Consonant Rhyme." Let's say them together three times.

Together (three times):
>   **B** stands for /b/ in /b/, /b/, ***bat.***
>   **C** stands for /k/ in /k/, /k/, ***cat.***
>   **D** stands for /d/ in /d/, /d/, ***dog.***
>   **F** stands for /f/ in /f/, /f/, ***fog.***
>   **G** stands for /g/ in /g/, /g/, ***gum.***
>   **H** stands for /h/ in /h/, /h/, ***hum.***
>   **J** stands for /j/ in /j/, /j/, ***Jeep.***
>   **K** stands for /k/ in /k/, /k/, ***keep.***
>   **L** stands for /l/ in /l/, /l/, ***lap.***
>   **M** stands for /m/ in /m/, /m/, ***map.***
>   **N** stands for /n/ in /n/, /n/, ***net.***
>   **P** stands for /p/ in /p/, /p/, ***pet.***
>   **Qu** stands for /kw/ in /kw/, /kw/, ***quack.***
>   **R** stands for /r/ in /r/, /r/, ***rack.***
>   **S** stands for /s/ in /s/, /s/, ***sip.***

Instructor: Now I will show you the consonant cards from the previous lessons. I will say the sound each consonant represents, and you will repeat that sound after me.

Instructor: I am going to ask you some questions about the sounds of the consonants. You will answer me with a line from the poem.

Point to each consonant card in order and ask the child, "For what sound does the letter *(insert consonant)* stand?"

New

Instructor: Today we are going to learn the consonant **t**. This is the big **T** and the little **t**:

T   t

Instructor:	I will write the big **T** and the little **t** on a card for you.
Instructor:	The letter **t** usually stands for the sound /t/. The sound /t/ is an unvoiced consonant sound because you do not use your voice to pronounce the sound. You just use air. I will point to the letter **t** card and say the consonant sound five times.
Instructor:	/t/, /t/, /t/, /t/, /t/. Now we will say the sound together.
Together:	/t/, /t/, /t/, /t/, /t/.
Instructor:	Listen as I say these words that begin with the sound /t/: *tip*, *tan*, *tug*. Now repeat after me: /t/, /t/, *tip.*
Child:	/t/, /t/, *tip.*
Instructor:	/t/, /t/, ***tug.***
Child:	/t/, /t/, *tug.*
Instructor:	Listen as I say these words that end with the sound /t/: ***hat***, ***yet***, ***lot***. Now repeat after me: ***hat.***
Child:	*hat.*
Instructor:	***yet.***
Child:	*yet.*
Instructor:	Now I am going to teach you the next line of the poem "The Consonant Rhyme." This is the sixteenth line:
	T stands for /t/ in /t/, /t/, ***tip***.
Instructor:	I will say this to you three more times.
Instructor:	Repeat after me: "**T** stands for /t/ in /t/, /t/, ***tip***."
Child:	***T*** *stands for /t/ in /t/, /t/, tip.*
Instructor:	Let's say that together three times.
Together (three times):	
	T stands for /t/ in /t/, /t/, ***tip***.
Instructor:	Let's add that line to the lines you have already learned. Let's say these lines together three times.

Together (three times):

> **B** stands for /b/ in /b/, /b/, **bat**.
> **C** stands for /k/ in /k/, /k/, **cat**.
> **D** stands for /d/ in /d/, /d/, **dog**.
> **F** stands for /f/ in /f/, /f/, **fog**.
> **G** stands for /g/ in /g/, /g/, **gum**.
> **H** stands for /h/ in /h/, /h/, **hum**.
> **J** stands for /j/ in /j/, /j/, **Jeep**.
> **K** stands for /k/ in /k/, /k/, **keep**.
> **L** stands for /l/ in /l/, /l/, **lap**.
> **M** stands for /m/ in /m/, /m/, **map**.
> **N** stands for /n/ in /n/, /n/, **net**.
> **P** stands for /p/ in /p/, /p/, **pet**.
> **Qu** stands for /kw/ in /kw/, /kw/, **quack**.
> **R** stands for /r/ in /r/, /r/, **rack**.
> **S** stands for /s/ in /s/, /s/, **sip**.
> **T** stands for /t/ in /t/, /t/, **tip**.

Instructor: For what sound does the letter **t** stand?

Child: ***T*** *stands for /t/ in /t/, /t/, tip.*

Game: Consonant Pick-Up

Place the following four consonant cards on the table: **Qu qu**, **R r**, **S s**, and **T t**. Say the sound that one of the letters represents and ask the child to pick up the correct consonant card. If the child picks the right card, he gets the card; if he doesn't, the instructor gets the card. Once you have gone through all four cards, have the child practice the cards he missed. Then shuffle all the cards and begin the game again. Once the child shows mastery, add the vowel cards and the other consonant cards and play the game with all the cards.

Follow-Up:

The child should repeat the **t** line from the poem two more times during the day. Point out the letter **t** to the child whenever you see it (on signs, on food boxes or cans, in books you read aloud to him, etc...). Ask him to recite the line from this lesson to you.

Reminder:

Once again, I encourage you to spend as many days as necessary on each lesson until you feel the child has mastered the letter and the sound.

Lesson 22:   The Consonant V v

You will need the following: *the cards you used previously, a blank index card, and a pen.*

___

Review

Try this beginning exercise without using the vowel cards. If the child can't remember the names and sounds of the vowels, use the cards and review the poem "The Five Vowels" from Lesson 5.

Instructor: What are the *names* of the five vowels?

Child: **a, e, i, o, u.**

Instructor: What are the short *sounds* for these five vowels?

Child: /ă/, /ĕ/, /ĭ/, /ŏ/, /ŭ/.

Instructor: Let's practice the first sixteen lines of the poem "The Consonant Rhyme." Let's say them together three times.

Together (three times):
>**B** stands for /b/ in /b/, /b/, **bat**.
>**C** stands for /k/ in /k/, /k/, **cat**.
>**D** stands for /d/ in /d/, /d/, **dog**.
>**F** stands for /f/ in /f/, /f/, **fog**.
>**G** stands for /g/ in /g/, /g/, **gum**.
>**H** stands for /h/ in /h/, /h/, **hum**.
>**J** stands for /j/ in /j/, /j/, **Jeep**.
>**K** stands for /k/ in /k/, /k/, **keep**.
>**L** stands for /l/ in /l/, /l/, **lap**.
>**M** stands for /m/ in /m/, /m/, **map**.
>**N** stands for /n/ in /n/, /n/, **net**.
>**P** stands for /p/ in /p/, /p/, **pet**.
>**Qu** stands for /kw/ in /kw/, /kw/, **quack**.
>**R** stands for /r/ in /r/, /r/, **rack**.
>**S** stands for /s/ in /s/, /s/, **sip**.
>**T** stands for /t/ in /t/, /t/, **tip**.

Instructor: Now I will show you the consonant cards from the previous lessons. I will say the sound each consonant represents, and you will repeat that sound after me.

Instructor: I am going to ask you some questions about the sounds of the consonants. You will answer me with a line from the poem.

Point to each consonant card in order and ask the child, "For what sound does the letter *(insert consonant)* stand?"

Instructor: Today we are going to learn the consonant **v**. This is the big **V** and the little **v**:

V v

Instructor: I will write the big **V** and the little **v** on a card for you.

Instructor: The letter **v** stands for the sound /v/. The sound /v/ is a voiced consonant sound because you use your voice to pronounce the sound. I will point to the letter **v** card and say the consonant sound five times.

Do not say /vuh/. Let your front teeth rest lightly on your bottom lip as you make a voice sound. The vibration may tickle your lip: /v/.

Instructor: /v/, /v/, /v/, /v/, /v/. Now we will say the sound together.

Together: /v/, /v/, /v/, /v/, /v/.

Instructor: Listen as I say these words that begin with the sound /v/: **vet, van**. Now repeat after me: /v/, /v/, **vet.**

Child: /v/, /v/, vet.

Instructor: /v/, /v/, **van.**

Child: /v/, /v/, van.

Most words that end with the letter **v** are followed by an **e** that is not pronounced (the **e** is silent).

Instructor: Listen as I say these words that end with the sound /v/: **give, have, five**. Now repeat after me: **give**.

Child: give.

Instructor: **five.**

Child: five.

Instructor: Now I am going to teach you the next line of the poem "The Consonant Rhyme." This is the seventeenth line:

                V stands for /v/ in /v/, /v/, **vet.**

Instructor: I will say this to you three more times.

Instructor: Repeat after me: "**V** stands for /v/ in /v/, /v/, **vet.**"

Child: **V** *stands for /v/ in /v/, /v/, vet.*

Instructor: Let's say that together three times.

Together (three times):
                V stands for /v/ in /v/, /v/, **vet.**

Instructor: Let's add that line to the lines you have already learned. Let's say these lines together three times.

Together (three times):

        B stands for /b/ in /b/, /b/, *bat*.
        C stands for /k/ in /k/, /k/, *cat*.
        D stands for /d/ in /d/, /d/, *dog*.
        F stands for /f/ in /f/, /f/, *fog*.
        G stands for /g/ in /g/, /g/, *gum*.
        H stands for /h/ in /h/, /h/, *hum*.
        J stands for /j/ in /j/, /j/, *Jeep*.
        K stands for /k/ in /k/, /k/, *keep*.
        L stands for /l/ in /l/, /l/, *lap*.
        M stands for /m/ in /m/, /m/, *map*.
        N stands for /n/ in /n/, /n/, *net*.
        P stands for /p/ in /p/, /p/, *pet*.
        Qu stands for /kw/ in /kw/, /kw/, *quack*.
        R stands for /r/ in /r/, /r/, *rack*.
        S stands for /s/ in /s/, /s/, *sip*.
        T stands for /t/ in /t/, /t/, *tip*.
        V stands for /v/ in /v/, /v/, *vet*.

Instructor: For what sound does the letter **v** stand?

Child: ***V** stands for /v/ in /v/, /v/, vet.*

Game: Vowel Pick-Up

Place the vowel cards on the table. Say the short sound of one of the vowels and ask the child to pick up the correct vowel card. If the child picks the right card, he gets the card; if he doesn't, the instructor gets the card. Once you have gone through all five cards, have the child practice the cards he missed. Then shuffle all the cards and begin the game again.

Follow-Up:

The child should repeat the **v** line from the poem two more times during the day. Point out the letter **v** to the child whenever you see it (on signs, on food boxes or cans, in books you read aloud to him, etc…). Ask him to recite the line from this lesson to you.

Lesson 23:   The Consonant W w

You will need the following: *the cards you used previously, a blank index card, and a pen.*

Review

Instructor: What are the *names* of the five vowels?

Child: **a, e, i, o, u.**

Instructor: What are the short *sounds* for these five vowels?

Child: /ă/, /ĕ/, /ĭ/, /ŏ/, /ŭ/.

Instructor: Let's practice the first seventeen lines of the poem "The Consonant Rhyme." Let's say them together three times.

Together (three times):
>   **B** stands for /b/ in /b/, /b/, **bat.**
>   **C** stands for /k/ in /k/, /k/, **cat.**
>   **D** stands for /d/ in /d/, /d/, **dog.**
>   **F** stands for /f/ in /f/, /f/, **fog.**
>   **G** stands for /g/ in /g/, /g/, **gum.**
>   **H** stands for /h/ in /h/, /h/, **hum.**
>   **J** stands for /j/ in /j/, /j/, **Jeep.**
>   **K** stands for /k/ in /k/, /k/, **keep.**
>   **L** stands for /l/ in /l/, /l/, **lap.**
>   **M** stands for /m/ in /m/, /m/, **map.**
>   **N** stands for /n/ in /n/, /n/, **net.**
>   **P** stands for /p/ in /p/, /p/, **pet.**
>   **Qu** stands for /kw/ in /kw/, /kw/, **quack.**
>   **R** stands for /r/ in /r/, /r/, **rack.**
>   **S** stands for /s/ in /s/, /s/, **sip.**
>   **T** stands for /t/ in /t/, /t/, **tip.**
>   **V** stands for /v/ in /v/, /v/, **vet.**

Instructor: Now I will show you the consonant cards from the previous lessons. I will say the sound each consonant represents, and you will repeat the sound after me.

Instructor: I am going to ask you some questions about the sounds of the consonants. You will answer me with a line from the poem.

Point to each consonant card in order, and ask the child, "For what sound does the letter *(insert consonant)* stand?"

Instructor: Today we are going to learn the letter **w** as a *consonant.* This is the big **W** and the little **w**:

W w

Instructor: I will write the big **W** and the little **w** on a card for you.

Instructor: The letter **w** usually stands for the sound /w/. The sound /w/ is a voiced consonant sound because you use your voice to pronounce the sound. I will point to the letter **w** card and say the consonant sound five times.

Do not say /wuh/. Purse your lips (almost like you are going to whistle), but instead of blowing air to whistle, make a voice sound and then un-purse your lips: /w/.

Instructor: /w/, /w/, /w/, /w/, /w/. Now we will say the sound together.

Together: /w/, /w/, /w/, /w/, /w/.

Instructor: Listen as I say these words that begin with the sound /w/: *wet, was, won.* Now repeat after me: /w/, /w/, **wet.**

Child: /w/, /w/, wet.

Instructor: /w/, /w/, **was.**

Child: /w/, /w/, was.

There are no words that end with the consonant **w**. In words like *jaw* and *few*, **w** is part of a vowel pair and does not stand for the sound /w/.

Instructor: Now I am going to teach you the next line of the poem "The Consonant Rhyme." This is the eighteenth line:

  W stands for /w/ in /w/, /w/, **wet.**

Instructor: I will say this to you three more times.

Instructor: Repeat after me: "**W** stands for /w/ in /w/, /w/, **wet.**"

Child: **W** *stands for /w/ in /w/, /w/, wet.*

Instructor: Let's say that together three times.

Together (three times):
  W stands for /w/ in /w/, /w/, **wet.**

Instructor: Let's add that line to the lines you have already learned. Let's say these lines together three times.

Together (three times):

        B stands for /b/ in /b/, /b/, ***bat***.
        C stands for /k/ in /k/, /k/, ***cat***.
        D stands for /d/ in /d/, /d/, ***dog***.
        F stands for /f/ in /f/, /f/, ***fog***.
        G stands for /g/ in /g/, /g/, ***gum***.
        H stands for /h/ in /h/, /h/, ***hum***.
        J stands for /j/ in /j/, /j/, ***Jeep***.
        K stands for /k/ in /k/, /k/, ***keep***.
        L stands for /l/ in /l/, /l/, ***lap***.
        M stands for /m/ in /m/, /m/, ***map***.
        N stands for /n/ in /n/, /n/, ***net***.
        P stands for /p/ in /p/, /p/, ***pet***.
        Qu stands for /kw/ in /kw/, /kw/, ***quack***.
        R stands for /r/ in /r/, /r/, ***rack***.
        S stands for /s/ in /s/, /s/, ***sip***.
        T stands for /t/ in /t/, /t/, ***tip***.
        V stands for /v/ in /v/, /v/, ***vet***.
        W stands for /w/ in /w/, /w/, ***wet***.

Instructor: For what sound does the letter **w** stand?

Child: ***W*** *stands for /w/ in /w/, /w/, wet.*

Follow-Up:
The child should repeat the **w** line from the poem two more times during the day. Point out the letter **w** to the child whenever you see it (on signs, on food boxes or cans, in books you read aloud to him, etc...). Ask him to recite the line from this lesson to you.

Lesson 24: The Consonant X x

You will need the following: *the cards you used previously, a blank index card, and a pen.*

Review

Instructor: What are the *names* of the five vowels?

Child: **a, e, i, o, u.**

Instructor: What are the short *sounds* for these five vowels?

Child: /ă/, /ĕ/, /ĭ/, /ŏ/, /ŭ/.

Instructor: Let's practice the first eighteen lines of the poem "The Consonant Rhyme." Let's say them together three times.

Together (three times):
> **B** stands for /b/ in /b/, /b/, **bat**.
> **C** stands for /k/ in /k/, /k/, **cat**.
> **D** stands for /d/ in /d/, /d/, **dog**.
> **F** stands for /f/ in /f/, /f/, **fog**.
> **G** stands for /g/ in /g/, /g/, **gum**.
> **H** stands for /h/ in /h/, /h/, **hum**.
> **J** stands for /j/ in /j/, /j/, **Jeep**.
> **K** stands for /k/ in /k/, /k/, **keep**.
> **L** stands for /l/ in /l/, /l/, **lap**.
> **M** stands for /m/ in /m/, /m/, **map**.
> **N** stands for /n/ in /n/, /n/, **net**.
> **P** stands for /p/ in /p/, /p/, **pet**.
> **Qu** stands for /kw/ in /kw/, /kw/, **quack**.
> **R** stands for /r/ in /r/, /r/, **rack**.
> **S** stands for /s/ in /s/, /s/, **sip**.
> **T** stands for /t/ in /t/, /t/, **tip**.
> **V** stands for /v/ in /v/, /v/, **vet**.
> **W** stands for /w/ in /w/, /w/, **wet**.

Instructor: Now I will show you the consonant cards from the previous lessons. I will say the sound each consonant represents, and you will repeat that sound after me.

Instructor: I am going to ask you some questions about the sounds of the consonants. You will answer me with a line from the poem.

Point to each consonant card in order, and ask the child, "For what sound does the letter *(insert consonant)* stand?"

Instructor: Today we are going to learn the consonant **x**. This is the big **X** and the little **x**:

X   x

Instructor: I will write the big **X** and the little **x** on a card for you.

Instructor: The letter **x** usually stands for the sound /ks/. The sound /ks/ is an unvoiced consonant sound because you do not use your voice to pronounce the sound. You just use air. I will point to the letter **x** card and say the consonant sound five times.

The sound of the letter x, /ks/, is not pronounced like the name of the letter x. You do not use your voice to produce the sound /ks/.

Instructor: /ks/, /ks/, /ks/, /ks/, /ks/. Now we will say the sound together.

Together: /ks/, /ks/, /ks/, /ks/, /ks/.

Although the word **x-ray** begins with the letter x, it is the name of the letter and not the sound /ks/. There are no words that begin with the sound /ks/.

Instructor: Listen as I say these words that end with the sound /ks/: **box**, **tax**, **fox**. Now repeat after me: **box**.

Child: *box.*

Instructor: **tax.**

Child: *tax.*

Instructor: **fox.**

Child: *fox.*

Instructor: Now I am going to teach you the next two lines of the poem "The Consonant Rhyme." The letter **x** gets two lines to itself:

> **X** at the end of a word like **box**
> Stands for /ks/ like in **tax** and **fox**.

Instructor: I will say this to you three more times.

Instructor: Repeat after me: "**X** at the end of word like **box**"

Child: ***X** at the end of a word like box*

Instructor: Stands for /ks/ like in **tax** and **fox**.

Child: *Stands for /ks/ like in tax and fox.*

Instructor: Let's say both lines together three times.

Together (three times):

> **X** at the end of word like ***box***
> Stands for /ks/ like in ***tax*** and ***fox***.

Instructor: Let's add that line to the lines you have already learned. Let's say these lines together three times.

Together (three times):

> **B** stands for /b/ in /b/, /b/, ***bat***.
> **C** stands for /k/ in /k/, /k/, ***cat***.
> **D** stands for /d/ in /d/, /d/, ***dog***.
> **F** stands for /f/ in /f/, /f/, ***fog***.
> **G** stands for /g/ in /g/, /g/, ***gum***.
> **H** stands for /h/ in /h/, /h/, ***hum***.
> **J** stands for /j/ in /j/, /j/, ***Jeep***.
> **K** stands for /k/ in /k/, /k/, ***keep***.
> **L** stands for /l/ in /l/, /l/, ***lap***.
> **M** stands for /m/ in /m/, /m/, ***map***.
> **N** stands for /n/ in /n/, /n/, ***net***.
> **P** stands for /p/ in /p/, /p/, ***pet***.
> **Qu** stands for /kw/ in /kw/, /kw/, ***quack***.
> **R** stands for /r/ in /r/, /r/, ***rack***.
> **S** stands for /s/ in /s/, /s/, ***sip***.
> **T** stands for /t/ in /t/, /t/, ***tip***.
> **V** stands for /v/ in /v/, /v/, ***vet***.
> **W** stands for /w/ in /w/, /w/, ***wet***.
> **X** at the end of word like ***box***
> Stands for /ks/ like in ***tax*** and ***fox***.

Instructor: For what sound does the letter **x** stand? Answer me with the two lines of the poem you learned this lesson.

Child: *X at the end of word like box*
Stands for /ks/ like in tax and fox.

Game: Vowel Pick-Up

Place the five vowel cards on the table. Say the short sound of one of the vowels and ask the child to pick up the correct vowel card. If the child picks the right card, he gets the card; if he doesn't, the instructor gets the card. Once you have gone through all the cards, have the child practice the cards he missed. Then shuffle all the cards and begin the game again.

Follow-Up:

The child should repeat the **x** lines from the poem two more times during the day. Point out the letter **x** to the child whenever you see it (on signs, on food boxes or cans, in books you read aloud to him, etc...). Ask him to recite the line from this lesson to you.

Lesson 25: The Consonant Y y

You will need the following: *the cards you used previously, a blank index card, and a pen.*

Review

Instructor: What are the *names* of the five vowels?

Child: **a, e, i, o, u**.

Instructor: What are the short *sounds* for these five vowels?

Child: /ă/, /ĕ/, /ĭ/, /ŏ/, /ŭ/.

Instructor: Let's practice the first twenty lines of the poem "The Consonant Rhyme." Let's say them together three times.

Together (three times):
    B stands for /b/ in /b/, /b/, ***bat***.
    C stands for /k/ in /k/, /k/, ***cat***.
    D stands for /d/ in /d/, /d/, ***dog***.
    F stands for /f/ in /f/, /f/, ***fog***.
    G stands for /g/ in /g/, /g/, ***gum***.
    H stands for /h/ in /h/, /h/, ***hum***.
    J stands for /j/ in /j/, /j/, ***Jeep***.
    K stands for /k/ in /k/, /k/, ***keep***.
    L stands for /l/ in /l/, /l/, ***lap***.
    M stands for /m/ in /m/, /m/, ***map***.
    N stands for /n/ in /n/, /n/, ***net***.
    P stands for /p/ in /p/, /p/, ***pet***.
    Qu stands for /kw/ in /kw/, /kw/, ***quack***.
    R stands for /r/ in /r/, /r/, ***rack***.
    S stands for /s/ in /s/, /s/, ***sip***.
    T stands for /t/ in /t/, /t/, ***tip***.
    V stands for /v/ in /v/, /v/, ***vet***.
    W stands for /w/ in /w/, /w/, ***wet***.
    X at the end of word like ***box***
    Stands for /ks/ like in ***tax*** and ***fox***.

Instructor: Now I will show you the consonant cards from the previous lessons. I will say the sound of each consonant and you will repeat that sound after me.

Instructor: I am going to ask you some questions about the sounds of the consonants. You will answer me with a line from the poem.

Point to each consonant card in order, and ask the child, "For what sound does the letter *(insert consonant)* stand?"

Instructor: Today we are going to learn about the letter **y** as a *consonant*. This is the big **Y** and the little **y**:

Y y

Instructor: I will write the big **Y** and the little **y** on a card for you.

Instructor: The consonant letter **y** stands for the sound /y/ in *yes*. The sound /y/ is a voiced consonant sound because you use your voice to pronounce the sound. I will point to the letter **y** card and say the consonant sound five times.

Instructor: /y/, /y/, /y/, /y/, /y/. Now we will say the sound together.

Together: /y/, /y/, /y/, /y/, /y/.

Instructor: Listen as I say these words that begin with the sound /y/: *yip*, *yes*, *yet*. Now repeat after me: /y/, /y/, **yip.**

Child: */y/, /y/, yip.*

Instructor: /y/, /y/, **yes.**

Child: */y/, /y/, yes.*

Words that end in the letter **y** are words in which **y** acts as a vowel: **by**, **toy**, **key**. This will be discussed in later lessons and not taught at this time.

Instructor: Now I am going to teach you the next line of the poem "The Consonant Rhyme."

      Y stands for /y/ in /y/, /y/, **yip.**

Instructor: I will say this to you three more times.

Instructor: Repeat after me: "**Y** stands for /y/ in /y/, /y/, **yip.**"

Child: **Y** *stands for /y/ in /y/, /y/,* **yip.**

Instructor: Let's say that together three times.

Together (three times):
      Y stands for /y/ in /y/, /y/, **yip.**

Instructor: Let's add that line to the lines you have already learned. Let's say these lines together three times.

Together (three times):

> **B** stands for /b/ in /b/, /b/, ***bat***.
> **C** stands for /k/ in /k/, /k/, ***cat***.
> **D** stands for /d/ in /d/, /d/, ***dog***.
> **F** stands for /f/ in /f/, /f/, ***fog***.
> **G** stands for /g/ in /g/, /g/, ***gum***.
> **H** stands for /h/ in /h/, /h/, ***hum***.
> **J** stands for /j/ in /j/, /j/, ***Jeep***.
> **K** stands for /k/ in /k/, /k/, ***keep***.
> **L** stands for /l/ in /l/, /l/, ***lap***.
> **M** stands for /m/ in /m/, /m/, ***map***.
> **N** stands for /n/ in /n/, /n/, ***net***.
> **P** stands for /p/ in /p/, /p/, ***pet***.
> **Qu** stands for /kw/ in /kw/, /kw/, ***quack***.
> **R** stands for /r/ in /r/, /r/, ***rack***.
> **S** stands for /s/ in /s/, /s/, ***sip***.
> **T** stands for /t/ in /t/, /t/, ***tip***.
> **V** stands for /v/ in /v/, /v/, ***vet***.
> **W** stands for /w/ in /w/, /w/, ***wet***.
> **X** at the end of word like ***box***
> Stands for /ks/ like in ***tax*** and ***fox***.
> **Y** stands for /y/ in /y/, /y/, ***yip***.

Instructor: For what sound does the letter **y** stand?

Child: **Y** *stands for /y/ in /y/, /y/, yip.*

Follow-Up:
The child should repeat the **y** line from the poem two more times during the day. Point out the letter **y** to the child whenever you see it (on signs, on food boxes or cans, in books you read aloud to him, etc…). Ask him to recite the line from this lesson to you.

Lesson 26: The Consonant Z z

You will need the following: *the cards you used previously, a blank index card, and a pen.*

Review

Instructor: What are the *names* of the five vowels?

Child: **a, e, i, o, u**.

Instructor: What are the short *sounds* for these five vowels?

Child: /ă/, /ĕ/, /ĭ/, /ŏ/, /ŭ/.

Instructor: Let's practice the first twenty-one lines of the poem "The Consonant Rhyme." Let's say them together three times.

Together (three times):
   B stands for /b/ in /b/, /b/, **bat**.
   C stands for /k/ in /k/, /k/, **cat**.
   D stands for /d/ in /d/, /d/, **dog**.
   F stands for /f/ in /f/, /f/, **fog**.
   G stands for /g/ in /g/, /g/, **gum**.
   H stands for /h/ in /h/, /h/, **hum**.
   J stands for /j/ in /j/, /j/, **Jeep**.
   K stands for /k/ in /k/, /k/, **keep**.
   L stands for /l/ in /l/, /l/, **lap**.
   M stands for /m/ in /m/, /m/, **map**.
   N stands for /n/ in /n/, /n/, **net**.
   P stands for /p/ in /p/, /p/, **pet**.
   Qu stands for /kw/ in /kw/, /kw/, **quack**.
   R stands for /r/ in /r/, /r/, **rack**.
   S stands for /s/ in /s/, /s/, **sip**.
   T stands for /t/ in /t/, /t/, **tip**.
   V stands for /v/ in /v/, /v/, **vet**.
   W stands for /w/ in /w/, /w/, **wet**.
   X at the end of word like **box**
   Stands for /ks/ like in **tax** and **fox**.
   Y stands for /y/ in /y/, /y/, **yip**.

Instructor: Now I will show you the consonant cards from the previous lessons. I will say the sound each consonant represents, and you will repeat that sound after me.

Instructor: I am going to ask you some questions about the sounds of the consonants. You will answer me with a line from the poem.

Point to each consonant card in order, and ask the child, "For what sound does the letter *(insert consonant)* represent?"

Instructor: Today we are going to learn the consonant **z**. **Z** is the final letter in the alphabet. This is the big **Z** and the little **z**:

Z z

Instructor: I will write the big **Z** and the little **z** on a card for you.

Instructor: The letter **z** stands for the sound /z/. The sound /z/ is a voiced consonant sound because you use your voice to pronounce the sound. I will point to the letter **z** card and say the consonant sound five times.

Do not say /zuh/. Put your teeth together and make a vibrating voice sound as you buzz like a bee: /z/.

Instructor: /z/, /z/, /z/, /z/, /z/. Now we will say the sound together.

Together: /z/, /z/, /z/, /z/, /z/.

Instructor: Listen as I say these words that begin with the sound /z/: *zip, zap*. Now repeat after me: /z/, /z/, *zip*.

Child: /z/, /z/, *zip*.

Instructor: /z/, /z/, *zap*.

Child: /z/, /z/, *zap*.

Instructor: Listen as I say these words that end with the sound /z/: *fizz, buzz, jazz*. Now repeat after me: *fizz*.

Child: *fizz*.

Instructor: *buzz*.

Child: *buzz*.

Instructor: Now I am going to teach you the final line of "The Consonant Rhyme."

Z stands for /z/ in /z/, /z/, *zip*.

Instructor: I will say this to you three more times.

Instructor: Repeat after me: "**Z** stands for /z/ in /z/, /z/, *zip*."

Child: *Z stands for /z/ in /z/, /z/, zip*.

Instructor: Let's say that together three times.

Together (three times):
   Z stands for /z/ in /z/, /z/, *zip*.

Instructor: Let's add that line to the lines you have already learned. You can now say the entire poem. Let's say the "The Consonant Rhyme" together three times.

Together (three times):

B stands for /b/ in /b/, /b/, **bat**.
C stands for /k/ in /k/, /k/, **cat**.
D stands for /d/ in /d/, /d/, **dog**.
F stands for /f/ in /f/, /f/, **fog**.
G stands for /g/ in /g/, /g/, **gum**.
H stands for /h/ in /h/, /h/, **hum**.
J stands for /j/ in /j/, /j/, **Jeep**.
K stands for /k/ in /k/, /k/, **keep**.
L stands for /l/ in /l/, /l/, **lap**.
M stands for /m/ in /m/, /m/, **map**.
N stands for /n/ in /n/, /n/, **net**.
P stands for /p/ in /p/, /p/, **pet**.
Qu stands for /kw/ in /kw/, /kw/, **quack**.
R stands for /r/ in /r/, /r/, **rack**.
S stands for /s/ in /s/, /s/, **sip**.
T stands for /t/ in /t/, /t/, **tip**.
V stands for /v/ in /v/, /v/, **vet**.
W stands for /w/ in /w/, /w/, **wet**.
X at the end of word like **box**
Stands for /ks/ like in **tax** and **fox**.
Y stands for /y/ in /y/, /y/, **yip**.
Z stands for /z/ in /z/, /z/, **zip**.

Instructor: For what sound does the letter **z** stand?

Child: **Z** *stands for /z/ in /z/, /z/, zip.*

Game: Consonant Pick-Up
Place the following five consonant cards on the table: **V v**, **W w**, **X x**, **Y y**, and **Z z**. Say the sound that one of the letters represents and ask the child to pick up the correct consonant card. If the child picks the right card, he gets the card; if he doesn't, the instructor gets the card. Once you have gone through all five cards, have the child practice the cards he missed. Then shuffle all the cards and begin the game again. Once the child shows mastery, add the vowel cards and the other consonant cards and play the game with all the cards.

Follow-Up:
The child should repeat the **z** line from the poem two more times during the day. Point out the letter **z** to the child whenever you see it (on signs, on food boxes or cans, in books you read aloud to him, etc...). Ask him to recite the line from this lesson to you.

Section 3

SHORT-VOWEL WORDS

About Sight Words:

I am philosophically in favor of a pure phonics program, but to encourage the child that he is reading real and meaningful sentences, and to make content more interesting, *I have included a few common words that either do not follow regular phonetic patterns or they follow patterns that will be introduced later in the book.* These "sight words" (which should be memorized) are introduced just before they are used in real sentences. Each time your child learns a new sight word, write it on an index card and save it in your collection of sight word cards (these sight wordd cards are in the cards available for purchase).

Lesson 27: Words with the Short-A Vowel Sound

You will need the following: *the consonant cards* **T t**, **M m**, **N n**, *and* **D d** *as well as the five vowel cards for this lesson. If you do the optional activity at the end of this lesson, you will need the magnetic alphabet board.*

Review

Instructor: Point to each of the vowel cards and say the *name* of each vowel: **a, e, i, o, u**. Now point to each vowel card again and say the *short-vowel sound* of each vowel: /ă/ /ĕ/ /ĭ/ /ŏ/ /ŭ/. Now we will turn these cards over so you can say these short-vowel sounds from memory.

Instructor: I am going to show you four consonant cards and review their sounds with you.

Point to the following consonant cards: **T t**, **N n**, **M m**, and **D d**. Ask the child to say the sound for which the letter stands. If the child has difficulty remembering a letter sound, repeat that specific verse of "The Consonant Rhyme" (see Lesson 26) as a review.

New

Instructor: Now you are going to start reading. The words I am going to show you all begin with the short-vowel sound of the letter **a**: /ă/. I am going to read you the first word. First I will look at the beginning letter and say the sound for which it stands. Then I will look at the next letter and the say the sound for which that letter stands. This is called "sounding out" a word.

Begin by reading the word **at** using the following technique: Cover the **t** with your index finger so the child only sees the first letter, **a**. Say the /ă/ sound, then uncover the **t** as you pronounce the /t/ sound. Do not separate the letter sounds but sustain your voice to blend the sounds seamlessly into the word **at**.

at

Instructor: Let's read this word together. We do not stop our voice between letters. We blend, or combine, the sounds together to say a word.

The lesson continues on the following page.

As you did before, use your finger to reveal the letters as you and the child say their sounds together. Remember to sustain your voice!

at

Instructor: Now you are going to read this word on your own. I will use my finger as a guide to help you.

Have the child sound out the word on his own, but continue to use your finger to reveal the letters. If the child resists your finger being over the word, stand firm! The purpose of this exercise is to make the child habitually read from left to right. I think many children are misdiagnosed as having dyslexia, when the problem is that their eyes have not been trained to move from left to right. So continue to use your finger to guide the child's eye movement from left to right until you are absolutely sure he is not reading anything backwards or just memorizing whole words.

at

Instructor: Now we are going to read some more words that start with the short-vowel sound of **a**: the sound /ă/.

Repeat the procedure you used for *at* with each of the remaining words: *am*, *an*, and *ad*. First, you read the word, then you and the child read the word together, then the child reads the word alone. Remember to sustain your voice and use your finger to reveal the letters each time.

am   an   ad

Instructor: Next lesson we are going to add a letter before the word *at* to make a new word. Then you will be reading three-letter words!

Optional Follow-Up:
Have the magnetic letters **a**, **t**, **n**, and **m** on hand. Give the child the necessary letters to form the first word in this lesson (in this case, *at*). Ask the child to sound out the word as he places the letters that you give him on the magnetic alphabet board. Do this for all of the words from this lesson.

Lesson 28: Words with the Short-A Vowel Sound

You will need the following: *the consonant cards P p, C c, S s, B b, R r, H h, V v, and F f. If you do the optional activity at the end of this lesson, you will need the magnetic alphabet board.*

Review

Instructor: I am going to show you seven consonant cards and review their sounds with you.

Point to the following consonant cards: **P p, C c, S s, B b, R r, H h, V v,** and **F f**. Ask the child to say the sound for which the letter stands. If the child has difficulty remembering a letter sound, repeat that specific verse of "The Consonant Rhyme" (see Lesson 26) as a review.

Instructor: Last lesson you read the words *at*, *ad*, *an*, and *am*. Read these words again with me.

Sound out the words with the child, and use your finger as a guide.

at   ad   an   am

New

Instructor: Now we are going to read words that do not begin with the letter **a**. I will read each word first. These words all contain the short-vowel sound of the letter **a**: the sound /ă/. First I will read each word. Then we will read that same word together. Then you will read that word by yourself.

Read the following list of words one at a time, *going across to train the child's eyes to read from left to right*. Use a folded sheet of plain paper to cover the line below the one you and the child are reading. This is to prevent the possibility of the child's eyes wandering down rather than moving habitually through a line.

Again, use your finger to uncover letters as the child says each letter sound. In the beginning the child will be saying each letter sound separately. Quickly begin teaching the child not to stop between sounds but to sustain the voice in order to blend the sounds seamlessly into a word. Assist the child as necessary until he gains confidence.

pat   fat   sat   bat

rat   cat   hat   mat

Optional Follow-Up:
Have the magnetic letters **a, t, m, p, c, s, b, r, h,** and **f** on hand. Give the child the necessary letters to form the first new word in this lesson (in this case, *pat*). Ask the child to sound out the word as he places the letters that you give him on the magnetic alphabet board. Do this for all of the new words from this lesson.

Lesson 29: Words with the Short-A Vowel Sound
Sight Word: the

You will need the following: *a blank index card and a pen. You will need the magnetic alphabet board if you do the optional activity at the end of the lesson.*

Review

Instructor: Let's review the words you have read the past two lessons. Read these words to me.

Use your finger to uncover letters as the child says each letter sound. Remind the child to sustain his voice and blend the sounds together. Assist the child as necessary to read the words. I suggest placing a sheet of plain, folded paper to cover the line below the one you and the child are reading.

am	an	ad	at
rat	pat	sat	cat
fat	mat	bat	hat

Instructor: Read the following word again as a review.

an

New

Instructor: Now you are going to read a list of words that all start with different letters. These words all contain the letter **a** that stands for the short-**a** vowel sound: /ă/. First I will read each word. Then we will read that same word together. Then you will read that word by yourself.

man	fan	ban	ran
can	van	tan	

Instructor: Now let's read some words that begin with big letters. The first word in a sentence and the names of people always begin with a big letter. First I will read each word. Then we will read that same word together. Then you will read that word by yourself.

Pat	Dan	Fan	Nan

Instructor: The best way to learn to read is to sound out words letter-sound by letter-sound. However, there are a few words that you will need to memorize. You will learn one of those words right now.

Although the rule is that the word *the* is pronounced /thuh/ before words beginning with consonants and /thee/ before words beginning with vowels, teach the child to say /thee/ in beginning reading. The child will pick up the standard pronunciations as you read to him and talk to him.

Instructor: The word is *the*. You do not yet know how to sound out this word, so we will just memorize the word. The word *the* is written with a big **T** when it is the first word in a sentence.

The

Instructor: The word *the* is written with a little **t** when it is inside a sentence.

the

Instructor: I will write **The** and **the** on a card for you.

Point to the card. Tell the child the word, and then turn the card over. The child should pick up the card, read the word, and turn the card over again. The child should do this three times. This will be the first card in the stack of sight word cards. Keep this card with your reading materials.

Instructor: Now you are ready to read real sentences. We are going to use the word you just learned, *the*, in the following story. Each sentence ends with a mark of punctuation. Punctuation marks help make clear the meaning of what is written. The sentences in this story all end with a type of punctuation mark called a *period*. A period is like a stop sign at the end of a sentence. When you see a period, you stop. I will point out the period when you get to the end of each sentence.

The child will begin to read the sentences below. Assist him as necessary. With the exception of the sight word *the*, cover the words in the following sentences with your finger and reveal the letters one at a time. Continue to use your finger to guide the child's eye movement from left to right until you are absolutely sure he is not reading anything backwards. As the child progresses in his reading, he may use own finger to keep his place. He will stop this practice on his own when he no longer needs the crutch. At any time if the child is having trouble staying on a line, place a folded piece of paper under the line he is reading. Point out the period at the end of each line. Remind the child that the period is like a stop sign—you stop when you see it.

Pat the fat cat.

Nan can pat the fat cat.

Nan can fan the tan cat.

Optional Follow-Up:
Give the child the necessary letters to form the first new word in this lesson. Ask the child to sound out the word as he places the letters that you give him on the magnetic alphabet board. Do this for all of the new words from this lesson. As the child gains confidence in placing letters to make individual words, you may wish to give him letters, one word at a time, to form sentences from the lesson.

Lesson 30: Words with the Short-A Vowel Sound

You will need the following: *the magnetic alphabet board if you do the optional activity at the end of this lesson.*

Review

Instructor: Read this word for me. This is the word that you memorized; you do not sound it out.

the

Instructor: Now do sound out this word for me. You have already read it before.

ad

New

Instructor: Now we are going to read words that have another letter before the **a**. I will read each word first. Then we will read it together. Then you will read that same word by yourself. I will place a folded piece of paper under each row to help you keep your place.

pad	had	mad	dad
sad	bad	Tad	

Instructor: Now we are going to read a story that contains words you have read.

The child will begin to read the sentences below. Assist him as necessary. Continue to use your finger to guide the child's eye movement from left to right until you are absolutely sure he is not reading anything backwards. As the child progresses in his reading, he may use own finger to keep his place. He will stop this practice on his own when he no longer needs the crutch. At any time if the child is having trouble staying on a line, place a folded piece of paper under the line he is reading.

Dan can bat.
Dan ran.
Dad can bat.
Dad ran.
The man ran.
Tad can bat.
Tad sat.

Optional Follow-Up:
Give the child the necessary letters to form the first new word in this lesson. Ask the child to sound out the word as he places the letters that you give him on the magnetic alphabet board. Do this for all of the new words from this lesson. As the child gains confidence in placing letters to make individual words, you may wish to give him letters, one word at a time, to form sentences from the lesson.

Lesson 31: Words with the Short-A Vowel Sound
Sight Word: I

You will need the following: *the J j consonant card, one blank index card, and a pen.*

Review

Instructor: I am going to show you a consonant card and I want you to tell me the sound for which the consonant stands.

Point to the **J j** consonant card. Ask the child to say the sound for which the letter stands. If the child has difficulty remembering the letter sound, repeat that specific verse of "The Consonant Rhyme" (see Lesson 26) as a review.

Instructor: Read this word for me. You have already read it before.

Let the child sound out the word as you use your finger as a guide. Help him as necessary.

am

New

Instructor: Now we are going to read words that have another letter before the **a**. I will read each word first. Then we will read that word together. Then you will read that same word by yourself.

ham   jam   Pam   Sam

Instructor: Remember, the best way to learn to read is to sound out words letter-sound by letter-sound. However, there are a few words that you will need to memorize. You have already learned the word *the*. Today, you will learn another word: the word *I*. This is an easy word because it is the name of a letter. What is this big letter?

I

Instructor: You just read the word! The word *I* is always written with a big letter. I will write this word on a card for you.

Point to the card. The child should pick up the card, read the word, and turn the card over again. The child should do this one more time. Keep this card with the sight word *the* card and put them in the place you will be keeping your sight word cards.

Instructor: Now we are going to read a story that contains words you have read as well as the word *I*.

I am Dad.
I ran.
I sat.
I had ham.
Pam had jam.

Lesson 32: Words with the Short-E Vowel Sound

You will need the following: *the consonant cards* **L l, G g, W w,** *and* **Y y** *as well as the five vowel cards. If you do the optional activity at the end of this lesson, you will need the magnetic alphabet board.*

Review

Lay out the five vowel cards: **A a, E e, I i, O o,** and **U u** in that order.

Instructor: Point to each of the vowel cards and say the *name* of each vowel: **a, e, i, o, u.** Now point to each vowel card again and say the *short-vowel sound* of each vowel: /ă/ /ĕ/ /ĭ/ /ŏ/ /ŭ/. Now we will turn these cards over so you can say these short-vowel sounds from memory.

If the child can't remember the names and sounds of the vowels, review the poem "The Five Vowels" from Lesson 5.

Instructor: I am going to show you four consonant cards and review the sounds with you.

Point to the following consonant cards: **L l, G g, W w,** and **Y y**. Ask the child to say the sound for which the letter stands. If the child has difficulty remembering a letter sound, repeat that specific verse of "The Consonant Rhyme" (see Lesson 26) as a review.

New

Instructor: Now you are going to start reading words that contain the letter **e** when it stands for the short-**e** vowel sound: /ĕ/. I will read a part of a word to you. Then we will read it together. Then you will read it all by yourself.

Ideally, I like to have the child read real words that mean something to them. However, there are no two-letter common nouns that start with the /ĕ/ sound. As you did before, use your finger to reveal the letters as you and the child say their sounds together. Remember to sustain the voice!

ed

Instructor: Now we will learn some words with a letter before the **ed**. I will read each word first. Then we will read that word together. Then you will read that same word by yourself.

red	bed	fed
led	Ned	Ted

Instructor: Now you will read a story that uses words you have read. This story contains words with both the short-**a** and short-**e** vowel sound.

With the exception of the sight word *the*, cover the words in the sentences on the next page with your finger and reveal the letters one at a time. If the child has difficulty distinguishing between the short-vowel sounds of **a** and **e**, practice chanting the sounds of the vowels using the vowel cards.

The tan cat ran.
Ned fed the tan cat.
The tan cat had ham.

Instructor: Now we will read a list of words that contain the letter **e** that stands for the short-**e** vowel sound: /ĕ/. The words end with **et**, but they all begin with a different consonant letter. I will read each word first. Then we will read that same word together. Then you will read that word by yourself.

Use your finger to uncover letters as you or the child says each letter sound. Don't forget to sustain the voice to blend the sounds into a word.

pet	get	bet	let	set
met	net	jet	wet	yet

Instructor: Now you will read a story that uses words you have read. This story also contains a mark of punctuation called a *comma*. When you see a comma, you pause and continue reading the sentence. I will point out the comma when you get to it in the story.

Be sure to place a folded sheet of plain paper under each line to encourage the child's eyes to move from left to right through each sentence.

Let Ted get the wet pet.
Set the wet pet cat at the mat.
Pet the sad, wet cat.
Ted can pat the fat, wet cat.

Optional Follow-Up:
Give the child the necessary letters to form the first new word in this lesson: *red*. Ask the child to sound out the word as he places the letters that you give him on the magnetic alphabet board. Do this for all of the new words from this lesson. As the child gains confidence in placing letters to make individual words, you may wish to give him letters, one word at a time, to form sentences from the lesson.

Lesson 33: Words with the Short-E Vowel Sound

You will need the following: *a pen and a blank index card.*

Review

Instructor: Last lesson you read these words. First I will read each word to you. Then you will read each word yourself. I will use my finger to reveal the letters as you read each word from left to right.

pet	get	bet	let	set
met	net	jet	wet	yet

New

Instructor: Now we will read another list of words that contain the letter **e** that stands for the short-**e** vowel sound: /ĕ/. The words end with **en**, but they all begin with a different consonant letter. I will read each word first. Then we will read that same word together. Then you will read that word by yourself.

hen	pen	ten	Ken	Ben

Instructor: Now you will read some stories.

Assist the child as necessary to read the sentences below. Remember to use your finger to uncover the letters as the child reads (unless the child is able to do it on his own). If at any time the child has trouble staying on a line, place a folded piece of paper under the line he is reading.

Ken fed the fat hen at the pen.
Ken fed the tan hen at ten.
Pet the fat hen.

Ben had a red van.
The red van ran.
Dad let Ben get the tan jet.

Instructor: Now we are going to read one more word. The word is the answer to this question: Is the sky blue? Try to read this word by yourself first. I will help you if you need it.

yes

Instructor: Yes, the sky is blue! And, *yes*, we are done with the lesson.

Write the word **yes** on an index card. Throughout the day, whenever the child makes a request that could be answered with **yes**, show him the card and have him read the word for himself.

Lesson 34: Words with the Short-I Vowel Sound

You will need the following: *the vowel cards. If you do the optional activity at the end of this lesson, you will need the magnetic alphabet board.*

Review

Lay out the five vowel cards: **A a**, **E e**, **I i**, **O o**, and **U u** in that order.

Instructor: Point to each of the vowel cards and say the name of each vowel: **a, e, i, o, u**. Now point to each vowel card again and say the short-vowel sound of each vowel: /ă/ /ĕ/ /ĭ/ /ŏ/ /ŭ/. Now we will turn these cards over so you can say these short-vowel sounds from memory.

New

Instructor: Now we are going to start reading words that contain the letter **i** that stands for the short-**i** vowel sound: /ĭ/. I am going to read the word. Then we will read the word together. Then you will read the word by yourself.

Begin by reading the word *in* using the same technique you have used before: Cover the **n** with your index finger so the child only sees the first letter, **i**. Say the sound /ĭ/, and then uncover the **n** as you pronounce the /n/ sound. Remember to blend the letter sounds together to read the word *in*.

in

Instructor: Now we are going to read words that have a consonant before the **in**. I am going to read each word. Then we will read that word together. Then you will read that same word by yourself.

pin   tin   win   fin

In the following instructions to the child, emphasize the word *it* each time it occurs. Make it fun as you exaggerate.

Instructor: Now you are going to read another word that contains the /ĭ/ sound. *It* is a very common word. *It* is spoken all the time. I wonder what *it* could be. You are going to read this word by yourself. What word is *it*?

it

Instructor: *It* is it! Now we are going to read words that have another letter before the **it**. I am going to read each word. Then we will read it together. Then you will read that same word by yourself.

sit   fit   hit

bit   pit   Kit

Instructor: Now you will read two very short stories that use some of the words you just read. The first story contains a mark of punctuation called an *exclamation point*. When you see an exclamation point at the end of a sentence, you say the sentence with sudden or strong feeling. I will point out the exclamation point when you get to it in the story.

Assist the child, only as necessary, to sound out the words in the sentences below. Move your finger under the words to help the child read from left to right. When you get to the second line, point out the exclamation point to the child. The child should read the sentence. Then read that sentence back to the child with strong feeling. Have him repeat the sentence back to you, using his voice to communicate strong feeling.

Kit hit the pin.
Win it, Kit!

Ben had the sad, wet cat.
Sam let the wet cat in the den.
Ben and Sam fed the cat ham.

Optional Follow-Up:
Give the child the necessary letters to form five to ten words from this lesson and five to ten words from Lesson 33. Ask the child to sound out each word as he places the letters that you give him on the magnetic alphabet board. As the child gains confidence in placing letters to make individual words, you may wish to give him letters, one word at a time, to form sentences from the lessons.

Lesson 35: Words with the Short-I Vowel Sound

You will need the following: *the consonant cards **X x**, **Y y**, **Z z**, **F f**, **G g**, and **R r** for the lesson. You will need twelve index cards, two markers of different colors, and scissors for the optional activity.*

Review

Instructor: I am going to show you six consonant cards and review their sounds with you.

Point to the following consonant cards: **X x**, **Y y**, **Z z**, **F f**, **G g**, and **R r**. Ask the child to say the sound for which the letter stands. If the child has difficulty remembering a letter sound, repeat that specific verse of "The Consonant Rhyme" (see Lesson 26) as a review.

New

Instructor: Last lesson you read words that contain the letter **i** that stands for the short-vowel sound of **i**: /ĭ/. Now we are going to read more words that contain the /ĭ/ sound. First I will read each word. Then we will read that same word together. Then you will read that word by yourself. Then you will read a sentence by yourself.

Read the following lists of words using your finger to reveal the letters each time. Then run your finger under each word in the sentence to guide the child to read from left to right. Place a folded piece of paper under the line the child is reading to help him keep his place.

if   fib   bib

I am sad if I fib.

him   dim   rim   Kim

Kim let him sit in the den.

six   fix

The six men can fix the van.

big   pig   dig   wig

The big pig can dig.

The lesson continues on the following page.

tip   rip   lip   nip

zip   yip   hip

The big pig can zip.
It can nip.

bid   did   hid   lid   kid
I hid the lid in the bin.

Optional Follow-Up Game: "Mix and Match" Words
Cut twelve index cards in half crosswise so you have twenty-four cards that are 3 inches by 2 ½ inches. Using eight "half cards," write each letter combination below with one colored marker, one combination to a card. These will be the "word ending" cards.

ip   in   ib   it   im   id   ig   ix

Then, using sixteen "half cards," write each letter below with the other colored marker, one letter per card. These will be the "beginning letter" cards.

b   d   f   h   j   k   l   m

n   p   r   s   t   w   y   z

Take the word ending card with **it** written on it and place it face up in front of the child. Then gather these beginning letter cards: **s, h, f, b, k, l, p**. Turn over these beginning letter cards so you can't see the consonants. Then have the child select one of the beginning-letter cards. Flip that card over and slide it next to the **it** card (from left to right it should read, for example, *sit*). If the child reads the word correctly, he gets the beginning letter card. If he doesn't, turn the beginning letter card back over and mix it up in the pile. Continue playing until the child has all the beginning letter cards. Play this game using the other seven word-ending cards. Here is the list of all the beginning letter cards you should team with each word-ending card.

Word-Ending Card	Beginning-Letter Card
it	s, h, f, b, k, l, p
ig	b, d, f, j, p, w
id	k, l, d, h, r
im	d, h, r
ib	b, r, f
in	p, f, b, s, w, k, t, d
ip	l, r, s, t, h, d, n, z, y
ix	s, f, m

Lesson 36:   Words with the Short-I Vowel Sound
S Sounds Like /z/: is, his, as, has
Sight Word: a

You will need the following: *the Qu qu, S s, and Z z cards, a blank index card, and a pen. If you do the optional activity at the end of this lesson, you will need the magnetic alphabet board.*

Review

Instructor: I am going to show you a consonant card and review its sound with you.

Point to the **Qu qu** card. Ask the child to say the sound for which **qu** stands: /kw/. If the child has difficulty remembering the sound, repeat that specific verse of "The Consonant Rhyme" (see Lesson 26) as a review.

New

Instructor: Now we are going to read two words that begin with **qu** and contain the /ĭ/ sound. I will read each word. Then we will read that same word together. Then you will read that word by yourself.

Although you have been uncovering words letter-by-letter, you should uncover the **qu** as one letter-sound unit.

quit   quiz

Instructor: Now you will read few sentences. I will place a folded piece of paper under the line you are reading.

Quit it, Tim!

Get the quiz.
Set the quiz in the den.
Quiz him.

Review

Instructor: I am going to show two more consonant cards and review the sounds with you.

Point to the **S s** and **Z z** cards. Ask the child to say the sound for which each letter stands. If the child has difficulty, repeat the specific verse of "The Consonant Rhyme" as a review (see Lesson 26).

Instructor: The letter **s** stands for the sound /s/. This is like the sound of a snake hissing. I will hiss like a snake. Hissssssssssssssssss. Now you hiss like a snake. The letter **z** stands for the sound /z/. This is like the sound of a bee buzzing. I will buzz like a bee. Buzzzzzzzzzzzzzzzzzzzzzz. Now you can you buzz like a bee.

The lesson continues on the following page.

Instructor: Now there are some special words that you need to learn. These are words in which the **s** does not stand for the sound of a hissing snake: /s/. In these words, the letter **s** stands for the sound of a buzzing bee: /z/. Now I will read these words. Watch the word as I uncover it with my finger. I will read all the words by myself first. Then we will read each word together. Then you will read that same word by yourself.

Sustain your voice and emphasize the /z/ sound in each of the words.

is   his   as   has

Instructor: Now you will read a story that uses the words you just read.

Run your finger under the words as the child reads the story. The child may use his own finger if he is able.

Kip has a hat.
His hat is red.
It is as big as the hat Dad has.

Instructor: Remember, the best way to learn to read is to sound out words letter-sound by letter-sound. However, there are a few words that you will need to memorize. You have already learned the words *the* and *I* this way. Today, you will learn another word. This is an easy word because it is the name of a letter. What is this letter?

Beginning readers should pronounce this word like the name of the letter **a**.

a

Instructor: You just read the word! Now read the word when it is written with a big letter.

A

Write the word on an index card as both a big **A** and a little **a**. Point to the card. The child should pick up the card, read the word, and turn the card over again. The child should do this one more time. Keep this card with the other sight word cards.

Instructor: Now you are ready to read some stories. The first story also contains a mark of punctuation called a *question mark*. A question mark at the end of a sentence is a signal that you should raise the pitch of your voice so it sounds like a question. Listen to my voice as I ask these three questions. Where are you going? Do you like to eat ice cream? What is your name? I will point out the question mark when you get to it in the story.

When you get to the second line in the story, point out the question mark to the child. The child should read the sentence. Then read the question back to the child, raising the pitch of your voice at the end. Have him repeat the question back to you, raising the pitch of his voice to indicate a question.

Jim has a red wig.
Can the wig fit Jim?
Yes, his wig can fit him.

Instructor: Now you are going to read a silly story.

If the child has difficulty distinguishing between the short-vowel sounds of **a**, **e**, and **i**, practice chanting the sounds of the vowels using the vowel cards. It is normal for beginning readers to forget short vowels when they are mixed up in a story.

A pig has a big pig pen.
The pig is as big as a van.

The big pig bit a man in tan in the pen.
The man in tan hit the big pig.

The pig ran in his den.
The man in tan ran in the pen.

The mad man sat in the pen.
The big pig had jam in his den.
The big pig had a nap in his den.

Optional Follow-Up:
Give the child the necessary letters to form the first new word in this lesson. Ask the child to sound out the word as he places the letters that you give him on the magnetic alphabet board. Do this for all of the new words from this lesson. As the child gains confidence in placing letters to make individual words, you may wish to give him letters, one word at a time, to form sentences from the lessons.

STOP ! This is a good time to stop and check the child's progress. If you feel like it would help the child, do not go on to Lesson 37 tomorrow. Instead, stop at this time and do a previous lesson or practice with the magnetic alphabet board. The /ĕ/ and /ĭ/ sounds are difficult for many children. If the child still has trouble with these sounds, spend as many days as necessary for the child to be able to distinguish between these two sounds. Review the words and sentences in Lessons 32 through 36. Then start the next lesson, Lesson 37, the following day.

Lesson 37: Words with the Short-O Vowel Sound

You will need the following: *the vowel cards. For the next lesson, you will need two paper lunch bags.*

Review

Lay out the five vowel cards: **A a, E e, I i, O o,** and **U u** in that order.

Instructor: Point to each of the vowel cards and say the *name* of each vowel. Now point to each vowel card again and say the *short-vowel sound* of each vowel. Now we will turn these cards over so you can say these short-vowel sounds from memory.

New

Instructor: Now we are going to start reading words that contain the letter **o** that stands for the short-**o** vowel sound: /ŏ/. I am going to read a word. Then we will read the word together. Then you will read the word by yourself.

Begin by reading the word **ox** using the same technique you have used before: Cover the **x** with your index finger so the child only sees the first letter, **o**. Say the /ŏ/ sound, then uncover the **x** as you pronounce the /ks/ sound. Remember to blend the letter sounds together into the word **ox**.

OX

Instructor: Now we are going to read two words that have a consonant before the **o**. I will read each word. Then we will read that same word together. Then you will read that word by yourself.

box   fox

Instructor: Now I am going to read some more words that contain the /ŏ/ sound. First I will read each word. Then we will read that same word together. Then you will read that word by yourself. I will put a folded piece of paper under the line that you are reading to help you keep your place as you read across.

on	Don	Ron	
not	dot	hot	lot
got	pot	rot	

Instructor: Now you will read a story.

The fox is in a box.
The fox did nap in the box.
The fox got hot.
The fox did yip a lot.
The fox did rip the box.
The fox did sit on the lid.

Lesson 38:   Words with the Short-O Vowel Sound

You will need the following for the optional activities: *two paper lunch bags, a pen, paper, and the magnetic alphabet board.*

Instructor: Now I am going to read some more words that contain the letter **o** that stands for the short-o vowel sound: /ŏ/. First I will read each word. Then we will read that same word together. Then you will read that word by yourself.

Read the following list of words, following the same procedure you have been using: Reveal the letters with your finger, and sustain your voice to blend the sounds seamlessly together into a word.

dog	fog	hog	jog	log
hop	pop	sob	job	

Instructor: Now you are ready to read some stories that contain many of the words we just read.

Assist the child as necessary as he reads the sentences below. Remember to use your finger to uncover the letters as the child reads (or if the child can do it successfully himself, have him do it).

Bob has a dog at his job.
Wag is his dog.
Don has not got a dog.
Don has a big pet hog.
His hog is not at his job!

Jim did fix a hot dog.
Jim did pop a hot dog in a big pot.
Jim fed a hot dog to his pet dog.
His dog did beg a lot.
Quit it, dog!

Optional Follow-Up:
Just for fun, get two brown paper lunch bags. Write your child a note that says, "Pop a bag." Then show him what to do by taking one bag, blowing it up, gripping the open end, and popping the bag. Then blow up the second bag, and give it to the child to pop once he has correctly read the note aloud. Assist him as necessary.

Optional Follow-Up:
As you have done in previous lessons, give the child the necessary letters to form the new words from this lesson on the magnetic board. As the child gains confidence in placing letters to make individual words, you may give him letters, one word at a time, to form sentences from the lesson.

Lesson 39: Words with the Short-U Vowel Sound

You will need the following: *the vowel cards, drawing supplies, and paper. If you do the optional activity at the end of this lesson, you will need the magnetic alphabet board. For the next lesson, you will need twenty index cards and two markers of different colors for the optional game. You may want to write out the cards in advance of the next lesson.*

Review

Lay out the five vowel cards: **A a**, **E e**, **I i**, **O o**, and **U u** in that order.

Instructor: Point to each of the vowel cards and say the *name* of each vowel. Now point to each vowel card again and say the *short-vowel sound* of each vowel. Now we will turn these cards over so you can say these short-vowel sounds from memory.

New

Instructor: Now we are going to start reading words that contain the letter **u** and the short-**u** vowel sound: /ŭ/. I am going to read a word. Then we will read the word together. Then you will read the word by yourself.

Begin by reading the word *up* using the same technique you have used before: Cover the **p** with your index finger so the child only sees the first letter, **u**. Say the /ŭ/ sound, and then uncover the **p** as you pronounce the /p/ sound. Remember to blend the letter sounds together into the word *up*.

up

Instructor: We are going to read two words that have a consonant before the **up**. I will read each word first. Then we will read that same word together. Then you will read that word by yourself.

cup   pup

Instructor: Now we will read some more words that contain the /ŭ/ sound. First I will read each word. Then we will read that same word together. Then you will read that word by yourself.

For the following words and sentences, continue to use a folded piece of paper to help the child form the habit of reading left to right, one line at a time.

| us | bus | bug | dug |
| hug | rug | tug | mug |

Instructor: Now you are going to read a sentence. Then we'll draw a picture of what the sentence is saying.

Assist the child as necessary to read the sentence and to draw the picture. Make the picture simple. If the child wants to, he can embellish it later. Label the picture with the following sentence.

The bug is on the rug.

Instructor: Now I am going to read some more words that contain the /ŭ/ sound. First I will read each word. Then we will read that same word together. Then you will read that word by yourself.

sun   fun   run   gun

nut   hut   cut

Instructor: Now you are going to read two sentences. Then we'll draw a picture of what the sentences are saying.

Assist the child as necessary to read the sentence and draw the picture. Label the picture with the following sentences.

I run in the sun.
It is fun.

Instructor: Now I am going to read some more words that contain the /ŭ/ sound. First I will read the word. Then we will read the word together. Then you will read the word by yourself.

tub   rub   mud   bud

hum   sum   gum   yum

Instructor: Now you are going to read some sentences. Then we'll draw a picture of what the sentences are saying.

Assist the child as necessary to read the sentences and draw a picture of a child digging in the mud or taking a bath. You label the picture for him.

I dug in the mud.
I had mud on a leg.
I did hum and rub in the tub.

Optional Follow-Up:
As you have done in previous lessons, give the child the necessary letters to form the new words in this lesson on the magnetic board. As the child gains confidence in placing letters to make individual words, you may give him letters, one word at a time, to form sentences from the lesson.

Lesson 40: Review of the Short-Vowel Sounds of A, E, I, O, and U

If you choose to do the optional game, *this lesson will take two days. You will need twenty index cards and two markers of different colors.*

Instructor: Now you are ready to read some stories.

Assist the child as necessary as he reads the sentences below. Remember to use your finger to uncover the letters as the child reads (or if the child can do it successfully himself, have him do it). Encourage him to blend the letter sounds together. If at any time he has trouble staying on the line, use a folded piece of paper to cover the lines below the one he is reading. If you notice that his eyes are consistently wandering to sentences *above* the line he is reading, you can cut a window out of heavy paper that will reveal only one line at a time.

Gus has gum. Pop!
Gum is fun.

Gus has a pup.
Bud the pup is in the mud.
Bud got a bug on him in the mud.
Gus can tug on the bug on his pup.
Did Gus hug Bud the pup?
Yes!
The mud is on Gus.

Gus ran in the den.
Gus got on the bed.
Gus got mud on the bed.
Bud ran in the den.
Bud sat on the rug.
Did Bud rub mud on the rug?
Yes!
The pup got mud on the red rug.

Mom ran in the den.
The bed had mud on it.
The rug had mud on it.
Mom got mad!

Optional Game: *Who* Did *What*?

You will need twenty index cards and two markers of different colors (I will use "red" and "green"—do not use yellow because it is too hard to read). With the red marker, write the following subjects (the *who*) on index cards, one subject per card. With the green marker, write the following predicates (*what* the subject did) on index cards, one predicate per card.

Subject (red)	Predicate (green)
His mom	has on a big wig.
The fat cat	sat on a red mat.
The sad man	sat on a pin.
The tan hog	had a fit.
The hot dog	is in the box.
The red fox	did nab a hen.
Tom	fed his dog ham.
The pup	did yip a lot.
The big bus	is fun.
The bug	dug in the mud.

First, lay the cards out in the order you see above. Set the first pair, "His mom" and "has a big wig," in front of the child. Have the child read that sentence. Repeat the same process for the next nine sentences. Then shuffle all the cards, keeping the subject cards in one pile and the predicate cards in another. Let the child pick any subject card and pair it with any predicate card. Have fun reading the wacky sentences!

Section 4

TWO-CONSONANT BLENDS

Important Encouragement for the Instructor:
Learning to blend letter sounds into words for the first time is the most difficult stage of reading. Persist, and it will begin to click. You have to be patient until the break-through, but use common sense. If after you have worked on sounding out letters faithfully 10-15 minutes per day for Lessons 27-40, and the child still cannot sound out a word, stop formal instruction for a month or two, and continue to play phonics activities (see Part 2: "Preparing the Young Child to Be a Reader" and Lessons 1-26). Then come back to formal reading instruction (Lesson 27).

About the "Two Review and One New" Teaching Technique:
When the child has trouble mastering a lesson, put a Post-It on that page so you can quickly refer to the lesson in the future. At the beginning of certain reading lessons, first review the words or sentences from one of the lessons you have marked with a Post-It, and then review yesterday's lesson. This is called "Two Review." This should take about five minutes. If the child needs more review than this, take the time to do it before proceeding with the new lesson (this is the "One New"). I will tell you to do the "Two Review and One New" at the beginning of many lessons. Review is a critical part of teaching.

Lesson 41: Double Consonants

You will need the following: *the magnetic alphabet board if you do the optional activity.*

From now on, there will be many lessons practicing various consonant combinations. These words will contain short-vowel sounds. If the child is confident with the short-vowel sounds, you may not find it necessary to review the sounds as often. If your child needs extra practice with the short-vowel sounds, review them as needed.

Instructor: Sometimes certain letters appear as a pair at the end of a word, but they still represent just one sound. Watch as I point to these double letters.

Point to each letter pair and spell it aloud to the child.

ss	ll	gg	zz	ff	dd	tt

Instructor: Now we are going to read some words that end with double letters. Many of these words are going to be in a story that you will soon read! First I will read each word. Then we will read that same word together. Then you will read that word by yourself.

Reveal the double letters with your finger as one letter-sound unit. For example, when uncovering the word **pass**, first reveal the **p**, then the **a**, then the **ss** together. Use a folded piece of paper to reveal one line at a time.

pass	mess	miss	toss	fuss	moss	yell
fell	Bill	Jill	will	hill	egg	fuzz
huff	puff	off	odd	mitt		

Instructor: Now you are ready to read some stories containing those words that end with double letters.

Assist the child as necessary to read the sentences below. Remember to use your finger (or have the child use his own finger if he is able) to uncover the letters. Place a folded piece of paper underneath the line the child is reading if the child is having trouble keeping his place.

Bill will toss an egg.
The egg will pass Jill.
Jill will miss the egg.
The egg is a mess!
Bill will not yell.
Bill will not fuss.
Bill will nod.
Bill will hug Jill.

The red bug sat on a hill.
The bug had red fuzz on it.
It did buzz.
The red bug did buzz in the sun.
The bug fell off the hill.
The bug fell on the moss.
It did huff.
It did puff.
Will the bug hop up the hill?
Will the bug jog up the hill?

It is an odd bug.
The bug will get in a red van.
The van will zip up the hill.
The bug will nap on the hill in the sun.

Optional Follow-Up:
As you have done in previous lessons, give the child the necessary letters to form the new words in this lesson on the magnetic board. As the child gains confidence in placing letters to make individual words, you may give him letters, one word at a time, to form sentences.

Lesson 42: The CK Combination

You will need the following: *the C c and K k consonant cards.*

About Revealing Letters in Blends and Digraphs
In simple short-vowel words, the child simply moves from left to right, sounding out each letter as it is uncovered by your finger. When a group of letters stand for a single sound (in blends, digraphs, and the **ck** combination), uncover the *group* of letters that stand for that sound. For example, if the word to be read is ***thick***, uncover the digraph **th** (do not uncover the **t** and **h** separately), then uncover the **i**, and then the **ck** (both letters at the same time). If the child still stumbles or tries to sound out each individual letter of a blend or digraph, circle these units of sound to show the child that these letters are pronounced as a single sound. Then have the child try again.

Don't forget to do the "Two Review and One New"!

Review
Point to the **C c** card.

Instructor: For what sound does the letter **c** stand?

Child: ***C*** *stands for /k/ in /k/ /k/ cat.*

Point to the **K k** card.

Instructor: For what sound does the letter **k** stand?

Child: ***K*** *stands for /k/ in /k/ /k/ keep.*

New

Instructor: The letters **c** and **k** stand for the same sound: /k/. When a word ends with the sound /k/, it is written with the letters **c** and **k** side-by-side. **Ck** is not a double letter, but it acts like it is. When you see the letters **c** and **k** together, you say /k/. Listen to these words that end in **ck**: ***back, deck, lock***. Now we are going to read words that end in **ck**. Soon you will see these words in a story. I will read each word first. Then we will read that same word together. Then you will read that word on your own.

Uncover the letters **ck** as one letter-sound unit.

sack	pack	quack	peck	deck
pick	Rick	Nick	rock	duck

Instructor: Now you are ready to read a story with words that end in **ck**. You will see a new mark of punctuation in today's story. When the exact words a person says are written, a special set of marks are used. These marks are called *quotation marks*. When we get to the exact words that Rick and Nick say, I will point out the quotation marks to you.

Assist the child to read the sentences below as needed, using your finger or a folded piece of paper to help the child read left to right and keep his place.

Rick will pick up a big nut.
Rick will pack it in his sack.
Nick will set a mat on the deck.
Rick will sit on the mat.
Nick will get a bun.
Nick will lick the jam off the bun.

A duck on a rock will quack.
The duck will peck at the bun.
Rick and Nick will yell, "Quit it, duck!"

Lesson 43: The Ending Blends LK, LB, and LP

If your child needs extra practice in any lessons from 43-48, you may use the magnetic alphabet board as a follow-up activity for any of these lessons. Put the two letters of the consonant blend on the board, and have the child add and take away letters to form the words from that lesson.

Don't forget to do the "Two Review and One New"!

Instructor: Two consonant sounds pronounced together are called a *two-consonant blend*. When you say a two-consonant blend, just *blend* the sounds smoothly together.

There are many final two-consonant blends. Although each consonant retains its sound, it is more efficient to learn them as blends rather than individual sounds in order to prevent the child from inserting vowel sounds between the two consonants.

Instructor: When you place the consonants **l** and **k** next to one another, they represent a sound that you hear at the ends of these words: ***milk, silk, sulk***. Now we are going to read words that end with the **lk** consonant blend. First I will read each word. Then we will read that same word together. Then you will read that word by yourself.

Follow the same procedure that you have been using: Move your finger to reveal the letters in order and sustain your voice to blend the letter sounds seamlessly into a word. Reveal the **lk** as one letter-sound unit.

milk   silk   sulk

Instructor: Here are some more words that end in consonant blends. The first word ends in the **lb** consonant blend: ***bulb***. The next two words end with the **lp** consonant blends. First I will read each word. Then you will read that same word. Then you will read that word by yourself.

bulb   help   gulp

Instructor: Now you are ready to read a story with the words from this lesson.

Mick is sick.
Mom will get Mick his milk and a pill.
Milk will help.

Mick will not sulk.
Mom will hug Mick.
Mick can sit up.
Mick is well.

Lesson 44: The Ending Blends ST and NT

Don't forget to do the "Two Review and One New!"

Instructor: Now we are going to learn another two-consonant blend. When you place the consonants **s** and **t** next to one another, they represent a sound that you hear at the ends of these words: ***nest, fast, dust***. Now we are going to read words that end with the **st** consonant blend. First I will read each word. Then we will read that same word together. Then you will read that word by yourself.

Follow the same procedure that we have been using: move your finger to reveal the letters in order and sustain your voice to blend the letter sounds seamlessly into a word. Reveal the **st** blend as one letter-sound unit.

fast	last	mist	dust	rust
best	rest	cost	just	list

Instructor: Now we are going to learn another two-consonant blend. When you place the consonants **n** and **t** next to one another, they represent a sound that you hear at the ends of these words: ***dent, rent, went***. Now we are going to read words that end with the **nt** consonant blend. First I will read each word. Then we will read that same word together. Then you will read that word by yourself.

Follow the same procedure that you have been using: Move your finger to reveal the letters in order and sustain your voice to blend the letter sounds seamlessly into a word. Reveal the **nt** as one letter-sound unit.

rent	dent	went	lent	hunt

Instructor: Now you are ready to read stories with words that end in the **st** and **nt** blend.

As needed, assist the child with reading the sentences below, using your finger or a folded piece of paper to help the child read left to right, stay on a line, and keep his place.

The van ran in the mist.
It got stuck fast in the mud.
The van had rust on the fan.
A dent is in the tan van.
The van cost a lot.
Fix the van.
It will not just sit in the mud.

Mom went fast.
Mom will rent a red van.
Dad will fix the tan van.
Will the tan van last?
Yes!

Lesson 45: The Ending Blends FT, LT, CT, and PT

Don't forget to do the "Two Review and One New"!

Instructor: Now we are going to learn other two-consonant blends. When you place the consonants **f** and **t** next to one another, they represent a sound that you hear at the ends of these words: *gift*, *soft*, *left*. Now we are going to read words that end with the **ft** consonant blend. First I will read each word. Then we will read that same word together. Then you will read that word by yourself. Once we are finished reading the list, you will read the sentences that follow it.

Follow the same procedure that you have been using: Move your finger to reveal the letters in order and sustain your voice to blend the letter sounds seamlessly into a word. Reveal the **ft** as one letter-sound unit.

left   gift   lift   sift   soft

Jack got a soft pup as his gift.
Jack left milk in a cup in the box.

Instructor: Now we are going to learn another blend: **lt**. You hear the sound of this blend at the ends of these words: *quilt*, *felt*, *wilt*. Now we are going to read words that end with the **lt** blend. We'll follow the same procedure we used for the last blend.

felt   belt   melt   wilt   quilt

Mom felt the soft, silk quilt on the bed.

Instructor: Now we are going to learn another blend: **ct**. You hear the sound of this blend at the ends of these words: *act, fact*. Now we are going to read those words. We'll follow the same procedure we used for the last blend.

act   fact

It is a fact.
If I act fast, I can help him.

Instructor: The last blend you will learn today is **pt**. You hear the sound of this blend at the ends of these words: *kept, wept*. Now we are going to read those words. We'll follow the same procedure we used for the last blend.

kept   wept

Deb kept a red pet bug in a box.
Deb lost the bug.
Deb wept.

Lesson 46: The Ending Blends MP, SP, LF, and LM

Don't forget to do the "Two Review and One New"!

Instructor: Now we are going to learn another two-consonant blend. When you place the consonants **m** and **p** next to one another, they represent a sound that you hear at the ends of these words: *camp*, *dump*, *jump*. Now we are going to read words that end with the **mp** consonant blend. First I will read a word. Then we will read a word together. Then you will read the word by yourself.

Follow the same procedure that you have been using: Move your finger to reveal the letters in order and sustain your voice to blend the letter sounds seamlessly into a word. Reveal the **mp** as one letter-sound unit.

lamp   damp   camp   bump   jump

Instructor: Now you are ready to read some sentences with words that end in the **mp** blend.

As needed, assist the child with reading the sentences in this lesson, using your finger or a folded piece of paper to help the child read left to right, stay on a line, and keep his place.

Mom can set up the tent at camp.
The kid will not jump in the tent and bump the lamp.

Instructor: Now we are going to learn another two-consonant blend. When you place the consonants **s** and **p** next to one another, they represent a sound that you hear at the ends of these words: *gasp*, *lisp*. Now we are going to read words that end with the **sp** blend. First I will read a word. Then we will read a word together. Then you will read the word by yourself.

gasp   lisp

Instructor: Now you are ready to read a story with words that end in the **sp** blend. This story is fun to read. It ends with a mark of punctuation called an *ellipsis*. When you see an ellipsis, you know that words have been left out on purpose. When you see the three dots in this story, you are supposed to start the story again from the beginning.

The kid on the dock sat on a pin.
The kid did jump up and gasp.
The kid ran fast.
The kid did huff and puff up the ramp.
The kid did pant and gasp.
The kid sat on the dock…

This is an amusing, never-ending story. When the child has finished reading it once, start again from the beginning. Read the story as many times as the child wants to read it.

The lesson continues on the following page.

Instructor: Now we are going to learn another two-consonant blend. When you place the consonants **l** and **f** next to one another, they represent a sound that you hear at the ends of these words: *elf, self, golf*. Now we are going to read words that end with the **lf** consonant blend. First I will read each word. Then we will read that same word together. Then you will read that word by yourself.

elf   self   golf

Instructor: Now we are ready to read a sentence with words that end in the **lf** blend.

The elf will win in golf.

Instructor: The last consonant blend you will learn today is **lm**. When you place the consonants **l** and **m** next to one another, they represent a sound that you hear at the ends of these words: *elm, film*. Now we are going to read words that end with the **lm** blend. First I will read each word. Then we will read that same word together. Then you will read that word by yourself.

elm   film

Instructor: Now you are ready to read a sentence with words that end in the **lm** blend.

In the film, a big elm fell on the deck.

Lesson 47: The Ending Blends ND, SK, and XT

Don't forget to do the "Two Review and One New"!

Instructor: Now we are going to learn another two-consonant blend. When you place the consonants **n** and **d** next to one another, they represent a sound that you hear at the ends of these words: ***and**, **bend**, **pond***. Now we are going to read words that end with the **nd** consonant blend. First I will read each word. Then we will read that same word together. Then you will read that word by yourself.

Follow the same procedure that you have been using: Move your finger to reveal the letters in order and sustain your voice to blend the letter sounds seamlessly into a word. Reveal each blend in this lesson (**nd**, **sk**, and **xt**) as one letter-sound unit.

and   sand   land   send

bend   wind   pond

Instructor: Now we are going to learn another two-consonant blend. When you place the consonants **s** and **k** next to one another, they represent a sound that you hear at the ends of these words: ***ask**, **tusk**, **task***. Now we are going to read words that end with the **sk** consonant blend. First I will read each word. Then we will read that same word together. Then you will read that word by yourself.

ask   task   bask   tusk

Instructor: Now you will read one word that ends with the unusual consonant blend **xt**. First I will read the word. Then you will read the word.

next

Instructor: Now we are ready to read a story with words that end in the **nd**, **sk**, and **xt** blends.

As needed, assist the child with reading the sentences below, using your finger or a folded piece of paper to help the child read left to right, stay on a line, and keep his place.

The man is on the raft.
The sun is hot on the big pond.
The man has a task.
The man must stop and get on land.

The wind did send him fast on land.
The man did kiss the tan sand.
Next, the man did sit and bask in the sun.

Lesson 48: The Ending Blend NK

Don't forget to do the "Two Review and One New"!

The /nk/ sound is difficult for some children to hear and say if it is isolated and not a part of a syllable.

Instructor: Now are going to learn a very fun two-letter blend. It is formed from the letters **n** and **k**. It is at the ends of these words: ***bank***, ***rink***, ***honk***, ***junk***. When the /ă/ sound comes before the **nk** blend, it sounds like this: /ănk/. Repeat after me: /ănk/. When the /ĭ/ sound comes before **nk**, you say this sound: /ĭnk/. Repeat after me: /ĭnk/. When the /ŏ/ sound comes before **nk**, you say this sound: /ŏnk/. Repeat after me: /ŏnk/. When the /ŭ/ sound comes before **nk**, you say this sound: /ŭnk/. Repeat after me: /ŭnk/. When you string those sounds together, you get: /ănk/, /ĭnk/, /ŏnk/, /ŭnk/. I will say this three times: /ănk/, /ĭnk/, /ŏnk/, /ŭnk/ *(pause)*; /ănk/, /ĭnk/, /ŏnk/, /ŭnk/ *(pause)*; /ănk/, /ĭnk/, /ŏnk/, /ŭnk/. Now let's say that three times together.

Together (three times):
/ănk/, /ĭnk/, /ŏnk/, /ŭnk/.

Instructor: Now say it three times by yourself.

If the child has difficulty, have him repeat the chant after you several times more.

Child (three times):
/ănk/, /ĭnk/, /ŏnk/, /ŭnk/.

Instructor: Now let's read some words that contain the sounds /ănk/, /ĭnk/, /ŏnk/, or /ŭnk/. First I will read each word. Then we will read that same word together. Then you will read that word by yourself. I will use a folded piece of paper to help you read across, left to right, and to help you stay on the correct line.

bank	sank	tank	yank
sink	wink	link	pink
bonk	honk		
bunk	dunk	hunk	junk

Now you will read two stories that contain words that end with the **nk** blend. The first story contains the marks of punctuation called quotation marks. Remember, quotation marks indicate that these words are exactly what the men in the tank said. The second story is about a girl who values her doll.

The tank went on the bank.
It sank in the mud.
The man in the tank did honk.
The man in tan did yell, "Yank the tank!"

The men got a link on the tank.
The men did huff and puff.
Bonk! Mud got on the men.
"Yuck! Let the tank sink!" the men did huff.

The bunk bed is pink.
The doll is on the pink bunk bed.
I will flop the bunk bed.
It will bump the doll off the bed.
I will pick up the doll and hug it.
The doll is not junk!

Lesson 49: Adding the Letter S to Words

Don't forget to do the "Two Review and One New"!

Instructor: Today we are going to learn the meanings of two words: *singular* and *plural*. A naming word *(noun)* can be singular or plural. *Singular* means "one thing." Here is a *singular* naming word: *cat*. You might have one cat. Cat is a *singular* naming word *(noun)*. *Plural* means "more than one." Here is a plural word: *cats*. You might have two, three, or one million cats. *Cats* is a plural naming word. Plural words almost always end in the letter **s**. Listen as I say some more plural words. Can you hear the /s/ sound at the end of each word: *lamps*, *gifts*, *belts, socks*?

Emphasize the /s/ sound at the end of each word.

Instructor: Now let's read some words in both their singular and plural forms. First I will read each pair of words. Then we will read that same pair of words together. Then you will read that pair of words by yourself.

cat	lamp	gift	belt	sock
cats	lamps	gifts	belts	socks

kid	mitt	mint	bunk
kids	mitts	mints	bunks

Instructor: Now you will read some sentences that have both singular and plural words in them.

I had a cat.
Kit had six fat cats.
The cats will not fit in the big tub.

Jeb had a mint.
I will hand him ten mints.
Jeb will suck on the mints.
The mints will melt.

Cam is at camp.
The camp had ten bunks.
Cam will set his stuff on a bunk.

Lots of words that are not plural naming words *(nouns)* also end in the letter **s**. Let's read some of these action words *(verbs)* that end in the letter **s**. First I will read each pair of words. Then we will read that same pair of words together. Then you will read that pair of words by yourself.

pat	get	fit	run
pats	gets	fits	runs
sulk	peck	ask	gasp
sulks	pecks	asks	gasps

Instructor: Now you are ready to read a story that has lots of words that end in the letter **s**.

The kids get ten gifts.
Mick gets six mitts.
Mick gasps.

Jen gets a red belt.
Jan gets a pink hat.
Rick gets soft socks.
Rick sulks.

Nell got the best gift.
Nell got a silk quilt.
Will the quilt fit the bed?
Yes, it fits!

Lesson 50: The Beginning Blends BL, CL, FL, GL, PL, and SL
Sight Word: of

You will need the following: *one index card and a pen.*

Do the "Two Review and One New" today.

Instructor: You have already learned that two consonants pronounced together are called a two-consonant blend. When you say these two consonants, just blend the sounds of the two consonants smoothly together. You know how to read a two-consonant blend at the *end* of a word. Now you will learn how to read a two-consonant blend at the *beginning* of a word. When you place the consonants **b** and **l** next to one another, they represent a sound that you hear at the beginning of these words: ***black***, ***bless***, ***blob***. Let's read some words that begin with the **bl** consonant blend. First I will read each word. Then we will read that same word together. Then you will read that word by yourself.

Some children have difficulty with consonant blends. They will insert a vowel sound after the first consonant. For the word ***blob***, the incorrect pronunciation would sound like "*buh*-lob." Help the child to blend the two-consonants together without putting a vowel sound between them.

blob   black   blend   blot   bless

Instructor: Remember, the best way to learn to read is to sound out words letter-sound by letter-sound. However, there are a few words that you will need to memorize. You have already learned the words *the*, *I*, and *a* this way. Today, you will learn another word. You will need to memorize it.

of

Write the word *of* on an index card. Point to the card and pronounce the word. Have the child repeat the word after you. Then turn the card over. Let the child turn the card back over and say the word. Do this five times. Keep this card in the sight word stack.

Instructor: Now you are ready to read a sentence that has some words that begin with **bl** as well as the word *of*.

Blot the blob of black jam on the rug.

Instructor: Now we will learn the two-consonant blend: **cl**. You can hear the sound of this blend at the beginning of these words: ***club***, ***click***, ***clock***. Let's read words that begin with the **cl** consonant blend. First I will read each word; then we will read that same word together. Then you will read that word by yourself. Once we are finished reading the list, you will read the sentence that follows it.

clock   class   click   clack   club

Click, clack, tick, tock, went the clock in the club.

Instructor: When you place the consonants **f** and **l** next to one another, they represent a sound that you hear at the beginning of these words: ***flag***, ***flock***, ***flat***. Let's read some words that begin with the **fl** consonant blend. We will follow the same procedure we used for the last blend.

flock   flap   flat   flit   flag

Ducks in flocks flit and flap on the flat pond.

Instructor: When you place the consonants **g** and **l** next to one another, they represent a sound that you hear at the beginning of these words: *glad*, *glum*, *glass*. Let's read some words that begin with the **gl** consonant blend. We will follow the same procedure we used with the last blend.

glad   glass   glint   glum   Glen

Glen spots a glint of glass on the sand.

Instructor: When you place the consonants **p** and **l** next to one another, they represent a sound that you hear at the beginning of these words: *plum*, *plump*, *plus*. Let's read some words that begin with the **pl** consonant blend. We will follow the same procedure we used with the last blend.

plus   pluck   plump   plums   Plat

Instructor: Now let's read a silly sentence about a boy named Plat. This sentence contains *plenty* of words that begin with **pl**. It is a tongue twister! I will say the sentence slowly three times.

Plat will pluck plump plums plus fat figs.

Instructor: Now read the sentence with me as I run my finger under each word.

Read the sentence with the child. Read the sentence slowly several times together so the child can grasp the meaning. Once the child is comfortable reading the sentence slowly, make a game out of the child saying the sentence as fast as he can. Please giggle and laugh a lot!

Instructor: When you place the consonants **s** and **l** next to one another, they represent a sound that you hear at the beginning of these words: *slept*, *sled*, *slick*. Let's read some words that begin with the **sl** consonant blend. We will follow the same procedure we used with the last blend.

slim   sled   slick   slug   slept

Instructor: Now let's read a silly sentence about some slugs. Slugs are slimy creatures that look like chubby worms. This sentence contains lots of words that begin with **sl**. It is a tongue twister! I will say the sentence slowly three times.

Slim slugs slept on the slick sled.

Instructor: Now let's read the sentence together. I will run my finger under each word as we say it.

Read the sentence slowly several times together so the child can grasp the meaning. Then have the child read the sentence himself. Once the child is comfortable reading the sentence slowly, make a game out of the child saying the sentence as fast as he can. Enjoy!

Lesson 51: The Beginning Blends SM, SP, SC, SK, SN, and ST

Do the "Two Review and One New" today.

You will need the following: *the magnetic alphabet board if you do the optional activity.*

Instructor: Now we will learn more two-consonant blends. When you place the consonants **s** and **m** next to one another, they represent a sound that you hear at the beginning of these words: *smell*, *smog*, *smack*. Let's read some words that begin with the **sm** consonant blend. First I will read each word. Then we will read that same word together. Then you will read that word by yourself.

smell   smack   smug   smog

Instructor: Now you will read a sentence that uses words beginning with **sm**.

Mack smells and smacks his mint gum.

Instructor: When you place the consonants **s** and **p** next to one another, they represent a sound that you hear at the beginning of these words: *spend*, *spot*, *spill*. Let's read some words that begin with the **sp** consonant blend. First I will read each word. Then we will read that same word together. Then you will read that word by yourself.

spell   spin   spit   spank

spot   speck   spend   spill

Instructor: Sometimes a punctuation mark called a *hyphen* is used to join word parts. The following word has two hyphens in it. You read it the same way you would read any word. First I will read the word. Then you will read the word to me. I will point out the hyphens when we get to them.

spick-and-span

Instructor: Now you will read a sentence that contains words beginning in the **sp** consonant blend.

Did Glen spill specks of milk on the spick-and-span deck?

Instructor: When you place the consonants **s** and **c** next to one another, they represent a sound that you hear at the beginning of these words: *scan, scoff, scab*. Let's read some words that begin with the **sc** consonant blend. We will read the words as we did for the last blend. Once we have finished going through the list, you will read the sentence that follows it.

scab   scalp   scan   scant

scoff   Scamp   Scat

Scamp the dog and Scat the cat will flop on the dock.

Instructor: When you place the consonants **s** and **k** next to one another, they represent a sound that you hear at the beginning of these words: *skip, skunk, skin*. Let's read some words that begin with the **sk** consonant blend. We will follow the same procedure we used for the last blend.

skip   skim   skin   skunk

Skip will sip his skim milk.

Instructor: When you place the consonants **s** and **n** next to one another, they represent a sound that you hear at the beginning of these words: *snag, snack, sniff*. Let's read some words that begin with the **sn** consonant blend. We will follow the same procedure we used for the last blend.

snag   snack   sniff   snug

Scat the cat will sniff and snag a snack.

Instructor: When you place the consonants **s** and **t** next to one another, they represent a sound that you hear at the beginning of these words: *stop, stamp, step*. Let's read some words that begin with the **st** consonant blend. We will follow the same procedure we used for the last blend.

stop   stand   step   stick

stack   still   stamp   Stan

Instructor: Now you will read a sentence that contains words beginning in the **st** blend.

Stan will stop and stand on a stack of sticks.

Optional Follow-Up:
Give the child the necessary letters to form some of the words from this lesson on the magnetic alphabet board. The child will read each word once it is formed.

Lesson 52: The Beginning Blends BR, CR, DR, FR, GR, PR, and TR

You will need the following: *the magnetic alphabet board if you do the optional activity.*

Do the "Two Review and One New" today.

Instructor: Now we will learn more two-consonant blends. When you place the consonants **b** and **r** next to one another, they represent a sound that you hear at the beginning of these words: *brag*, *brand*, *brass*. Let's read some words that begin with the **br** consonant blend. First I will read each word. Then we will read that same word together. Then you will read that word by yourself.

brag   brand   brass   brick   Brad

Instructor: Now you will read a sentence that contains words beginning in the **br** blend.

Brad brags. Brad has the best brand of brass lamps.

Instructor: When you place the consonants **c** and **r** next to one another, they represent a sound that you hear at the beginning of these words: *crab*, *crisp*, *crack*. Let's read some words that begin with the **cr** consonant blend. First I will read each word. Then we will read that same word together. Then you will read that word by yourself.

crab   crack   crisp   crept   craft

Instructor: Now you will read a sentence that contains words beginning in the **cr** blend.

The crab crept in the crack of the rock.

Instructor: When you place the consonants **d** and **r** next to one another, they represent a sound that you hear at the beginning of these words: *drag*, *dress*, *drop*. Let's read some words that begin with the **dr** consonant blend. First I will read each word. Then we will read that same word together. Then you will read that word by yourself.

drag   dress   drill   drop   drum

Instructor: Now you will read a story that contains words beginning in the **br** blend.

Brent did not drop and drag his big drum on the fast drill up the hill.

Instructor: When you place the consonants **f** and **r** next to one another, they represent a sound that you hear at the beginning of these words: ***frill, frog, frost***. Let's read some words that begin with the **fr** consonant blend. First I will read each word. Then we will read that same word together. Then you will read that word by yourself.

Fred   frock   frill   frog   frost

Instructor: Now you will read a story that contains words beginning in the **fr** blend.

Jan has on a red dress.
Fred the frog will jump on the frill of the frock.

Instructor: When you place the consonants **g** and **r** next to one another, they represent a sound that you hear at the beginning of these words: ***grass, grin, grill***. Let's read some words that begin with the **gr** consonant blend. First I will read each word. Then we will read that same word together. Then you will read that word by yourself.

Greg   grasp   grill   grin   grass

Instructor: Now you will read a sentence that contains words beginning in the **gr** blend.

Greg will grasp a plump hot dog and grill it.

Instructor: When you place the consonants **p** and **r** next to one another, they represent a sound that you hear at the beginning of these words: ***prank, press, print***. Let's read some words that begin with the **pr** consonant blend. First I will read each word. Then we will read that same word together. Then you will read that word by yourself.

prank   press   prick   print   prod

Instructor: Now you will read a story that contains words beginning in the **pr** blend.

Frank did press his hands on the silk quilt.
Frank left the print of his hand on the quilt.

Instructor: When you place the consonants **t** and **r** next to one another, they represent a sound that you hear at the beginning of these words: ***track, trip, truck***. Let's read some words that begin with the **tr** consonant blend. First I will read each word. Then we will read that same word together. Then you will read that word by yourself.

truck   track   trim   trip   trap

Instructor: Now you will read a sentence that contains words beginning in the **tr** blend.

A truck will cross the track.

Optional Follow-Up:
Give the child the necessary letters to form words from this lesson on the magnetic alphabet board. The child will read each word once it is formed.

Lesson 53:   The Beginning Blends SQU, SW, and TW

You will need the following: *the magnetic board for the optional activity. For tomorrow's lesson you will need the following: thirteen index cards, scissors, a pen, metal paperclips, a dowel, a piece of string, and a magnet that can be tied to a piece of string.*

Don't forget to do the "Two Review and One New"!

Instructor: Now we will learn another two-consonant blend. As you already know, the letter **q** is always followed by the letter **u**. It is too afraid to go anywhere alone! When you place the consonant **s** before **qu**, you get the **squ** blend. **Squ** represents a sound that you hear at the beginning of these words: *squid, squint*. Let's read some words that begin with the **squ** consonant blend. First I will read each word. Then we will read that same word together. Then you will read that word by yourself. Once we have finished reading the words in the list, you will read three sentences.

squid   squint

I run in the sand.
I squint in the sun.
Yuck! Did I just step on a squid?

Instructor: Now we will learn another two-consonant blend. When you place the consonants **s** and **w** next to one another, they represent a sound that you hear at the beginning of these words: *swift, swell, swam*. First I will read each word with the **sw** consonant blend. Then we will read that same word together. Then you will read that word by yourself.

swift   swim   swam   swept

Instructor: Now you will read a little story that contains words beginning in the **sw** blend.

Skip fell in the pond and swam to the dock.
Skip did drip sand and mud on the dock.
Skip swept the sand and mud off the dock.
Skip is swift!

Instructor: Now we will learn the last two-consonant blend. When you place the consonants **t** and **w** next to one another, they represent a sound that you hear at the beginning of these words: *twig, twist, twin*. First I will read a word that begins with the **tw** consonant blend. Then we will read that word together. Then you will read that word by yourself. Then you will read a sentence that contains words beginning with the **tw** blend.

Twins   twist   twig   twill

The twins will twist the twig till it snaps.

Optional Follow-Up:
Give the child the necessary letters to form words from this lesson on the magnetic alphabet board. The child will read each word once it is formed.

Section 5

CONSONANT DIGRAPHS

Lesson 54: The Digraph NG

You will need the following for the optional follow-up game: *seventeen metal paperclips (without rubber coating), thirteen 3 x 5 index cards, scissors, a marker, a two- to three-foot length of string, a "fishing pole" (ruler, unsharpened pencil, dowel, etc…), and a lightweight magnet to which you can tie the string (a little one with a hole in the center is ideal).*

Instructor: Do you remember learning that the sounds /m/ and /n/ are called nasal consonant sounds *(Lessons 15 and 16)*? The word ***nasal*** refers to the nose; the sound /m/ and /n/ seem to come out of your nose! Well, the letter pair **ng** also stands for a nasal consonant sound. When you put short vowels in front of **ng**, the sounds are /ăng/, /ĕng/, /ĭng/, /ŏng/, /ŭng/.

Ng looks like a consonant blend (two distinct sounds blended together), but it is actually a consonant digraph (two letters that represent a single speech sound). The /ng/ sound is difficult for some children to hear and say if it is not a part of a syllable. Since most of the early words a child encounters when learning to read the /ng/ sound contain **a, i, o,** and **u** rather than **e**, a fun drill is to practice hearing the syllables /ăng/, /ĭng/, /ŏng/, and /ŭng/ as described below.

Instructor: These words all end with the letter pair **ng**: *bang, ring, song, hung.* So when the /ă/ sound comes before the letters **ng**, it sounds like this: /ăng/. Repeat after me: /ăng/. When the /ĭ/ sound comes before **ng**, you say this sound: /ĭng/. Repeat after me: /ĭng/. When the /ŏ/ sound comes before **ng**, you say this sound: /ŏng/. Repeat after me: /ŏng/. When the /ŭ/ sound comes before **ng**, you say this sound: /ŭng/. Repeat after me: /ŭng/. When you string those sounds together, you get: /ăng/, /ĭng/, /ŏng/, /ŭng/. I will say this three times:
/ăng/, /ĭng/, /ŏng/, /ŭng/ *(pause)*;
/ăng/, /ĭng/, /ŏng/, /ŭng/ *(pause)*;
/ăng/, /ĭng/, /ŏng/, /ŭng/.
Now let's say that three times together.

Together (three times):
/ăng/, /ĭng/, /ŏng/, /ŭng/.

Instructor: Now say it three times by yourself.

If the child has difficulty, have him repeat the chant after you several times more.

Child (three times):
/ăng/, /ĭng/, /ŏng/, /ŭng/.

The lesson continues on the following page.

Instructor: Now we will put these sounds into real words. Let's look at some words that end with the /ăng/ sound. I will read each word to you, and you will read it after me. Then I want you to try to read the list by yourself. I will help you if you need it.

Cover each word with your finger. After you reveal the first letter, reveal the **ang** as one letter-sound unit.

hang   bang   rang   sang

Instructor: Now let's look at some words that end with the /ĭng/ sound. I will read each word to you, and you will read it after me. Then I want you to try to read the list by yourself.

Cover each word with your finger. After you reveal the first letter, reveal the **ing** as one letter-sound unit.

king   ding   ring   sing

Instructor: Now let's look at some words that end with the /ŏng/ sound. I will read each word to you, and you will read it after me. Then I want you to try to read the list by yourself.

Cover each word with your finger. After you reveal the first letter, reveal the **ong** as one letter-sound unit.

dong   gong   long   song

Instructor: Now let's look at some words that end with the /ŭng/ sound. I will read each word to you, and you will read it after me. Then I want you to try to read the list by yourself.

Cover each word with your finger. After you reveal the first letter, reveal the **ung** as one letter-sound unit.

hung   lung   rung   sung

Instructor: I think /ăng/, /ĭng/, /ŏng/, /ŭng/ words are fun to say. Now I want you to read these words in two little stories.

Place a folded piece of paper under the line the child is reading. It is also okay for the child to move his finger under each word to help keep his place.

The man sang a long song.
The king did nap.

Ding went the bell.
Dong went the gong.
The king did yelp.
The king sat up.

Bang and clang went the drum.
Ding and dong rang the bell.
The kids in the band sang a glad song.

Optional Follow-Up Game: Catch That Sound!
Cut nine index cards in half (so you have eighteen 3 x 2.5 inch cards). Write the following letters or letter blends, one on each card. You will have one card left over.

h	b	f	r	s	p	cl	sl	w
k	d	z	sw	fl	br	g	l	

Clip a metal paperclip to each half-card. Then, using four full-sized index cards, write one of the following endings on each card:

ang   ing   ong   ung

Now construct your fishing pole: Tie one end of the string to your pole (pencil, ruler, etc...). Tie the other end to your magnet. To play the game, scatter the following half-sized cards on the floor, upside-down (so you can't see the letters): **h, b, f, r, s, p, cl,** and **sl**. Then set the **ang** card in front of the child. Then the child stands by the letter pile and lowers his pole. When he "hooks" a half-sized letter card, remove the card from the magnet and set the letter or letter blend in front of **ang**. The child then reads the word. If he reads the word successfully, you can give him a prize (perhaps a sticker, a goldfish cracker, or the half-sized letter card itself). Ask the child to make up a sentence using the word. Assist him to make real sentences. If he is unable to read the word, it gets thrown back into the "sea." Keep fishing until all the half-sized letters cards are "caught." Then play the game three more times using the **ing** or **ong** or **ung** cards . Here are the half-sized letter cards that should go into each "sea":

<u>ang</u>

h	b	f	r	s	p	cl	sl

<u>ing</u>

w	k	d	p	r	s	z	sw	cl
fl	sl	br						

<u>ong</u>

b	d	g	l	s

<u>ung</u>

h	l	r	s	fl	sw	sl

Lesson 55: The Digraph SH
The Digraph Blend SHR

You will need the following: *the magnetic alphabet board for the optional activity.*

Do the "Two Review and One New" today.

Instructor: Today we are going to learn about a special letter pair. When you see the letters **s** and **h** side-by-side, you should say /sh/. This is the sound that you would say when you lightly put your finger in front of your lips and whisper, "/Sh/, /sh/, /sh/, don't wake the baby!" Let's say that sentence together.

Together (putting your finger to your lips):
    /Sh/, /sh/, /sh/, don't wake the baby!

Instructor: You can hear this /sh/ sound at the beginning of words. We will read a list of words that all begin with the letter pair **sh** which stands for the sound /sh/. First I will read each word to you. Then you will read that same word back to me. Then you will begin the list again and read all of the words by yourself. I will help you if you need it.

Cover each word with your finger. Remember to reveal the **sh** as one letter-sound unit, and then uncover the rest of the letters, letter-sound by letter-sound.

ship   shop   shed   shut   Shem

shall   shack   shell   shelf

Instructor: Now let's read a sentence about a man at the beach who sells shells and toy ships at his store called the "Shell Shack." This sentence is a real tongue-twister. I will read it slowly to you three times. Then you will read it slowly three times.

Run your finger under the words as you read the sentence aloud. The child should run his finger under the words as he reads the sentence.

Shem shall shelf the ship in the shed and shut the Shell Shack shop.

Once the child can read the sentence and understand its meaning, have him say the sentence as fast as he can. Have fun!

Instructor: Now you will learn to blend the **sh** letter pair with the letter **r**. **Shr** is found in words like *shrug, shrink, shred*. Let's read some words that contain the blend **shr**. First I will read each word. Then you will repeat that same word back to me. Once we have finished, you will read the entire list by yourself. I will help you if you need it.

Cover each word with your finger. Remember to reveal the **shr** as one letter-sound unit.

shrug   shrink   shrank   shred   shrill

shrimp   shrub   shrunk

Instructor: Now you will read a story that contains many of the words from the list above.

The crab shrank back in the crack on the rock.
The shrimp swam in the crack.
Smack!
The crab had his shrimp snack in a flash.
Yum!

Optional Follow-Up:
Put **sh** and **shr** on the magnetic alphabet board. Then give the child the additional letters that will make words from this lesson. Help the child pronounce the word as he puts up the letters. He may look at the list from this lesson to help him form the words.

Lesson 56:   The Digraph SH

Don't forget to do the "Two Review and One New"!

Instructor: Last lesson, we learned that when we see the letter pair **sh**, we say the sound /sh/ in
"/Sh/, /sh/, /sh/, don't wake the baby!" Say that sentence with me.

Together (putting your finger to your lips):
/Sh/, /sh/, /sh/, don't wake the baby!

Instructor: Last lesson you read words that all began with **sh**. **Sh** can also come at the end of a word.
Let's read some words that end with **sh**, which stands for the sound /sh/. First I will read
each word to you. Then you will read that same word back to me. Then you will begin the
list again and read all of the words by yourself. I will help you if you need it. Read across.

Cover each word with your finger. Remember to reveal the **sh** as one letter-sound unit.

fish	wish	dish	rush
cash	stash	trash	flash
fresh	crash	Trish	swish

Instructor: Do you remember Shem at the Shell Shack from the last lesson? Well, Shem is closing up his
shop again today. His assistant, Trish, is closing up her side of the shop where fresh fish are
sold for supper. Two unexpected visitors come by. Read the story to find out what happens.

Place a folded sheet of paper under the line the child is reading.

The sun sets on the Shell Shack.
Shem shall shelf the ships in the shed.
Fish swish in the tank.
Trish shall wish she had a fresh fish in a dish.
Trish will stash the trash in a can.
Shem shall rush and shut the shop.

Scamp the dog and Scat the cat flop on the dock.
The smell of the trash in the can drifts past the pets.
Scat will smell the trash.
In a flash, Scamp and Scat will scan the dock.
Scamp will spot the fish in a dish.
Scamp and Scat will run fast.
Crash! The can of trash hits the deck.
Scamp and Scat will grab the fish trash and run!

Lesson 57: The Digraph CH

You will need the following: *the magnetic alphabet board for the optional activity.*

Don't forget to do the "Two Review and One New"!

Instructor: Today we are going to learn about another special letter pair. When you see the letters **c** and **h** side-by-side, you should say /ch/. /Ch/ is the sound of a "choo-choo" train slowly chugging uphill—/ch/, /ch/, /ch/, /ch/, /ch/. Let's say that train sound together slowly.

Together: /ch/, /ch/, /ch/, /ch/, /ch/.

Instructor: We will read a list of words that all begin with the letter pair **ch** which stands for the sound /ch/. First I will read each word to you. Then you will read that same word back to me. Then you will begin the list again and read all of the words by yourself.

Cover each word with your finger. Remember to reveal the **ch** as one letter-sound unit.

chat	chip	chin	chug	chum
Chet	check	chess	chill	chuck

Instructor: Now you are ready to read a story using lots of words beginning with **ch**.

Chet and Chan will get on a ship.
The ship will chug and chug.
Chet and his chum Chan will set up a chess set.
Chet will set his chin in his hand.
Chet will win at chess.
Chan will chuck the chess set off the ship.
Bad Chan!

Instructor: **Ch** can also come at the end of a word. Let's read some words that end with the letter pair **ch**, which stands for the sound /ch/. First I will read each word to you. Then you will read that same word back to me. Then you will read all of the words by yourself.

Cover each word with your finger. Remember to reveal the **ch** as one letter-sound unit.

rich   much   such

Instructor: Now you are ready to read a story using words that end with **ch**.

Chad sells such a lot of rings at his shop.
A rich man got a ring at the shop and spent much of his cash.

Optional Follow-Up:
Put **ch** on the board. Then give the child the additional letters that will make words from this lesson (but only the words that begin with **ch**). Help the child pronounce the word as he puts up the letters. He may look at the list from this lesson to help him form the words.

Lesson 58: The Digraph Blends TCH and NCH

You may need the following: *a piece of paper and a pen.*

Don't forget to do the "Two Review and One New"!

Review

Instructor: Do you remember that when you saw the letter pair **ch** in the last lesson, you made the sound of a train chugging uphill: /ch/, /ch/, /ch/, /ch/, /ch/? The train goes very slowly. Say that sound with me.

Together: /ch/, /ch/, /ch/, /ch/, /ch/.

New

Instructor: Now you are going to learn a three-letter blend that often comes at the ends of words. The blend combines the letter **t** with the letter pair **ch**. **Tch** is a very interesting blend because it stands for the same sound as the letter pair **ch**: /ch/. Listen as I say words that have the **tch** ending: *catch, match, pitch*. Can you hear the /ch/ sound: *catch, match, pitch*? Here is the interesting part: You cannot hear the sound of the letter **t** by itself. It is silent. So, when you see **tch** you say /ch/. Let's read the following list of words that end with **tch**. First I will read each word. Then you will repeat that same word back to me. Once we have finished going through the list together, you will read the entire list by yourself. I will help you if you need it.

As you uncover the words with your finger, remember to reveal **tch** as one letter-sound unit. Make sure the child is saying one-syllable words and not dividing the **t** into a separate syllable in his pronunciation (for example, in the word *catch*, he should not say "ca-tuh-ch"). Remind the child that the **t** is silent; it makes no sound of its own. If the child persists, write the list of words on a separate sheet of paper. Draw line through the letter **t** to remind the child not to pronounce it. Once the child catches on to the concept, read the words from the book.

catch	match	hatch	patch	batch
fetch	pitch	ditch	switch	twitch

Instructor: Now you will read a story that contains many of the words from the list above.

Rich will pitch the stick.
The stick will land in a ditch.
The dog will fetch the stick.
The dog will catch it and bring it back.

Instructor: In this lesson you will also learn about another ending blend. This blend combines the letter **n** with the letter pair **ch**. You can hear this blend at the ends of these words: *lunch, ranch, pinch*. Let's read some words that end with **nch**. First I will read each word. Then you will repeat that same word back to me. Once we have finished, you will read the entire list by yourself. I will help you if you need it.

Make sure the child is blending the sounds slowly together but pronouncing these words in one syllable.

ranch   pinch   lunch   bunch   munch

branch   clench   crunch   quench

Instructor: Now you will read a story that contains many of the words from the list above.

Tex will munch his lunch on the ranch.
Tex will clench his drink with his left hand.
Tex will crunch his thin chips and sip his soft drink.
Tex will pick up his trash and toss it in the can.

Lesson 59: The Digraph TH (Voiced)

Don't forget to do the "Two Review and One New"!

Children use **th** words naturally in their spoken vocabulary and have little difficulty replicating the voiced and unvoiced **th** once a word has been pronounced by the instructor. A child will pronounce the **th** as either voiced (as in *that*) or unvoiced (as in *thin*) because he has heard these words spoken many times before.

Instructor: Today we are going to learn about a very special letter pair: **th**. **Th** is a tricky letter pair because there are two slightly different sounds it represents. This lesson we will focus on one of those sounds. You can hear this sound in words like ***them, than, this***. You can make this sound by sticking the end of your tongue under your front teeth and adding your voice. This is a voiced sound.

The voiced sound of **th** is written phonetically like this: /<u>th</u>/.

Instructor: The voiced /<u>th</u>/ sounds like a race car going around a track: "/<u>th</u>/, /<u>th</u>/, /<u>th</u>/, there it goes!"

Put one hand above your eyes as if you are watching something in the distance.

Instructor: Let's say that together. Remember to use your voice to make the sound /<u>th</u>/!

Together (with hand shielding eyes):
    /th/, /th/, /th/, there it goes!

Instructor: The words in the following list all begin with a **th** which stands for the voiced sound /<u>th</u>/. Let's read this list together. First I will read each word to you. Then you will read that same word back to me. Then you will begin the list again and read all of the words by yourself. I will help you if you need it.

Cover each word with your finger. Remember to reveal the **th** as one letter-sound unit.

this   that   than   them   then

Instructor: Let's read a rhyming story containing words with the voiced /<u>th</u>/ sound.

This is a hog. That is a hen.
The man will set them in the pen.
Then the man will bring in a fish.
That fish will swish in the tan and red dish.

Optional Follow-Up:
After the child has read the poem, have him read it aloud until it seems easy to him. Then read the poem aloud with him, emphasizing the rhythm of the poetry.

Lesson 60: The Digraph TH (Unvoiced)
The Digraph Blends THR and NGTH

Don't forget to do the "Two Review and One New"!

The unvoiced sound of **th** (as in *thin*) is written /th/.

Instructor: Yesterday, you read words that contained the special letter pair **th**. All of these words make the voiced sound in /th/, /th/, /th/, *there* it goes! Today, you are going to learn the other sound the letter pair **th** can represent. The letters **t** and **h** side-by-side can stand for the sound /th/. This is an unvoiced consonant sound because you do not use your voice to make the sound. You only use air. This is the same sound you hear in /th/, /th/, *thumb*. You can make this sound by sticking the end of your tongue under your front teeth and blowing out your breath (it's very quiet, like a whisper). Let's practice this sound by saying /th/, /th/, *thumb* together.

When saying "/Th/, /th/, *thumb*," give the "thumbs up" sign.

Together (give the "thumbs up" sign):
/Th/, /th/, thumb.

Instructor: The words in the following list all begin with a **th** which stands for the unvoiced sound /th/. Let's read this list together. First I will read each word to you. Then you will read that same word back to me. Then you will begin the list again and read all of the words by yourself. I will help you if you need it.

Cover each word with your finger. Remember to reveal the **th** as one letter-sound unit.

thank	think	thin
thick	thing	Thad

Instructor: Now you will read some sentences that contain many of the words you just read. These sentences are about an athlete who uses a long pole to jump very high.

Thad thinks the thin stick will help Chip jump.
A thick stick is not the thing to help him.
Drop the thick stick, Chip.
Pick up the thin stick.
Run and jump, Chip!
Chip will thank Thad.

The lesson continues on the following page.

Instructor: **Th** is also found at the ends of words. Let's read another list of words. First I will read each word to you. Then you will read that same word back to me. Then you will begin the list again and read all of the words by yourself. I will help you if you need it.

Cover each word with your finger. Remember to reveal the **th** as one letter-sound unit.

path	bath	math
with	moth	cloth
Beth	Cath	Seth

Instructor: Now you will read a short story using some of the words you just read.

Beth will shop with Cath.
Cath will pick up pink cloth off a shelf.
Beth thinks Cath will get the thin cloth with the checks on it.
Beth will get the black, plush cloth.

The thin, silk cloth with checks costs a lot.
Cath had a class in math.
Cath will add up the cash and get much of the thin, silk cloth.

Instructor: Now you will learn to blend the **th** letter pair with the letter **r**. **Thr** is found in words like *thrill*, *thrash*, *throb*. Let's read some words that contain the blend **thr**. First I will read each word. Then you will read each word back to me. Once we have finished going through the list together, you will read the entire list by yourself. I will help you if you need it.

thrill	throb	thrust

Instructor: Now you will read a story that contains some of the words from the list above.

The kid thrust his hand in the crack.
A fish bit him!
His hand did throb.

Instructor: You will read two words that combine **eng** with the unvoiced letter pair: **th**. This is a little tongue twister! First I will read each word. Then you will read each word back to me. Once we have finished, you will read the two words by yourself.

length	strength

Instructor: Read these two sentences for me.

Fetch a length of thick, strong string.
Thick string has strength.

Lesson 61: The Digraphs WH and PH

You will need the following: *a pencil and paper for this lesson. You will need paper and drawing supplies for the follow-up activity.*

Don't forget to do the "Two Review and One New"!

Instructor: Today we are going to learn another special letter pair. When you see the letters **w** and **h** side-by-side, you make an unvoiced sound. This is the sound you make when you are blowing out candles on your birthday cake: /hw/.

The digraph **wh** represents the sound /hw/ in **whiff**. As you can see, the phonetic spelling of the sound is /hw/.

Instructor: Lightly put your finger in front of your lips and pretend that you are blowing out this candle (your finger).

Child (blowing at finger):
              /hw/

Instructor: This /hw/ sound comes at the beginning of these words: **whiff**, **when**, **whip**. The words in the following list all begin with **wh**, which stands for the unvoiced sound /hw/. Let's read this list together. First I will read each word to you. Then you will read that same word back to me. Then you will begin the list again and read all of the words by yourself. I will help you if you need it.

Cover each word with your finger. Remember to reveal the **wh** (as well as the **ch** in **which**) as one letter-sound unit.

when	Whim	whip	whiff
whack	whisk	which	whiz

Instructor: Now you will read a short poem about an elm tree that uses some of the words you just read.

When the wind whips,
The elm cracks and dips.
Its trunk cannot bend.
When will this wind end?

The child will practice the sound of **ph** in just a few words. There will be more practice with the digraph **ph** once the child can read words with long-vowel sounds.

Instructor: In this lesson we are going to learn another special letter pair. When you see the letters **p** and **h** side-by-side, you make as sound in /f/, /f/, **phone**.

Pretend to be on the phone when you say, "/f/, /f/, **phone**."

The lesson continues on the following page.

Instructor: This sound /f/ is the same sound that the letter **f** represents, but you won't see an **f**: only **ph**. Let's practice saying, "/f/, /f/, ***phone***" together.

Together (pretending to talk on the phone):
    /f/, /f/, ***phone***.

Instructor: Let's read a word that starts with **ph**. This word is a person's name. First I will read the word. Then you will read the word by yourself.

Cover the word with your finger. Remember to reveal the **ph** as one letter-sound unit.

Phil

Instructor: Now let's read two words that end with **ph**. First I will read each word. Then you will read that same word by yourself.

Remember to reveal the **ph** as on letter-sound unit.

Graph   Steph

Instructor: There are plenty of other words that contain the letter pair **ph**, and you will learn how to read those words in later lessons. For now, I will read the words to you, using my finger to move under a word as I read it. When you see **ph** and hear me make the sound /f/, circle the **ph** in the word.

If you want to reuse this book with another student, copy the following list onto another sheet of paper rather the circling the **ph** in the book.

Phone   photograph   phonics

Physical   graph   Ralph

Dolphin   alphabet   telephone

There is a delightful poem that contains all sorts of **ph** words (real words and not-so-real words) called "Eletelephony" by Laura Richards. You can find this poem on several internet sites or in the book *Favorite Poems Old and New* by Helen Ferris (Doubleday Books for Young Readers, 1957).

Follow-Up:
Have the child illustrate the poem "When the Wind Whips." You write the title for the child at the top of a piece of paper.

Lesson 62: Review the Ending Blend NK

Don't forget to do the "Two Review and One New"!

Instructor: Do you remember this chant: /ănk/, /ĭnk/, /ŏnk/, /ŭnk/? I will say this three times:

/ănk/, /ĭnk/, /ŏnk/, /ŭnk/. *(three times)*

Instructor: Now let's say that three times together.

Together (three times):
/ănk/, /ĭnk/, /ŏnk/, /ŭnk/.

Instructor: Now say it three times by yourself.

If the child has difficulty, have him repeat the chant after you several times more.

Child (three times):
/ănk/, /ĭnk/, /ŏnk/, /ŭnk/.

Instructor: Read these review words to me. Read across.

tank	Bank	sank	yank
link	Sink	pink	honk
bonk	Hunk	junk	bunk

Instructor: Now you will read two review stories that contain the words you just read. I will put a folded piece of paper under each line to help you keep your place.

The tank went on the bank.
It sank in the mud.
The man in the tank did honk.
The man in tan did yell, "Yank the tank!"
The men put a link on the tank.
They did huff and puff.
Bonk! A hunk of mud got on the men.
"Yuck! Let the tank sink!" the men did huff.

The doll is on the pink bunk bed.
If I jump and romp on the bunk bed I will dump the doll off.
The doll is left on the rug.
She is not junk!
I will pick up the doll and hug it.

Section 6

THREE-CONSONANT BEGINNING BLENDS

Lesson 63: The Three-Consonant Blends SCR and STR

Instructor: Do you remember that two consonant sounds pronounced together are called a two-consonant blend? Today you are going to start reading three-consonant blends in which three consonants are pronounced together. Each letter in a three-consonant blend still keeps its own sound. The first blend is **scr**. Scr is found in words like *scram, scrub, scrap*. Let's read some words that contain the three-consonant blend **scr**. First I will read each word. Then you will read each word back to me. Once we have finished going through the list together, you will read the entire list by yourself. I will help you if you need it.

Cover each word with your finger. Remember to reveal the **scr** as one letter-sound unit.

scram   Scrap   script   scrub   scruff

Instructor: Now you will read a story using some of the words you just read.

I will scrub Scruff the dog in the tub.
Scruff has a scrap of mud on his neck.
I will rub it with suds.
Scruff will scram fast!

Instructor: Now you will learn the three-consonant blend **str**. Str is found in words like *strap, strong, stress*. Let's read some words that contain the three-consonant blend **str**. First I will read each word. Then you will read each word back to me. Once we have finished going through the list together, you will read the entire list by yourself. I will help you if you need it.

Cover each word with your finger. Remember to reveal the **str** (as well as the **ong** in *strong* and the **ing** in *string*) as one letter-sound unit.

strap   Strand   strong   stress   strict

string   Strut   struck   strip

Instructor: Now you will read a sentence that uses some words you just read.

Gramps will strap a strong string on the box.

Lesson 64: The Three-Consonant Blends SPL and SPR

Don't forget to do the "Two Review and One New"!

Instructor: In this lesson you will learn the three-consonant blend **spl**. **Spl** is found in words like *split, splash, splat*. Let's read some words that contain the three-consonant blend **spl**. First I will read each word. Then you will read each word back to me. Once we have finished going through the list together, you will read the entire list by yourself. I will help you if you need it.

Cover each word with your finger. Remember to reveal the **spl** (as well as the **sh** in *splash*) as one letter-sound unit.

split   Splat   splint   splash

Instructor: In the last lesson you read a story about a boy who was washing his dog, Scruff. Scruff escaped from the tub! Now you will read the rest of the story. This story uses words you just read.

When Scruff splits, I will grab him.
Splat! I will stick him back in the tub.
Scruff the dog will splash when I scrub him in the tub.

Instructor: The last three-letter blend that we will learn is **spr**. **Spr** is found in words like *sprint, sprung, spring*. Let's read some words that contain the three-consonant blend **spr**. First I will read each word. Then you will read each word back to me. Once we have finished going through the list together, you will read the entire list by yourself. I will help you if you need it.

Cover each word with your finger. Remember to reveal the **spr** (as well as the **ing**, **ang**, and **ung** in *spring*, *sprang*, and *sprung*) as one letter-sound unit.

sprig   Sprint   spring   sprang   sprung

Instructor: Now you will read a sentence that uses some words you just read.

A sprig of grass sprang up in the spring.

Section 7

Long Vowel, Silent-E Words

Important Note to the Instructor:

Many children seem to struggle when the instruction moves from short-vowel words to words with long-vowel sounds and silent letters. Go very slowly at this time. In new, long-vowel word instruction, don't be afraid to *help the child sound out the words with which he struggles*. Review these troublesome words the next day or as long as necessary to build confidence. Since the change to long-vowel sounds is difficult for many children, do not do the "Two Review and One New" until it resumes in Lesson 84.

Lesson 65: Words with the Long-A Vowel Sound

The long-vowel sound of **a** (as in **acorn**) is written /ā/. The line over the **a** is called a macron.

Review

Instructor: You know the short sounds of all the vowels: /ă/, /ĕ/, /ĭ/, /ŏ/, /ŭ/. Say that with me.

Together: /ă/, /ĕ/, /ĭ/, /ŏ/, /ŭ/.

New

Instructor: In this lesson, you are going to learn another sound for the letter **a**. This sound is also the *name* of the letter: /ā/. Now isn't that easy? Listen to these words that all have this sound, called the *long*-vowel sound of **a**: *made, plane, cape*. Read the word below; this is a word that you have read many times before. It does *not* have the long-vowel sound of **a**.

mad

Instructor: Now let's change that word. If I add a letter **e** to the end of this word, it changes the short-vowel sound to a long-vowel sound: /ā/. The **e** at the end of the word has no sound of its own; it is silent. I will read this new word for you.

made

Instructor: Do you see how this works? If I add a silent **e** to the end of a short word with only one vowel, this changes the short-vowel sound to a long-vowel sound. Remember, the long-vowel sound of **a** sounds exactly like the name of the vowel: /ā/. Let me read you some pairs of words. First I will read a short-vowel word. Then I will read a word that has a silent **e** added onto the end. Listen to how the vowel sound changes once that silent **e** has been tacked on to the end of the word.

Read the following pairs of words to the child. Run your finger under each word so the child can follow along.

mad	at	cap	can
made	ate	cape	cane
Sam	tap	pan	rat
same	tape	pane	rate
gap	fat	past	plan
gape	fate	paste	plane

Instructor: Now let's read that same list again. I will read each short-vowel word and then the long-vowel word that is made when **e** is added; then you will read both words. I will help you if you need it. Once we have finished reading each word pair in the list together, you will go back to the beginning and the read the entire list of word pairs yourself.

Read the above list of words with the child. Explain that the word ***gape*** means "to stare with an open mouth." You should also explain that ***pane*** means "the glass in a window," not "something that hurts."

Instructor: Now you will read some of these words in a story about a broken window.

I tap the pane.
I gape at a gap in the pane.
I will get wet.
A pan will catch the drip.
I will tape the split pane.
The tape will stop the drip.

Lesson 66: Words with the Long-A Vowel Sound
   Sight Word: have

You will need the following: *one index card, a pen, and the magnetic alphabet board.*

Review

Instructor: Last lesson you learned how to change a short-vowel word into a long-vowel word. If you add a letter **e** to the end of some short-vowel words, it changes the short-vowel sound to a long-vowel sound: /ā/. The **e** is silent. Read these word pairs to me as a review.

rat	mad	Sam
rate	made	same

Instructor: Now you will read these words in sentences.

The rat made Sam mad.
That same rat ran at a quick rate.

New

Instructor: There is a common word that looks like the words you have been reading. It contains the vowel **a** and ends with a silent **e**. According to the pattern, it should have the long-**a** vowel sound. But this word is a "disobedient" word: it refuses to follow the pattern! It has a short-**a** vowel sound instead of a long-**a** vowel sound. I will write this word on a card for you.

have

Say the word to the child, and then turn the card over so the child cannot see the word. Have the child flip the card over and back several times, saying the word. Add this word card to your sight word stack.

Instructor: Read this sentence to me.

I have the same cap and cape as Sam.

Use the magnetic board to practice the following word pairs. Form the short-vowel word for the child. Have the child read the word. Then ask the child to put an **e** at the end of the word. Have the child read this new word with the long-vowel sound. Then have the child take the **e** off and read the word as a short-vowel word. Repeat this "adding and taking away" of the letter **e** until the child can read the words easily.

mad	at	cap	can
made	ate	cape	cane
Sam	tap	pan	rat
same	tape	pane	rate
gap	fat	past	plan
gape	fate	paste	plane

Lesson 67: Words with the Long-E Vowel Sound

You will need the following: *the magnetic alphabet board.*

There are very few words that have the long-e vowel sound that are formed by adding a silent **e** to the end of a short-vowel word. The long vowel sound of **e** (as in *equal*) is written /ē/.

Review

Instructor: Let's review the sounds of the short vowels: /ă/, /ĕ/, /ĭ/, /ŏ/, /ŭ/. Say those sounds with me.

Together: /ă/, /ĕ/, /ĭ/, /ŏ/, /ŭ/.

Instructor: Now let's say the vowel names: **a, e, i, o, u**. Say those names with me.

Together: **a, e, i, o, u.**

New

Instructor: Do you remember that the long-vowel sound of the letter **a** is the same as the *name* of the letter: /ā/? In this lesson, you are going to practice the long-vowel sound for the letter **e** in words. This sound sounds exactly like the *name* of the letter: /ē/. Now isn't that easy? Listen to these words that all have the long-vowel sound of **e**: *Pete, eve, these.* Read the word below. This is a word that you have read many times before. It does *not* have the long-vowel sound of **e**.

pet

Instructor: Now let's change the word. If I add a letter **e** to the end of this word, it changes the short-vowel sound to a long-vowel sound: /ē/. The **e** at the end has no sound of its own; it is silent. I will read this new word for you.

Pete

Instructor: Now let's read some pairs of words. First I will read each pair of words. Then you will read that same pair back to me. Once we have finished going through them together, you will go back to the beginning and read all three pairs yourself. I will help you if you need it.

pet	fat	at
Pete	fate	ate

Instructor: Now you will read a story that uses the words you just read.

The lesson continues on the following page.

Pete had a pet pig.
The pet pig had a bad fate.
The pet pig ate at a big pan.
The pet pig ate and ate and ate.
Pete will have a big, fat pig.
It is fate!

Take out the magnetic alphabet board. Go through the following list of word pairs. Form a short-vowel word for the child. Have the child read the word. Then ask the child to put an **e** at the end of the word. Have the child read this new word with the long-vowel sound. Then have the child take the **e** off and read the word as a short-vowel word. Repeat this "adding and taking away" of the letter **e** until the child can read the words easily.

mad	at	plan	Sam
made	ate	plane	same
mat	can	tap	pet
mate	cane	tape	Pete

Lesson 68: Words with the Long-E Vowel Sound

Instructor: Here is another time when the letter **e** stands for the long-**e** vowel sound. If **e** is the last letter and the only vowel in a very short word, it stands for the long **e** vowel sound: /ē/. I will read these words to you.

Me	he	we
She	be	the

Instructor: Did you recognize that last word in the list? You memorized the word *the* when you first started reading. Now you know all the words that follow this same pattern. Let's go back through the list together. I will read each little word to you. Then you will read each little word back to me. Once we have finished reading each of these tiny words together, you will go back to the beginning and read the whole list yourself.

Instructor: Now you will read a story that uses these little words.

Will Kate be at the match?
Yes, she and Kat will be at the match.

When will Pete get in?
He will get in at six.
He will be with me at the track.
We will have fun.
We will run ten laps!

Instructor: Let's review some short- and long-vowel words. Read this list of word pairs by yourself. I will help you if you need it.

cap	plan	past
cape	plane	paste
mad	can	pet
made	cane	Pete

Lesson 69: Words with the Long-I Vowel Sound

The long-i vowel sound (as in *ice*) is written /ī/.

Review

Instructor: Let's review the sounds of the short vowels: /ă/, /ĕ/, /ĭ/, /ŏ/, /ŭ/. Say those sounds with me.

Together: /ă/, /ĕ/, /ĭ/, /ŏ/, /ŭ/.

Instructor: Now let's say the vowel names: **a, e, i, o, u**. Say those names with me.

Together: **a, e, i, o, u.**

New

Instructor: Do you remember that the long-vowel sounds of the letters **a** and **e** sound exactly like the names of the letters: /ā/ and /ē/? In this lesson, you are going to practice the long-vowel sound for the letter **i** in words. This sound is the *name* of the letter: /ī/. That is easy to remember! Listen to these words that all have the long-vowel sound of **i**: *ride, bite, fine*. Read the word below; this is a word that you have read many times before. It does not contain the long-vowel sound of **i**.

bit

Instructor: Now let's change the word. If I add a letter **e** to the end of this word, it changes the short-vowel sound to a long-vowel sound: /ī/. The **e** is silent. I will read this new word for you.

bite

Instructor: I will read each pair of words below. Then you will read that same pair back to me. Once we have finished going through the list together, you will read the entire list of pairs by yourself.

| bit | rip | fin | hid | din |
| bite | ripe | fine | hide | dine |

| rid | kit | pin | dim | sit |
| ride | kite | pine | dime | site |

| Tim | Liv | shin | spin | quit |
| time | live | shine | spine | quite |

Instructor: Here is another time when the letter **i** stands for the long-i vowel sound. If **i** is the last letter and the only vowel in a very short word, it stands for the long **i** vowel sound. I will read this word to you, and then you will read the word by yourself

hi

Instructor: Now you and I will read a little play. We must pretend to talk on the phone to perform this play. I will read my sentence. Then I will point to your sentence. Let's practice this once, and then we will read it again and pretend to be on the phone with each other.

136

Instructor (pretends to pick up the phone):
    Ring! Ring!

Child (pretends to pick up the phone):

Hi!

Instructor: Hi! Is this (child's name)?

Have the child read the correct line below, depending on whether the child is a boy or a girl.

Child:

Yes, this is he.   Yes, this is she.

Instructor: Will you come and play with me?

Child:

I have to ask Mom and Dad.

Instructor: Okay. Will you call me back?

Child:

Yes, I will call back.

(Child and Instructor pretend to hang up the phones.)

Child (picks up pretend phone):

Ring! Ring!

Instructor (pretends to pick up phone):
    Hi!

Child:

Hi! Mom will let me.

Instructor: I am so glad! See you soon!

Child:

That is fine!

(Instructor and Child pretend to hang up the phones.)

Lesson 70: **Words with the Long-I Vowel Sound**
Review Long-A and Long-E Vowel Sounds
Sight Word: give

You will need the following: *one index card and a pen. You will also need the magnetic board if you do the optional activity at the end of the lesson.*

Review

Instructor: We will review a few of the long-vowel words that are made when we add a silent **e** to the ends of short-vowel words. First I will read each pair of words, and you will read that pair back to me. Once we have read all the pairs, you will read them all by yourself.

Tim	kit	sit
time	kite	site

Instructor: Now you will read these words in a story.

Tim had a kite kit.
Tim made the kite with cloth and string.
His kite will catch the wind in time.
Tim will sit at a site on a hill with his kite.

Instructor: Now let's review another set of words.

bit	at	fin
bite	ate	fine

din	mad	Jan
dine	made	Jane

New

Instructor: Before you read a story, you will learn new long-vowel words that end in **e** but do not have a short vowel partner word. I will read the word first. Then you will read the word back to me.

line   Plate   late   Steve

Instructor: Now you will read these words in a story.

Steve cast his line at the dock.
Did a fine fish bite?
Yes! A fish bit on his line.
Steve did grab the fish fin and set the fish in the net.
Steve can dine on a fine plate of fish back at the tent.

His kids made a din.
Jan and Jane made a din.
Steve got mad.
Steve made them stop.
Steve and Jan and Jane ate fish.

Instructor: Read the list of words and then read the sentence that follows the list.

Liv   pet   have
live   Pete

Pete and Liv have a live fish as a pet.

Instructor: There is a word that looks exactly like one of the words you just read. This word is spelled
                the same as the word *live* (a *live* fish), but it is pronounced with the short-**i** vowel sound: *live*
                (*live* your life). Read these sentences for me. You will need to decide which word (and its
                different pronunciation) makes sense in each sentence.

Sam spots a live snake in the tank.

Will the plant in the pot live?

I hope my dog will live a long time.

He sings the song live.
It is not on tape.

Instructor: There is another common word that looks like the long-**i** words but has the short-**i** vowel
                sound. I will write this word on a card for you.

give

Say the word to the child. Then turn the card over so he cannot see the word. Have the child flip over the
card and say the word. Do this until the child is comfortable. Add this word card to your sight word stack.

Instructor: Read this sentence.

Give me a pen.

Optional Follow-Up:
Take out the magnetic alphabet board. Go through the long-i word pairs from this lesson. Form the short-
vowel word for the child. Have the child read the word. Then ask the child to put an **e** at the end of the
word. Have the child read this new word with the long-vowel sound. Then have the child take the **e** off
and read the word as a short-vowel word. Repeat this "adding and taking away" of the letter **e** until the
child can read the words easily.

Lesson 71: Words with the Long-O Vowel Sound
Review Words with the Long Vowel Sounds of A, E, and I

You will need the following: *the magnetic board if you do the optional activity at the end of the lesson.*

The long-**o** vowel sound (as in *old*) is written /ō/.

Review

Instructor: Before you read a story, you will learn new long-vowel words that end in **e** but do not have a short-vowel partner word. I will read the word first. Then you will read the word back to me.

take   Prize   late   case

Instructor: Now you are ready to read a story.

Dad, Steve, and I take a fine trip in a plane.
We get a bite.
Dad gives a dime to Steve.
Steve spends his dime to get a prize.

Then we ride on the bus.
We must not be late.
We have time to rest as we stand in line at the plane.
A man with a big, black case is quite late.
We will have a fine time on the plane ride.

Instructor: Let's review the sounds of the short vowels: /ă/, /ĕ/, /ĭ/, /ŏ/, /ŭ/. Say those sounds with me.

Together: /ă/, /ĕ/, /ĭ/, /ŏ/, /ŭ/.

Instructor: Now let's say the vowel names: **a, e, i, o, u**. Say those names with me.

Together: **a, e, i, o, u.**

New

Instructor: Do you remember that the long-vowel sounds of the letters **a**, **e**, and **i** sound exactly like the names of the letters: /ā/, /ē/, /ī/? In this lesson, you are going to practice the long-vowel sound for the letter **o** in words. This sound is the *name* of the letter: /ō/. That is easy to remember! Listen to these words that all have this sound, called the long-vowel sound of **o**: *note, hope, globe*. Read the word below. This is a word that you have read many times before. It does not have the long-vowel sound.

not

Instructor: Now let's change the word. If I add a letter **e** to the end of this word, it changes the short-vowel sound to a long-vowel sound: /ō/. The **e** at the end has no sound of its own; it is silent. I will read this new word for you.

note

Instructor: Now let's read pairs of words. First I will read each pair. Then you will read each pair back to me. Once we have finished going through all of them together, you will go back to the beginning and read them all by yourself. I will help you if you need it.

not	hop	rob	mop	rod
note	hope	robe	mope	rode
cop	cod	con	glob	slop
cope	code	cone	globe	slope

Optional Follow-Up:
Take out the magnetic alphabet board. Go through the pairs of words above. Form the short-vowel word for the child. Have the child read the word. Then ask the child to put an **e** at the end of the word. Have the child read this new word with the long-vowel sound. Then have the child take the **e** off and read the word as a short-vowel word. Repeat this "adding and taking away" of the letter **e** until the child can read the words easily.

Lesson 72: Review Words with the Long Vowel Sounds of A, E, I, and O

Review

Instructor: In this lesson we will review more long-vowel words that are made when we add a silent **e** to the ends of short-vowel words. Then we will read these words in sentences. Let's begin by reading the following pairs of words. First I will read each pair. Then you will read each pair back to me. Once we have finished going through all of them together, you will go back to the beginning and read all of the word pairs by yourself. I will help you if you need it.

mop	Rob	glob	bad	not	past
mope	robe	globe	bade	note	paste

New

Instructor: Before you read a story, you will learn new long-vowel words that end in **e** but do not have a short-vowel partner word. I will read the word first. Then you will read the word back to me.

Shane   Home   Zeke   phone   game

Instructor: Now you will read these words in a story.

Mom left Shane, Rob, and Zeke at home.
Rob had on his red robe.
He had a glob of gum stuck on his robe and on the globe.
He must fix this mess!

Mom left a note.
Mom did ask that Shane mop the deck.
Shane did mope.
Shane had spilt paste on the deck.
Shane went past the paste and did not mop it up.

Mom bade big Zeke help Shane and Rob.
Bad Zeke did not help Shane and Rob.
Zeke did chat on the phone.
When Mom got home, she did spot the gum and the paste.
She made Zeke help them fix the mess.

Lesson 73: Words with the Long-O Vowel Sound

Instructor: Here is another time when the letter **o** stands for the long-**o** vowel sound. If **o** is the last letter and the only vowel in a very short word, it stands for the long-**o** vowel sound: /ō/. First I will read these words to you.

go   so   no   pro   yo-yo

Instructor: Now I will read each little word to you. Then you will read each little word back to me. Once we have finished reading these tiny words together, you will go back to the beginning and read the whole list yourself.

Read the list above with the child.

Instructor: Now you will read some stories that use these little words.

Hal is a golf pro.
He swings his golf club with so much strength!
Will Hal the golf pro win the match?
No, he will not go.
He has no time.

Trish is a yo-yo pro.
She can swish and twist the yo-yo so fast!
Trish can fling the length of string and then catch the yo-yo.
She is a whiz!
She can stretch the string and then toss and swing the yo-yo.
The yo-yo springs back.
I think it is such fun.

Lesson 74: Words with the Long-U Vowel Sound

You will need the following: *the magnetic board if you do the optional activity.*

The long-**u** vowel sound (as in *use*) is written /ū/.

Review

Instructor: Let's review the sounds of the short vowels: /ă/, /ĕ/, /ĭ/, /ŏ/, /ŭ/. Say those sounds with me.

Together: /ă/, /ĕ/, /ĭ/, /ŏ/, /ŭ/.

Instructor: Now let's say the vowel names: **a**, **e**, **i**, **o**, **u**. Say those names with me.

Together: **a, e, i, o, u**

New

Instructor: Let's begin this lesson by reading new long-vowel words that end in "e" but do not have a short-vowel partner word. I will read each word first. Then you will read the word back to me.

hole   side   make   cake   bike

Instructor: Do you remember that the long-vowel sounds of the letters **a**, **e**, **i**, and **o** sound exactly like the names of the letters: /ā/, /ē/, /ī/, /ō/? In this lesson, you are going to practice the long-vowel sound for the letter **u** in words. This sound sounds exactly like the *name* of the letter: /ū/. Isn't that easy? Listen to these words that all have this sound, called the long-vowel sound of **u**: *use, cute, cube*. Read the word below. You have read it many times before. It does *not* have the long-vowel sound.

us

Instructor: Now let's change the word. If I add a letter **e** to the end of this word, it changes the short-vowel sound to a long-vowel sound: /ū/. The **e** at the end has no sound of its own; it is silent. I will read this new word for you.

use

Instructor: Now let's read a list of words. First I will read each pair of words. Then you will read each pair of words back to me. Once we have finished going through the list together, you will go back to the beginning and read the entire list of word pairs by yourself. I will help you if you need it.

There are some differences in the regional pronunciations of certain long-u words. Some people may pronounce the long-u in *tube* as /ōo/ in *food*. We encourage you to use the long-u pronunciation.

us	cub	cut	tub
use	cube	cute	tube

Instructor: Now you will read sentences that use some of the words you just read.

The cute cub sits on a big red cube.
The cube has a hole cut in the side.

Jed has the use of the club.
He will ask us if we will go with him.

Pete did drop his tube of paste in the tub.
He must pick it up and then make use of it.

Instructor: Now you will read new long-**u** words that end in **e** but do not have a short-vowel partner word. I will read the word first. Then you will read the word back to me.

mute   mule   June   tune   Jude   Duke

Instructor: Now you will read a story that uses some of the words you just read.

Jude likes to sing a tune.
He made a tape.
Which tune did he sing on the tape?
He sang "The Duke and the Mule."
It is a cute tune.
He did not miss a note.
He sang two songs.
He will sing the songs to help his sis, June, rest.
Then he will mute the tune.

Optional Follow-Up:
Take out the magnetic alphabet board. Go through the list of long-**u** word pairs in the lesson. Form the short-vowel word for the child. Have the child read the word. Then ask the child to put an **e** at the end of the word. Have the child read this new word with the long-vowel sound. Then have the child take the **e** off and read the word as a short-vowel word. Repeat this "adding and taking away" of the letter **e** until the child can read the words easily.

Lesson 75: Long-Vowel Words: CK to KE

You will need the following: *the magnetic alphabet board for the optional activity.*

Instructor: Small, short-vowel words that end in **ck** also have long-vowel partner words. I will read this short-vowel word to you.

back

Instructor: Now I will read the long-vowel partner word.

bake

Instructor: The silent **e** has been added to the end of the word, making the **a** stand for the long-vowel sound: /ā/. Do you notice something else that has changed? The **c** has been dropped! Since **ck** is pronounced /k/, just like **k** is pronounced /k/, the **c** is not needed to correctly pronounce this word. Now let's read a list of words that follow this pattern. First I will read each pair of words. Then you will read each pair back to me. Once we have finished going through the list together, you will go back to the beginning and read the entire list of pairs by yourself. I will help you if you need it.

lack	tack	back	snack	stack
lake	take	bake	snake	stake

sack	shack	Mick	hick	lick
sake	shake	Mike	hike	like

Instructor: Now you will read a story that uses some of the words you just read.

Mack, Mike, and I will go on a trip.
We will live in a shack at the lake.
We will take a hike and spot a grass snake.
Mike will catch the snake and bring it back with us.
The sack will shake.
Will he bake the snake?
Will he make snake cake?
I hope not!
With luck, Mack and I will get a snack of chips and not snake.
I think of the chips and I lick my lips.
I will tell Mike to let the snake go.
I like to camp at the lake with Mack and Mike.

Optional Follow-Up:
Play with the magnetic letter board. The instructor should form the short **ck** word, and then the child reads that word. The child then removes the **c** and adds the silent **e** and reads the long-vowel word. Do this for the words in this lesson.

Lesson 76: Sight Words: to, two, too

You will need the following: *three index cards and a pen.*

Instructor: In this lesson you will memorize three tiny words. These words are all pronounced the same. That's simple! I will write these words on cards for you.

Write each of the following words on separate index cards. After this lesson, store these three cards in the sight word stack.

to   too   two

Lay all three cards out for the child to see. Tell the child they are all pronounced the same but they are used in different ways. Explain that *two* always means the number two; *too* means "also" or "very." The word *to* is one of the most common words in the English language and it often means "in the direction of." Have the child read the following sentences.

Mike has two hands.

He has two legs.

I like you, too.

I can go, too.

I ate too much.

I slept too late.

I will go to the shop.

She has to be at home.

Instructor: Now I will read sentences that each have a missing word. Each sentence will be missing one of the words on your cards: *to*, *too*, or *two*. *(Point to cards.)* When I get to the missing word, I will say *(to)* and point to the blank. Once I have read the entire sentence, you will pick up the correct spelling for the word *to*. If you pick up the right card, you will read the completed sentence by yourself.

Use a piece of folded paper to cover the sentences in the Answer Key. Read each of the sentences below for the child but let the child follow along. Reveal each sentence in the Answer Key only after the child has selected the correct card. Then the child will read the completed sentence in the Answer Key.

1. Luke has on ____ socks.

2. He is ____ late. He will miss the bus.

3. She will go ___ the bank.

4. I ate lunch. Jane ate lunch, ____.

5. I will take the trash ___ the dump.

6. I got six gifts, but Will got _____ gifts.

7. I will take the time ___ brush the dog.

Answer Key

1. Luke has on <u>two</u> socks.

2. He is <u>too</u> late. He will miss the bus.

3. She will go <u>to</u> the bank.

4. I ate lunch. Jane ate lunch, <u>too</u>.

5. I will take the trash <u>to</u> the dump.

6. I got six gifts, but Will got <u>two</u> gifts.

7. I will take the time <u>to</u> brush the dog.

Instructor: Now you will read these words in some short sentences.

I will go to bed.
Mom will go to bed, too.

I will go to the shop.
I will get two games.

Fred has two hats.
Ike has two hats, too.

Instructor: Now you will read some sentences. Each sentence contains all three words: *to*, *two*, and *too*!

I like to go to two games, too.

Two cakes will be too much to eat.

I like to lick two cones, too.

I am too late to go to the match at two.

Lesson 77: The Hard and Soft Sounds of C

Review

Instructor: I am going to read you a list of words that all begin with the letter **c**. I will point to each word as I read it. Follow along with your eyes.

Point to the **c** and the vowel that follows it in each word as you read it. Read across.

cat	catch	cane	cost
cot	cone	cut	cute

Instructor: The letter **c** stands for the sound /k/ in the words I just read. The sound /k/ is called the *hard* sound of the letter **c**. This is the way **c** is pronounced when it comes before an **a**, **o**, or **u**. Now I want you to read the words I just read. I will point to the **a**, **o**, or **u** in each word. Remember, **c** stands for the hard sound /k/ when it comes before **a**, **o**, or **u**.

The letter **c** also stands for the hard sound /k/ when it comes before a consonant. Since the child learned **cl**, **cr**, and **ct** as blends, that will not be discussed here.

New

Instructor: The letter **c** does not always stand for the /k/ sound. Sometimes it stands for the sound /s/. This is called the *soft* sound of the letter **c**. Repeat after me.

Say the sentence quite slowly, drawing out the sound /s/, and emphasizing the /s/ sound in the beginning of the words **soft** and **sound**.

Instructor: /S/ is the soft sound of **c**.

Child: */S/ is the soft sound of **c**.*

Instructor: When the letter **c** is followed by **e**, **i**, or **y**, the **c** is pronounced with the soft sound: /s/. You can hear this sound at the beginning of these words: ***cell, cent, cinch.*** Read the words below. Notice in these words, the letter **c** is followed by the vowel **e** or **i**. That is why the **c** stands for the soft sound: /s/.

Explain to the child that the word **cinch** means "an easy thing" (as in "It is a **cinch** to sing the Alphabet Song.").

cell	cent	cite	cinch

Instructor: Now you will read some sentences by yourself. I will help you if you need it.

I use a cell phone to call Dad.

A pack of gum costs ten cents.

It is a cinch to ride a bike!

The lesson continues on the following page.

Instructor: Now we are going to read some words where the letter **c** comes before **e** at the very ends of words. These words end in a silent letter **e**, which is a signal that the words all have long-vowel sounds. First I will read each word. Then you will read each word back to me. Once we have finished going through the list together, you will go back to the beginning and read the entire list yourself. I will help you if you need it. Remember, the **c** is pronounced with its soft sound /s/ in all of these words because it is followed by an **e**. I will put a piece of folded paper under the line you are reading to help you keep your place.

race	face	place	space
brace	trace	grace	mice
rice	spice	slice	price

Instructor: Now you will read four sentences that contain some of the words you just read.

Put the folded piece of paper under the line the child is reading.

We will drop an ice cube in the drink.
We will add a spice to the drink.

Two white mice hid in the space.
The cute, white mice snack on rice.

Lesson 78:   The Hard and Soft Sounds of G

You will need the following for tomorrow's lesson: *twelve index cards and a pen. You should also have the following items available in the room: rice, a penny, a slice of bread, a pencil, and a sheet of paper on which the child will trace his hand. You may wish to write the words on cards beforehand.*

Instructor: I am going to read you words that all begin with the letter **g**. I will point to each word as I read it. Follow along with your eyes.

Point to the **g** and the vowel that follows it in each word as you read it.

gap	game	go	got
God	gum	gun	gulf

Instructor: The letter **g** stands for the sound /g/ in the words I just read. The sound /g/ is called the *hard* sound of the letter **g**. This is the way **g** is pronounced when it comes before an **a**, **o**, or **u**. Now I want you to read the words I just read. I will point to the **a**, **o**, or **u** in each word. Remember, **g** stands for the hard sound /g/ when it comes before **a**, **o**, or **u**.

The letter **g** also stands for the hard sound /g/ when it comes before a consonant. Since the child learned **gl** and **gr** as blends, that will not be discussed here.

Instructor: The letter **g** does not always stand for the /g/ sound. Sometimes it stands for the sound /j/. This is called the *soft* sound of the letter **g**. When the letter **g** is followed by **e**, **i**, or **y**, the **g** is usually pronounced with the soft sound: /j/. You can hear this sound at the beginning of these words: *gel, gem, gist*. Read the words below. Notice in these words, the letter **g** is followed by the vowel **e** or **i**. That is why the **g** stands for the soft sound: /j/.

Explain to the child that the word *gist* means "the main point of something" (in "the *gist* of the conversation…").

gel	gem	Gene	gist

Instructor: Now you will read sentences that use some of the words you just read. I will put a folded piece of paper under the line you are reading to help you keep your place.

The gem is on the ring.
It will shine in the sun.

Gene will fix a hole in the shelf at his home.
Gene will rub a glob of gel in the hole.
The gel will crust and hide the hole.
It is a cinch!

The lesson continues on the following page.

Instructor: Now we are going to read some words where the letter **g** comes before **e** at the very *ends* of words. These words end in a silent letter **e**, which is a signal that the words all have long-vowel sounds. First I will read each word. Then you will read each word back to me. Once we have finished going through the words together, you will go back to the beginning and read them all yourself. I will help you if you need it. Remember, the **g** is pronounced with its soft sound /j/ in all of these words because it is followed by an **e**.

age   cage   page   rage

huge   strange   change   stage

Instructor: Now you will read a story that uses some of the words you just read.

The snake in the cage is strange and huge.
He slides to a log in the cage.
The tag on the cage tells the age of the snake.
The snake is two.
The man in white will change the cage of the snake.
I hope that the snake will not be in a rage!

Lesson 79: Review of the Soft Sounds of C and G

You will need the following: *twelve index cards and a pen. You should also have the following items available in the room: rice, a penny, a slice of bread, a pencil, and a sheet of paper on which the child will trace his hand.*

Game: Command Cards
Using seventeen index cards, write each of the following words on a card. **Keep them in order as you go across the page from left to right.**

face	place	trace	age	change	strange
cent	cell	rice	slice	mice	huge

Read the following sentences to the child. When you get to the word in bold print, **do not read it out loud**. Instead, hold up the appropriate index card so the child can read it. Once the child has correctly read the words, he may do what the sentence commands.

Make a silly **face**.
Do seven jumping jacks in **place**.
Trace your hand on a piece of paper.
Hold up the number of fingers that tell your **age**.
Change your voice to pretend you are a baby.
Do a **strange** dance.
Balance one **cent** on your head.
Pretend to call me on a **cell** phone.
Hold the **rice** in both hands.
Nibble a **slice** of bread.
Let's pretend we are **mice** escaping from a cat.
Pretend you are catching a **huge** fish.

When you have finished playing the game, shuffle the cards and give them to the child. Have him read each card. If he has difficulty with any of the words, put those cards in a pile to review over the next few days.

Lesson 80: Long-Vowel Words: S Stands for the /z/ Sound

Instructor: Read these words for me. You have already read them many times before.

as   has   is   his

Instructor: These words have something in common: the **s** in the word sounds like /z/. The **s** "buzzes" like a bee; it does not "hiss" like a snake. You are going to read some more words in which the **s** buzzes like a bee. **S** often stands for the sound /z/ when it is followed by an **e**, as in the words *rose* and *wise*. Let's read the following words. First I will read each word. Then you will read each word back to me. Once we have finished going through the words together, you will go back to the beginning and read the entire list yourself. I will help you if you need it. Remember, the letter **s** in these words is pronounced /z/. The silent **e** at the end of each word is a signal that these words all contain long-vowel sounds.

The verb **use** (pronounced with a /z/ sound) is included in this list. The noun **use** (that the child has read previously) is pronounced with a /s/ sound. Place a folded piece of paper under line the child is reading to help train his eyes to move across a page from left to right.

wise	rise	rose	pose
nose	chose	close	use
fuse	these	those	phrase

Instructor: You will read a story that uses some of the words you just read. I will place a folded sheet of paper under the line you are reading.

Trace chose a huge, red rose at the shop.
A tag on the rose tells its price.
Trace will use these snips to clip the rose.

Trace will lift the rose to his face.
Trace will sniff the rose with his nose.
It smells nice.
He will take the rose to his Mom.
She will hug him.

Lesson 81: Adding S to the Ends of Words

Instructor: You already know how to read short-vowel words ending in the letter **s**. In these words, the letter **s** stands for the sound /s/ (like the hissing of a snake). Read these words for me.

kits   grins

Instructor: You also know how to read long-vowel words that end in a silent **e**. You can also add an **s** to the ends of these words. Read each word pair to me.

pile	grape	date	lime
piles	grapes	dates	limes

Instructor: Now you will read some sentences that contain the words you just read.

A cloth is set on the grass.
Piles of grapes, dates, and limes sit on plates.

Instructor: Let's read more words. Read these words to me.

name	state	drive
names	states	drives

Instructor: Now you will read a sentence that contains the words you just read.

I spot the names of six states on the van that drives past us.

Instructor: Let's read even more words! Read these words to me.

chime	wake	pane	flake
chimes	wakes	panes	flakes

pipe	scrape	sale
pipes	scrapes	sales

Instructor: Now you will read a story that uses the many of the words you just read.

The bell chimes.
It wakes me up.
Ice clings to the panes of glass.
Flakes drift past the pane.
I must scrape the ice off the panes and check if the pipes froze.
I get a chill when I think of it.
I will go to the sales and get thick socks!

Lesson 82: Review of Long-Vowel Words

Instructor: Let's read a list of long-vowel words that end in silent **e**. First I will read each word. Then you will read each word back to me. Once we have finished going through the list together, you will go back to the beginning and read the entire list yourself. I will help you if you need it. Then you will read a story using these words. I will put a folded piece of paper under the line you are reading to help you read across the correct line. The letter s in the word *close* (*you are* ***close*** *to me*) is pronounced /s/. It does not stand for the sound /z/.

nine	shape	close	side	gaze	whale
white	five	twice	size	stride	wide
while	strike	game	smile		

Instructor: Some of the words in the following list add an **s** to the long-vowel, silent **e** form of a word. First I will read each pair of words. Then you will read that same pair to me. Once we have finished going through them together, you will go back to the beginning and read each pair of words by yourself.

shine	stripe	make	wave	shake
shines	stripes	makes	waves	shakes

Instructor: Now you will read a story about a giant whale! I will put a folded piece of paper under the line you are reading to help you keep your place.

The nine men on the ship spot a huge shape.
The shape shines in the sun.
The shape drifts close to the side of the ship.
The men gaze at the shape.
It is a whale!
It is a strange white whale with five stripes on its back.
It is twice the size of the ship!

The nine men yell and stride on the deck.
Then the whale swims in a wide path.
The whale dives and makes two huge waves while it swims.
The waves strike the ship twice and the ship shakes.
This is a game to the whale!
The whale swims off, and the men smile.
That was close!

Lesson 83:   Review of Long-Vowel Words

Instructor: Let's read some long-vowel words that end in silent **e**. First I will read each word or pair of words. Then you will read each word or pair of words back to me. Once we have finished going through the words together, you will go back to the beginning and read all of them by yourself. I will help you if you need it.

wife	came	bride	name	plate	shine
state	brave	flame	mile	wide	save
life	maze	slice	rope	prize	

throne	line
thrones	lines

Instructor: Let's practice a couple of difficult words. Then you will be able to read them with ease when you encounter them in the story.

quest	depth
quests	depths

Instructor: Now you will read a story that uses the words you have read in this lesson. This story is about a king who has an announcement to make. Find out what this king says to the people of his kingdom. I will point out the quotation marks when you get to them in the story.

The rich king and his wife came up the path.
Then the king and his bride sat on thrones.
The thrones had lines of red gems on them.
The king had a name plate on his throne that did shine in the sun.
The king rose.

The king did state, "I shall test a brave man of strength.
I shall send him on a quest.
Can he quench the flame that is a mile wide?
Can he save the life of the man stuck in the Black Depths?
Can he run the maze and slice the strong rope that no man can cut?
I shall grant a prize to this man.
He shall be the next king!"

Section 8

COMMON SPELLINGS FOR THE LONG-A SOUND

"Two Review and One New" Starts Again Here.

It's time to do daily reviews again! *Each day* at the beginning of your reading lesson, you should briefly review the last lesson and any concepts from previous lessons with which the child has had difficulty. This generally should take about five minutes. If the child needs more review, stop and do it before proceeding with the next lesson. After you are finished with the "Two Review," begin the new lesson. I will remind you of the "Two Review and One New" at the beginning of many lessons.

Now that the child is familiar with words that have one long-vowel sound and end with silent **e**, the child will begin to recognize other spellings of the long-vowel sounds.

Lesson 84: The Vowel Pair AI as /ā/

Review

Instructor: Read the following three words. You have read these words many times before.

to   two   too

Instructor: These are three different words with three different meanings spelled three different ways, but they are all pronounced alike. There are a lot of words like this in our language: words that sound the same, but have different spellings and different meanings. You will read some of these words in this lesson. You already know how to read words that have the long-**a** vowel sound and end with silent **e**. Read the following words for me. Read across the line.

made   plane   tale   male   sale

pale   pane   mane   waste   gale

New

Instructor: There are other spellings for this same long-vowel sound of **a**. You will learn them in the next few lessons. Today, you learn that when the vowels **a** and **i** are paired together in a word, you say /ā/. First I will read each word to you. Then you will read each word to me. Once we have finished reading the list together, you will go back to the beginning and read all the words yourself. I will help you if you need it.

Cover the words with your finger and reveal **ai** as one letter-sound unit.

maid   plain   tail   mail   sail

pail   pain   main   waist   Gail

158

Instructor: Now you will read a little story that contains some of the words you just read.

Gail is a cute maid.
Gail has a plain belt on her thin waist.
She will take a pail and get the mail.
The cat with the black tail will go, too.
She will run back home when she has the mail.

Instructor: Now you can read two different kinds of words with the long-**a** vowel sound. Read the next two words for me.

maid
made

Instructor: The words you just read may be spelled differently, but they are pronounced the same way: *maid* and *made*. Each word means something different.

Point to *maid* (above).

Instructor: This word, *maid*, means "a female servant" in "The *maid* cleaned the room." It can also mean "an unmarried woman" in "The young *maid* braided her hair for the party."

Point to *made* (above).

Instructor: This word, *made*, means "created or put together" as "I *made* a tower out of blocks." It can also mean "forced to" in "Mother *made* me pick up the mess." So you see, the words *maid* and *made* may sound the same, but they are spelled differently and have different meanings. I will point to each pair as you read the words.

Maid and *made* are homophones. The term is described in Lesson 227. Do not discuss the term "homophone" with the child yet.

Instructor: Now you will read pairs of words that sound the same but are spelled differently and have different meanings.

Discuss the different meanings of each of the words with your child. Use each word in a sentence.

maid	plain	tail	mail	sail
made	plane	tale	male	sale
pail	main	waist	Gail	
pale	mane	waste	gale	

The lesson continues on the following page.

Instructor: Now you will read some sentences. Each sentence contains a pair of words that sound the same, but are spelled differently and have different meanings. Can you find them?

Gail, the maid, made the bed.

Twain, the plain man, rode in the plane.

Did she tell you the tale of when the fox lost his tail?

His soft, long mane is his main pride.

She had a pail of fresh, pale white milk.

The ship with the big red sail is on sale.

The male dog yaps at the man when he brings us the mail.

It is not a waste of time to cinch the belt on your waist.

Lesson 85: The Vowel Pair AI as /ā/

Don't forget to do the "Two Review and One New"!

Instructor: In this lesson you will read more words that have the **ai** vowel pair. Let's read the following words. First I will read each word to you. Then you will read each word after me. Once we have finished reading all the words together, you will go back to the beginning and read the entire list yourself. I will place a folded piece of paper under the line you are reading to remind you to read all the way across the line.

rain	pain	vain	rail	nail
snail	frail	trail	train	brain
chain	sprain	Spain	wait	faith

Instructor: Sometimes words with a vowel pair such as **ai** still end with a silent **e**. Since the **ai** stands for the long-**a** sound anyway, the silent **e** does not change the sound of the vowel. The words we are about to read also contain an **s** which stands for the /z/ sound. Let's read these two words. First I will read the two words; then you will read the two words.

raise   praise

Instructor: Now you will read a story that uses some of the words you have read in this lesson.

Gail is quite frail.
She has a sprain.
She waits with Steph and Ralph to take the train to the job.
She has faith that the train will stop.
Hiss, hiss, hiss.
The train slides like a snail to a stop.

Steph and Ralph help raise Gail so she can get on the train.
Gail grips the rail as she steps up.
The train chugs to life.
A chain of smoke trails in the wind as the train zips off.

Lesson 86: The Vowel Pair AY as /ā/

Don't forget to do the "Two Review and One New" today!

Review

Instructor: Let's begin by saying the names of the five vowels together.

Together: **a, e, i, o, u**.

Instructor: **A**, **e**, **i**, **o**, and **u** are the five main vowels. Today you are going to learn about a letter that is *sometimes* a vowel and *sometimes* a consonant. The letter **y** acts like a consonant when it is at the beginning of a word. Read this list of words for me that all begin with the letter **y**.

| yes | yet | yap | yam | yoke |

New

Instructor: As I mentioned before, sometimes **y** acts like a vowel. Today you will read words that contain the vowel pair **ay**. When you see **ay** in a word, you say /ā/. The vowel pairs **ay** and **ai** both stand for the same sound: /ā/. Let's read a list of words that all contain the vowel pair **ay**. First I will read each word. Then you will read each word to me. Once we have finished, you will go back to the beginning and read the words by yourself. Read across from left to right.

day	way	pay	ray	say
bay	gray	clay	stay	play
stray	Fay	Clay	May	Kay

Instructor: Now you will read a story that contains many of the words you just read.

Fay, Kay, and Clay will stay at a home on the bay for two days.
Fay will play games with Clay and Kay on a nice day in May.
Kay and Clay will play ping-pong.

Fay will lay a cloth on the sand and bask in the rays of sun.
These kids will swim and splash in the bay.
Fay, Kay, and Clay will go back home when it rains.

The word *gray* can be spelled two different ways. Americans spell the word *gray*, while the British spell the word *grey*. Since many children's books use the British spelling, *grey* will be taught in the next lesson.

Lesson 87: The Vowel Pairs EA, EI and EY as /ā/

You will need the following: *paper and drawing supplies for the optional activity. For the next lesson, you will need twenty index cards, a pen, and clear tape. You may wish to write the words on cards before the next lesson.*

Don't forget to do the "Two Review and One New" today!

Instructor: In this lesson you will learn about other long-**a** vowel pairs. The vowel pair **ea** stands for the sound /ā/ in these three words: *great, break, steak*. That's not too many words! Let's read those three words. First I will read each word. Then you will read each word. You will then read all three words in a sentence.

great   break   steak

I will take a break and munch on a great steak.

Instructor: Now you will learn another long-**a** vowel pair: **ei**. When you see the vowels **e** and **i** together in a word, you will also say /ā/. Let's read a few words and the sentences that follow them. We will use the same procedure we have been using.

Explain to the child that **reins** are the straps with which you guide a horse (or reindeer!).

veil   vein   rein

The bride will flick the reins and set off to be wed.
The veil will trail in the wind.

Instructor: Do you remember learning that **y** sometimes acts like a vowel in the vowel pair **ay** *(Lesson 86)*? There is another vowel pair that contains the vowel **y**. That pair is **ey**. When you see the vowels **e** and **y** together in the following words, you say /ā/. Let's read a few words, and then you will read the story that follows the words.

hey   prey   grey   they

Instructor: Now let's read a story about a big, black snake. This story uses all of the words you just read.

The black snake did wish that he had a snack of mice.
The snake did scan the grass to prey on mice.
The grey mice sat on the rock and ate nuts.
The snake came to the rock.
Hey! The mice fled.
They hid in holes.
The snake will have no snack this day.

Optional Follow-Up:
Have the child draw a picture illustrating the above story, making sure to include the following items: snake, mice, grass, nuts, rock, hole. Once he has finished, you label the items in the picture.

Lesson 88: Review of the Long-A Vowel Pairs

You will need the following: *twenty index cards, a pen, and clear tape.*

Game: Scavenger Hunt Cards
Write each of the following words on an index card. **Keep the cards in order as you go across each line from left to right.** Have plenty of clear tape nearby.

bake	shake	made	place	face
game	page	waist	plain	rail
train	nail	brain	May	play
ray	break	great	veins	grey

For this game, you will read each sentence below to the child. When you get to the word in the bold print, **do not read it aloud**. Instead, point to the word card. The child will read the card. You finish the sentence. Then have the child stick the card to the thing or place the sentence commands. Help your child to figure out where to place each card. When you are finished playing the game, you can either leave the cards up around the house, or take them down, reading the words as you do so. Save the cards to play the game again or to use as review cards if your child needs extra practice on these words.

Put this card on the place where you would **bake**.
Put this card on something that **shakes**.
Put this card on something you have **made**.
Put this card on the **place** you sit at dinner.
Put this card on the **face** of a toy.
Put this card on a **game**.
Put this card on this **page** I am reading.
Put this card on your **waist**.
Put this card on a **plain** piece of paper.
Put this card on the **rail** by the steps.
Put this card on a toy **train**.
Put this card on my thumb **nail**.
Put this card over your **brain**.
Put this card on the calendar at the month of **May**.
Put this card at your favorite place to **play**.
Put this card on a place where you see a **ray** of light.
Put this card *near* something that could **break**.
Put this card on something you think is **great**.
Put this card on one of your **veins**.
Put this card on something that is the color **grey**.

Section 9

COMMON SPELLINGS FOR THE LONG-E SOUND

Lesson 89: The Vowel Pair EE as /ē/

Review

Instructor: You already know how to read words that have the long-**e** vowel sound and end with a silent **e**. Read this list of words for me.

these   theme   eve   Steve   Pete   Zeke

New

Instructor: In this lesson you are going to read words that contain a double **e**. When you see **ee**, you say /ē/. **Ee** words are so easy! Would you like to try to read these words by yourself? If you have trouble I will help you. Remember, whenever you see **ee**, you say /ē/.

see   seed   peek   peep   tree   green

sleep   creep   sweet   queen   three   street

Instructor: Occasionally words with vowel pairs like **ee** also have a silent **e** at the end. This does not change the way you pronounce the word. Read these words for me. Remember, the **e** at the end of the word is silent.

breeze   sneeze   freeze

Instructor: Now you are ready to read a story that uses many of the words you have read.

The queen creeps to a sweet plum tree.
She sits on the green grass.
Plop! Three seeds drop on the queen.
The queen peeks at the strange seeds.
The seeds make the queen sneeze.

The queen bites a seed. Bad queen!
The seed makes the queen sleep.
The queen wakes up and peeps.
The nap has made the queen late!
She has to rush to get home on time.

Lesson 90:   The Vowel Pair EA as /ē/

You will need the following: *sixteen index cards, a pen, and four edible treats (cheese, raisins, candy, etc…).*

Don't forget to do the "Two Review and One New" today!

Review

Instructor: In this lesson you will review words that contain the vowel pair **ea**: *great*, *break*, *steak*. Read aloud these sentences that use three words in which the **ea** stands for the /ā/ sound.

I will take a break and munch on a great steak.
Break up that great steak so that I may take a bite!

New

Instructor: In the words *steak*, *great*, and *break*, the vowel pair **ea** stands for the long-**a** vowel sound. However, there are many more words that contain the vowel pair **ea**. In most of *these* words, the **ea** stands for the long-**e** vowel sound. Let's read the following list of words together. First I will read each word. Then you will read each word after me. Once we have finished reading all the words, you will go back to the beginning and read the list by yourself. I will put a folded piece of paper under the line you are reading to help you keep your place.

eat	meat	seat	beat	treat	tea
team	read	leaf	lean	clean	each
beach	cheap	speak	dream	steam	stream

Instructor: The following words also have the letter combination **ea** which stands for the long-**e** vowel sound. Three of these words end with the letter **s** followed by the silent letter **e**. Remember to say /z/ when you see the **s**.

ease	tease	please	breathe

Follow-Up Game: Eat a Treat
Using sixteen blank index cards, write each of the following words or phrases on a card. Shuffle the cards.

beach	cheap	clean	dream	leaf	meat
read	scream	speak	stream	team	seat
eat a treat	eat a treat	eat a treat	eat a treat		

Put four treats on the table (candy, cookies, cheese, etc…). Put the cards face down on the table. Have the child select a card and read it aloud. If he correctly reads the card he gets to keep it. If he does not, it goes back on the table in a different place. If the child gets an "eat a treat" card, he must read it aloud correctly before getting the treat.

166

Lesson 91: Review the Vowel Pair EA
Sight Words: do, who

You will need the following: *two blank index cards, a pen, and the* **to** *sight word card.*

Don't forget to do the "Two Review and One New" today!

Review

Instructor: Let's review some words that contain the **ea** vowel pair. Remember, **ea** is pronounced differently in different words. Try to read these words by yourself. I will help you if you need it.

great	steak	seat	steam	clean
please	eat	scream	lean	speak
meat	tea	tease	read	meal

Instructor: Now you will read a list of instructions that use **ea** words. This list tells you things to do and things not to do at meal time.

Sit still in the seat.
Please eat the beets.
Do not scream.
Do not whine.
Eat beets with a smile.
Cut the great, lean steak.
Do not speak while you chomp on the meat.

Do not play with that glass.
Please sip the tea.
Do not gulp it.
It is not nice to tease Sis.
Do not toss grapes at Sis.
Do not read in the seat while you eat.
Wait till the end of the meal and then read.

The lesson continues on the following page.

Instructor: Read this tiny word for me. You have read this word many, many times in stories.

to

New

Instructor: The word *to* is similar to a few other small words. These words all rhyme. I will read these words to you.

to   **do**   **who**

Take out the **to** card from the sight word stack. Write the words **do** and **who** on index cards. Have the child practice reading all three of the words until he can do it quickly. Remember to mix up the cards often. Add these cards to your sight word stack.

Instructor: Now let's review some other tiny words. You have already read these words before *(Lesson 73)*. These words also end in **o**, but the **o** stands for the sound /ō/.

go   **no**   **so**   **pro**   **yo-yo**

Instructor: Now you will read some sentences that use the words *to*, *do*, and *who* as well as *go*, *so*, *no*, *pro*, and *yo-yo*.

Who beats the rug with ease?
I do!
Who eats lean meat?
I do!
Who cleans the pane like a pro?
I do!
Who swings and flings the yo-yo so well?
I do!
Who likes to play a game?
I do!
Who likes to win a prize?
I do!
Shall I stop?
No!
Shall I go on?
Yes!

Follow-Up:
For variety, have the child go back and re-read the sentences. Have him change his voice for the questions and answers, pretending he is two different people.

Lesson 92: The Vowel Pair IE as /ē/
Sight Word: friend

You will need the following: *an index card and a pen.*

Don't forget to do the "Two Review and One New" today!

Review

Instructor: Let's review three words that contain the vowel pair **ei**. The **e** comes before the **i** in this vowel pair. When you see **ei** in these words, you say the long-**a** vowel sound *(Lesson 87)*.

veil   vein   rein

New

Instructor: In this lesson you are going to learn a new vowel pair that, at first glance, looks a lot like the **ei** vowel pair. This vowel pair is **ie**: the vowel **i** comes *before* the vowel **e**. When you see the vowel pair **ie** in the following list of words, you say /ē/. First I will read each word, and then you will read each word. When we are finished, you will read the entire list yourself.

field   yield   brief   grief   thief

chief   priest   shield   shriek

Instructor: Now you will read two more **ie** words in which the **ie** stands for the long-**e** vowel sound. These words end with a silent **e**. This silent **e** at the end of each word is a signal that the **c** in the word stands for the soft sound: /s/. Try to read these words by yourself. I will help you if you need it.

piece   niece

Instructor: Now let's learn a very common word. This word contains the vowel pair **ie**, but *it is not pronounced like the other words*. I will write it on a card for you.

friend

Read the word card to the child and have the child repeat the word after you until he knows it. Add this card to your sight word stack.

Instructor: Now you are ready to read a story using many of the words you have read in this lesson.

My niece of the chief is my friend.
She gave me a piece of cake.
I went to eat it in a field.
A strange snake made me shriek.
The brief shriek made the snake slide back to its hole. I ran!
I will yield that field to the snake.

Lesson 93:   Review of the Long-E Vowel Pairs

You will need the following: *the magnetic alphabet board.*

Instructor: Now you have learned all the vowel pairs that stand for the long-**e** vowel sound. Read these
words as a review. Later in the lesson you will read these words in a story.

Dee	deep	sleep	peeps	weeps	creep
flees	glee	Jean	speak	dream	breathes
steal	brief	shriek	thief	grief	

Instructor: Read the following three words. These words do not have the long-**e** vowel sound.

Remind the child that he cannot sound out the word ***friend***.

break   great   friend

Instructor: Now you will read a story about two girls with overactive imaginations. I will place a folded
piece of paper under the line that you are reading.

Jean and Dee lay in bed, deep in sleep.
CRASH! Jean wakes up with a brief shriek.
Dee jumps up, too.
Jean and Dee speak with a hush.
"Is this a dream?" asks Jean.
"Is this a thief who will break in and steal the cash?" breathes Jean.
Jean weeps with grief.
"I do not think it is a friend, Dee," peeps Jean.

"Jean, hush. I will creep to the phone.
I will see if it is safe." states Dee.
Just then they spot the great, grey pet.
It flees past the beds.
He is on a quest for white mice.
Jean and Dee gasp as they gaze at the cat.
"It is not a thief! It is a cat!" Jean yells with glee.
Jean and Dee smile and go back to sleep.

Optional Follow-Up:
Give the child the necessary letters to form some of the words from the list in this lesson. The child
should read each word once it is formed.

Section 10

COMMON SPELLINGS FOR THE LONG-I SOUND

Lesson 94: The Vowel Pair IE as /ī/
              Y Alone as /ī/

You will need the following for tomorrow's lesson: *eighteen index cards and a pen. You may wish to prepare the cards before that lesson.*

Review

Instructor: You already know how to read words with the vowel pair **ie**. When you see the **ie** in these words, you say the long-**e** vowel sound. Read the following words for me.

chief   shield   priest   field   piece

Instructor: Now you will read two sentences that use some of the words you just read.

The chief held up his shield.
The priest did cross the field to get to the chief.

New

Instructor: In this lesson you will read more words that contain the **ie** vowel pair. In these few, short words, the **ie** vowel pair stands for the long-**i** vowel sound: /ī/. I will read the whole list to you. Then I will point to different words in the list. Say the word as I point to it.

Do not point in order.

die   pie   tie   lie

Instructor: Now you are ready to read a short story.

I will die if I do not eat that piece of pie!
That is a joke, but I do like pie.
And that is no lie!

The lesson continues on the following page.

171

Do you remember that the letter **y** sometimes acts like a vowel? Next you are going to read, words that contain the vowel **y**. In these words, the **y** stands for the long-**i** vowel sound. When you see the vowel **y** in these short words, you say /ī/. Let's read these words together. First I will read each word. Then you will read each word. Once we have finished reading the words, you will go back and read all of them by yourself. Read across each line from left to right.

my	by	fly	sly	cry
dry	fry	try	sky	spy
shy	why			

Instructor: Now you will read a little play about a boy who has never worn a tie. There are two characters: a mom and her son. First you will read the lines for the son. Do not read the word son, just read the sentences that follow it. I will read the part of the mother.

Son: Mom, my tie will choke my neck and make me cry.
I do not lie!
Why must I keep this tie on?
It is just lunch with Dad and Sis.
I will be shy in a tie.

Mom: It will be fine.

The son pretends to put on the tie.

Son: I am cute in this tie!
In fact, it is quite nice.
I bet we will have pie at lunch.
Will the pie spot my tie?
No! Not that!
I will keep my tie clean and dry.

Mom: You look so handsome in that tie. Dad and I will be proud to be with you.

Lesson 95: Y Plus a Silent E as /ī/
Sight Word: eye

You will need the following: *eighteen index cards (seventeen for the game and one for the sight word) and a pen.*

Don't forget to do the "Two Review and One New" today!

Instructor: In the last lesson you read words that end in the vowel **y**. Sometimes words that contain the vowel **y** end with silent **e**. The silent **e** does not change the way you say the word. Let's read this line of words together. I will read the entire line for you. Then you will read the entire line for me.

dye   bye   rye   type   style

Instructor: There is another word that rhymes with the words you just read. It doesn't follow the same pattern as the others, but it is still pronounced the same. I will read it to you and then I want you to look at the word and say it back to me.

Make a sight word card, and practice the word with the child until he knows it. Keep the card in the sight word stack.

eye

Game: I Spy...
Write "I spy with my eye a thing that" on an index card. Try to get it all on one line while still keeping the print large enough to read. Using the remaining sixteen index cards, write each of the following sentence endings on a card.

is dry.	can fly.	will cry.	is black.
gleams.	is a treat.	I can feed.	is great.
is wide.	shakes.	I made.	I can play with.
is by me.	is white.	I can eat.	is a seat.

Place the "I spy..." card in front of the child. Give him the stack of sentence ending cards as well. The child pairs the "I spy" card with the first ending card. He reads the sentence. Help him as necessary to find something in the room that meets the description. Repeat these steps with each sentence ending card.

Review

Instructor: Read the following story that contains short- and long-i vowel sounds.

Lil, Jean, Steve, Bliss, and Phil will plan a great play.
It will be a treat to make a play with a script.
Jean plays the boss at a place to eat.
Steve and Bliss sit in seats.
Bliss reads, "I will eat fish, rice, and a side of peas."
Steve reads, "I will buy a slice of pie."
Phil will say, "Please give me a tip."

Phil will sneeze on the pie.
Who will eat that pie?
Steve drops the pie.
Lil pipes up, "I will clean that mess!"
Bliss thanks Lil.
Mom tells Bliss to switch roles with Phil.
When the play ends, Mom smiles with pride.

New

Instructor: In the story you just read, there are two types of words with the vowel **i** in them. There are words where **i** is the only vowel: *will*, *switch*, and *script*. When you see the **i** in these words you know to say the short-**i** vowel sound: /ĭ/. There are also words that contain the vowel **i** and end with the silent letter **e**: *smile*, *pipes*, and *pride*. When you see the **i** in these words you know to say the long-**i** vowel sound: /ī/. There are certain words that don't follow either pattern. These words are "disobedient words" because they refuse to follow the patterns. These words have only one vowel: **i**. They are not followed by a silent **e**. Yet in these words, the letter **i** still stands for the long-**i** vowel sound. Let's read this list of words together. I will read each word to you; then you will read each word. Once we have finished going through the list together, you will go back to the beginning and read the whole list yourself. I will help you if you need it. Remember, in these words, the single **i** stands for the long-**i** vowel sound.

rind	kind	mind	find	blind
grind	wild	mild	child	

Instructor: Those words all have something in common: they end in the blend **nd** or **ld**. Now I will show you a word. This word has the *short*-**i** vowel sound /ĭ/. I will read the word for you.

The following word is **wind**, as in "the wind blows."

wind

Instructor: Read this word in a sentence.

The wind is strong.

Instructor: Now I will show you another word that looks exactly like the word **wind** (as in "the wind blows") but is pronounced differently. This word has the long-**i** vowel sound, like the words **mind** and **kind**. I will read this word to you.

wind

Instructor: Now you will read this word in a sentence.

I will wind the string of the kite.

Instructor: You cannot tell the words **wind** and **wind** apart just by looking at them—they are spelled exactly the same! You need to read the sentence, try both pronunciations, and choose the one that makes sense in the sentence. Read the following two sentences, and try both pronunciations to decide if the word is **wind** (as in rushing air) or **wind** (as in to turn or roll-up).

The wind whips past the trees.

I must wind up this string.

Instructor: Now you will read a story.

The kind man will take the string off the bag of limes.
He will wind the string on his hand so it will not fly off in the wind.

The kind man will take a lime to the shy child.
The child will peel the rind off the lime.
The lime tastes quite mild.

Lesson 97:   Review of the Long-I Vowel Pairs and Patterns
Sight Word: buy

You will need the following: *a blank index card and a pen. If you do the optional activity, you will need several sheets of paper and drawing supplies.*

Review

Instructor: We have been reading different spellings for the long-i vowel sound. Two lessons ago we read words that end in **y** and have the long-i vowel sound. Read this word for me.

by

New

Instructor: Now you will read a word that is pronounced the same as the word you just read: **by**. This word also ends in the vowel **y**, but it contains a silent letter **u** before the **y**. I will read this word to you.

buy

Instructor: This word means "to purchase." I will write the word *buy* on a card for you.

Write *buy* on an index card. Lay the card in front of the child. Tell him that he is to say the word on the card when you point to the card. Use the word *buy* in simple sentences (for example, "I will go to the store and *buy* two apples," and "I will *buy* you a gift for your birthday," and "Will you *buy* me a book?"). Keep the card in the sight word stack.

Instructor: Now you will read a short story.

The man will go by the sweet shop and buy a cream pie.
The price is not cheap.
It is quite steep.
He will pay and take it home.

Instructor: The following poem is about a train with colorful cars full of things that all have the long-i vowel sound. It is called "The Long-I Line." Listen as I read this poem to you without your looking at it. Then you will look at the poem as I go back and slowly read it again. This time you will help me by reading all the words in bold print.

I sit at the stop and **I** gaze at the track.
I hear it approaching: click, clack, click, click, clack.

I squint my **eyes** tight so I can read the sign.
It says in **white** letters: "The Long-I **Line**."

Five cars on that train have a strange shape and **size**.
I blink, and I wink, and I rub **my** two **eyes**.

The first car is pink filled with **shy**, little **mice**.
They squiggle and wiggle and **dine** on **white rice**.

An odd **kind** of car makes me stop and look **twice**.
It's filled to the brim with peach **pie** by the **slice**.

The third car is blue, stocked with **kites** you can **fly**,
A few have escaped and now float in the **sky**.

The fourth car is red, packed with fruit that's **quite ripe**—
Limes, grapes, and oranges of every good **type**.

The car last in the **line** has black **stripes** on its **side**.
Wild zebras and tigers can blend in and **hide**.

The train pulls away in the fast fading light.
I wave it "good-**bye**" as it travels from sight.

Optional Follow-Up:
Have the child draw a picture of a train with five cars (guide the child to make the cars quite large—you may need to tape several pieces of paper together). Write a name on each car as follows:

Shy Mice
Pie by the Slice
Kites That Fly
Limes and Grapes
Things with Stripes

Have the child read each name of the car. Then the child can draw the contents of each car and color the picture. Title it "The Long-I Line."

Section 11

COMMON SPELLINGS FOR THE LONG-O SOUND

Lesson 98: The Vowel Pair OA as /ō/

Review

Instructor: You already know how to read words that contain the vowel **o** and end with silent **e**. These words are pronounced with a long-**o** vowel sound. Read this list of words as a review.

cone	globe	hope	nose	chose	those

New

Instructor: In this lesson you will learn another long-**o** vowel pair. When you see the vowels **o** and **a** together in a word, you say the long-**o** vowel sound: /ō/. Let's read this list of words. First I will read each word. Then you will read each word. Once we have finished going through the list together, you will go back to the beginning and read the entire list yourself.

oat	boat	float	throat	soak	Joan
groan	road	loaf	goal	soap	toast

Instructor: Now you will read a story about an exciting soccer game. I will place a folded piece of paper under the line that you are reading.

May and Joan pay to go see a game.
May and Joan sit in the stands.
The home team is in red.
The team on the left is in black.

The red team runs on the field.
They dash by the black team.
A man on the red team kicks a goal.
May and Joan clap and scream and cheer.

A man on the black team zips by the red team.
May and Joan moan and groan.
Is the game lost? Will we tie?
No! We win!

Lesson 99:   The Vowel Pair OW as /ō/
       Sight Word: was

You will need the following: *one index card and a pen.*

Don't forget to do the "Two Review and One New" today!

Review

Instructor: Let's begin by saying the names of the five vowels together.

Together: **a, e, i, o, u.**

Instructor: Do you remember that the letter **y** sometimes acts like a vowel *(Lesson 86)*? There is one more letter that *sometimes* acts like a vowel and *sometimes* acts like a consonant. Read this list of words that all begin with the letter **w** which is acting like a consonant.

wag	wet	win	wait	week	wave

New

Instructor: When the letter **w** follows a vowel such as **o**, it becomes part of a vowel pair. When you see the vowel pair **ow** in a word, you say /ō/. Let's read a list of words that all contain the vowel pair **ow**. First I will read each word, and you will read it after me. Once we have finished, you will go back to the beginning and read the whole list by yourself.

low	glow	slow	blow	snow	throw
bowl	own	grow	grown	show	shown

Instructor: Before you read a story about a snowy night, you will memorize a new word.

was

Write the word *was* on a card, pronounce the word, and give it to the child. Have him turn it over to hide the word. Then flip it back over several times until he is familiar with the way the word looks. Then lay the card face-up in front of the child. Tell the child that when he gets to the word in the story below, he should slap his hand on the card. At the end of this lesson, add this card to the sight word stack.

The wind was strong.
The white snow did blow in the sky.
It did glow in the street lamp.
It was so nice to see.
We had to scrape the ice and snow off the truck.

I was shown my own place to play in the snow.
I did not throw snow and blow snow.
My face was like a sheet of ice!
I went back in the den to sip hot tea.

Lesson 100: The Vowel Pair OE as /ō/
Sight Word: shoe

You will need the following: *one index card and a pen. The child should be wearing shoes for this lesson.*

Don't forget to do the "Two Review and One New" today.

Instructor: In this lesson you are going to learn about another vowel pair: **oe**. When you see the vowels **o** and **e** together, you say the long-**o** vowel sound. First I will read each word. Then you will read each word to me. Once we have finished, you will go back to the beginning and read the whole list by yourself.

doe	toe	hoe	woe
foe	Joe	Moe	goes

Instructor: Now you are going to read a word that looks like the words you just read, but it is pronounced differently. You will have to memorize the word. I will write this word on a card for you.

shoe

Write the word on a card and read it to the child. Then put the card on the floor and have the child say the word as he steps on it. Do this several times. If you wish you may tape the word to the child's shoe for the rest of today's reading lesson. After the lesson, put this word with the other sight word cards.

Instructor: Now you will read a story.

Joe goes to the shop to buy a hoe.
On his way in the shop, he stubs his toe on a step.
He grabs his shoe and hops.
"Woe is me!" Joe moans.

Joe wails.
"My toe throbs!" Joe groans.
The men at the shop help Joe.
Joe wipes his eyes and limps home with his hoe.

Lesson 101: O Alone as /ō/

You will need the following for tomorrow's lesson: *twenty index cards, a pen, a pencil, and blank paper. You may wish to write out the cards before tomorrow's lesson.*

Review

Instructor: Read the following story about a boy named Cole who does not stay and play with someone who is unkind. This story uses words with short- and long-**o** vowel sounds.

Todd and Cole tromp on a slope of soft moss close to the lake.
Todd yells that he will toss Cole in the lake.
Then Todd acts like it is just a joke.
Cole strides off to the phone.
He will tell his Mom to pick him up.

New

Instructor: In the story you just read, there are two types of words with the vowel **o** in them. There are words in which **o** is the only vowel: ***soft***, ***moss***, and ***tromp***. In these words you say the short-**o** vowel sound: /ŏ/. There are also words that contain the vowel **o** and end with the silent letter **e**: ***joke***, ***close***, and ***slope***. In these words you say the long-**o** vowel sound: /ō/. In this lesson you will read "disobedient words" that refuse to follow these patterns. They have only one vowel: **o**. They are not followed by a silent **e**. Yet, the letter **o** still makes the long-**o** vowel sound. First I will read each word in the list to you, and you will read each word after me. Once we have finished reading all the words, you will read the list by yourself. Remember, in these words, the single **o** stands for the long-**o** vowel sound.

old	bold	cold	gold	mold	told
sold	roll	stroll	gross	most	both

Instructor: Now you will read a story about a conversation between two friends who are on a long hike.

It is so cold!
My toes froze a mile back.
This trail seems like a ten-mile hike.
I was told it was just five miles long.
It was bold of us to take this trip.
When will we be home?

I need to munch. What is in the sack?
I will not eat that old roll!
It is so old it has grown mold.
It has green slime with specks of white fuzz on it.
It is too gross to eat!
Let us go home!

Lesson 102: Review of the Long-O Vowel Pairs and Patterns

You will need the following: *twenty index cards, a pen, a pencil, and plenty of blank paper.*

Game: Guess What I Am Drawing
Using twenty index cards, write one of the following words or phrases on each card:

boat on the sea	bow	bowl of grapes	coat on a child
an ice cream cone	hole in the mud	home	nose on a face
pole with a flag	phone	roach	road
rope	rose	smoke	flakes of snow
toad	toast on a plate	toe	an old, gross troll

Have plenty of scratch paper and a pencil ready. Put five cards at a time in front of the child. Have the child read them aloud. Then you pick one of the five cards (in your mind) and draw a simple picture of the words. The child has to guess which card you are drawing. After you have finished playing the game with all of the cards, turn all the cards over so you cannot see the words. Then have the child pick a card, read it to himself, and then draw a picture of it for you. You try to guess what the child is drawing. If the child is reading the words incorrectly, go through half the stack with him. Let him choose words from that stack.

Section 12

COMMON SPELLINGS FOR THE LONG-U SOUND

Lesson 103: The Vowel Pair UE as /ū/

You will need the following: *the magnetic alphabet board.*

Review

Instructor: You already know how to read words that contain the vowel **u** and end with silent **e**. These words are pronounced with a long-**u** vowel sound. Read this list of words for me.

use   cute   cube   tube   huge   June

New

Instructor: In this lesson you will learn about another vowel pair. When you see the vowels **u** and **e** together in a word, you say the long-**u** vowel sound: /ū/. Let's read this list of words. First I will read each word. Then you will read each word.

Explain to the child that *cue* means "a signal." The child will read more words that follow this pattern (in *rescue* and *continue*) when he is reading words of more than one syllable.

cue   due

Instructor: Now you will read these words in a sentence.

A note in the mail is the cue that the bill is due.

In the following instruction to the child, point to the words *due* and *cue* in the list above as you read them.

Instructor: I think that you are *due* for a break. This is your *cue* that today's reading lesson is over!

Lesson 104: The Vowel Pair EW as /ū/

You will need the following: *the magnetic alphabet board. For tomorrow's lesson you will need twenty-seven index cards and a pen. You may wish to write out the cards before tomorrow's lesson.*

Do the "Two Review and One New" today.

Review

Instructor: Do you remember that the letter **w** sometimes acts like a vowel *(Lesson 99)*? When the letter **w** follows a vowel, such as **o**, it becomes part of a vowel pair. When you see the vowel pair **ow**, you say /ō/. Let's review some of these words.

low   slow   grow   show

New

Instructor: The letter **w** also acts like a vowel when it is a part of the vowel pair **ew**. When you see the vowels **e** and **w** together in a word, you say the long-**u** vowel sound: /ū/. Let's read this list of words. First I will read each word. Then you will read each word. Once we have finished going through the list together, you will go back to the beginning and read the entire list yourself.

few   new   mew   stew

Instructor: Read the following sentences.

Few like the stew.

The new colt may bolt when the cat mews.

Follow-Up:
Take out the magnetic alphabet board. Have the child construct the following words with the long-**u** vowel sound. Give the child the necessary letters to form each word, letting him look at the word in the list. Once he has constructed the word, he will read it aloud.

use   cute   cube   tube   huge   June

cue   due   few   new   mew   stew

Lesson 105: Review of the Long-U Vowel Pairs and Patterns

You will need the following: *twenty-seven index cards and a pen.*

Game: Cross the River
Using nine index cards, write one of the following words on each card:

cube	cute	tube	tune	mule	due
few	new	stew			

Using eighteen cards, write other words with which your child has had difficulty (not words that contain the long-**u** vowel sound). If you can't think of these words offhand, here is a list of eighteen of the more difficult words you could use.

shown	wait	throat	child	buy	strength
priest	piece	please	scream	break	vein
praise	smile	twice	those	change	snatch

Lay out nine rows of three cards each on the floor. In each row, one card should be a word that contains the long-**u** vowel sound. The other two cards in that row should be other words of your choice (or from the list above). Tell the child he has to get from one side of the river to the other. The river is covered with stones, but the only safe stones have words with the long-**u** vowel sound. He starts at the edge of the "river" and reads the first row of cards. When he figures out which word card contains the long-**u** vowel sound, he may hop on that card. Then he reads the next row of word cards and hops on the next safe "stone." If he hops on the wrong "stone", the child must go back to the beginning and start over. See if he can safely cross the river!

Section 13

COMMON SPELLINGS FOR OTHER VOWEL SOUNDS

Lesson 106: The Vowel Pair OO as /ōō/

The long-**oo** vowel sound (that you hear in the words **too** and **cool**) is written /ōō/.

Instructor: Read these words for me. They are all pronounced the same way.

to   two   too

Instructor: Look at the last word in the list above. The word too has two **o**'s side-by-side. In this lesson we are going to read words with this letter pair: **oo**. When you see the letter pair **oo**, you know to make the sound in "/ōō/, /ōō/, oozing slime." Say that with me.

Together: /ōō/, /ōō/ oozing slime.

Instructor: This is the same sound you hear in these words: **choo-choo** train, **zoo**, and **tooth**. This is called the long-**oo** sound. It is not the name of any one vowel; it is a brand-new sound. Let's read a list of words together. First I will read each word. Then you will read each word. Once we have finished going through the list together, you will go back to the beginning and read the whole list yourself. Read across each line from left to right. I will put a folded piece of paper under the line you are reading to help you keep your place.

tooth	zoo	mood	smooth	spoon
scoop	room	broom	food	roof
cool	stool	moon	soon	oops

Instructor: Now you are ready to read a story using many of the words you just read.

I am in the mood.
May I get a smooth, cold treat?
Two scoops will do.
May I get it soon?

I sit on a stool in this huge room.
I eat this cool food with a spoon.

Instructor: Now let's read a list of words that contain the long-**oo** sound and end with silent **e**. Notice that in one of these words, ***choose***, the letter **s** sounds like /z/. First I will read each word; then you will read each word. Then you will read the whole list by yourself.

goose   loose   ooze   choose

Instructor: Now you will read a short story using all four words you just read.

When it rains, the mud will ooze in the goose pen.
So I choose to let the goose loose.

Lesson 107: The Vowel Pair OU as /o͞o/

Don't forget to do the "Two Review and One New" today!

Review

Instructor: In the last lesson you learned a brand-new sound: the long-**oo** sound. This is the sound in "/o͞o/, /o͞o/, oozing slime" (*or alternately, the sound in* **choo-choo** *train*). Say that with me.

Together: /o͞o/, /o͞o/, oozing slime.

Instructor: When you see the vowel pair **oo** in some words, you say the long-**oo** vowel sound: /o͞o/. Read these sentences that use a few words with the vowel pair **oo**.

My tooth is loose.

I will choose a tool.
I will use it to hit a loose nail on the roof.

New

Instructor: In this lesson you will learn another vowel pair. When you see the vowels **o** and **u** together in the following list of words, you say: /o͞o/. Let's read this list of words with the vowel pair **ou**. First I will read each word. Then you will read each word. Once we have finished going through the list together, you will go back to beginning and read the whole list yourself.

you   group   soup   youth   wound

Instructor: Now you will read a sentence that uses some of the words you just read.

Do you see the group of youths who sip the soup?

Lesson 108: U Plus a Silent E as /o͞o/
Single O as /o͞o/

Don't forget to do the "Two Review and One New" today!

Review

Instructor: You already know how to read words that contain the vowel **u** and end with a silent **e**. These words have the long-**u** vowel sound: /ū/. The long-**u** sounds exactly like the name of the vowel **u**. Read the following words and sentences for me:

use   huge   cube   cute

Do you need ice?
Use that huge cube of ice in the glass with the cute frogs on it.

New

Instructor: In this lesson you will read more words that contain the vowel **u** and end with the silent **e**. These words look like the words you just read, except they are pronounced differently. In these words, the vowel **u** stands for the long-**oo** vowel sound: /o͞o/. First I will read each word to you, and you will read it after me. Once we have read all the words, you will read all of them by yourself.

rude   rule   plume   brute   flute   spruce

Instructor: Now you will read some sentences that use the words you just read.

The rude brute breaks the rules.

Jen can tune the flute and play it by the old spruce tree.

Instructor: Read this list of words for me. You have already read these words many times before.

to   do   who

Instructor: You learned these words by memorizing them. The vowel **o** in these words stands for the long-**oo** vowel sound. Here are a few more words in which the vowel **o** represents that sound. You would think that because these words contain a single **o** and end with a silent **e**, they would be pronounced with the long-**o** vowel sound. However, these words are "disobedient." They do not follow the pattern! The words contain the long-**oo** sound instead.

lose   move   prove

Instructor: Now you will read these words in sentences.

I must not lose my strength.
To prove I am strong, I will move those huge stones.

Review

Instructor: Read each group of words with the long-**oo** sound as well as the sentence that follows each group as a review.

zoo   room   food   spoon   tooth

I can eat soft food with a spoon.

you   group   soup   youth

Do you sip soup with a spoon?

do   who   lose   move   prove

If I move do I lose my place in line?

Instructor: Now read these words with the vowel pair **ue** which stands for the long-**u** vowel sound. Read these two words for me.

cue   due

New

Instructor: In the two words you just read, the vowel pair **ue** stands for the long-**u** vowel sound. In this lesson, you will read more words that contain this same vowel pair. These words look similar to the words **cue** and **due**, but they contain the long-**oo** vowel sound. Let's read this list of words in which the vowel pair **ue** stands for the long-**oo** vowel sound. I will read each word. Then you will read each word. Once we have finished reading the list, you will go back to the beginning and read the word yourself.

true   blue   glue   clue   Sue

Instructor: Now you will read these words in a sentence.

Is it true that Sue will glue the blue and gold bow to the new dress?

Lesson 110: The Vowel Pair EW as /ōō/

Don't forget to do the "Two Review and One New" today!

Review

Instructor: You have already read words with the vowel pair **ew** in them. Read this sentence for me as a review.

Few like the new soup.
Most like the old stew.

New

Instructor: In the words *few*, *new*, and *stew*, the **ew** vowel pair stands for the long-**u** vowel sound. In this lesson you will read more words that contain the **ew** vowel pair. When you see the vowel pair **ew** in these new words, you say the long-**oo** vowel sound. Let's read this list of words together. First I will read each word. Then you will read each word. Once we are finished going through the list together, you will go back to the beginning and read the list yourself.

grew   drew   crew   blew

flew   chew   threw   screw

Instructor: Now you will read two stories. I will put a folded piece of paper under the line that you are reading to help you keep your place.

You may need to explain to your child that a gull is a bird that lives near the seashore, and eats fish.

The strong gusts of wind blew the sails of the ship.
Each man on the crew flew to his post.
Huge swells of waves did crash on the deck.
The crew drew up the sails.

The crew did wind up the ropes.
The crew drew in the net of fish.
The fish did flop and jump on the slick deck.
The gulls flew down to scoop up the trash fish.
The crew threw fish scraps off the deck.

191

Lesson 111: The Vowel Pair UI as /o͞o/

Don't forget to do the "Two Review and One New" today!

Instructor: In this lesson you will learn another vowel pair: **ui**. When you see the vowels **u** and **i** together in a word, you say the long-**oo** vowel sound. Let's read this list of words together. Some of these words end in silent **e**, but that does not affect the pronunciation of the word. First I will read each word. Then you will read each word. Once we have finished going through the list together, you will go back to the beginning and read the entire list yourself.

suit   fruit   juice   bruise   cruise

Instructor: Now you will read a story that uses some of the words you just read.

We drink fruit juice on the cruise.
I spill a bit of juice on the deck.
A man in a grey silk suit slips on the juice and scrapes his hand.
Oops!
I hope he will not get a bruise.
The man is not too mad, but his new suit is quite wet.

Lesson 112: Review of Words with the /o͞o/ Sound

You will need the following: *paper, a pen, and drawing supplies for the optional activity.*

Instructor: In this lesson you are going to read a very silly story that uses many words with the long-**oo** vowel sound.

I had a dream in which I had a strange and wild lunch.
It is true that in this dream bits of food flew by me.
I sat in my same stool at lunch in this dream.
Soon I did spy a prune fly by.
Which brute threw his piece of fruit at me?
This room is a zoo!

Just then I did see a slice of pie and a scoop of blue ice cream fly in the sky.
As I got up, a bowl of hot soup did slosh on my leg.
I did cruise past a chunk of meat and step on a steak.
Whoops!

Then I was hit by a group of fish that stank.
That was not my wish.
I did groan and moan.
Then I woke up.

I still do not eat fish.

Optional Follow-Up:
Have the child draw a picture of this story; make sure he includes the following items: ***stool***, ***prune***, ***fruit***, ***scoop of blue ice cream***, ***bowl of soup***, and ***group of fish***. Once the child has drawn the picture, label the items for him and have him read them to you.

Lesson 113: The Vowel Pair OO as /ŏŏ/

You will need the following: *the magnetic alphabet board.*

The short-**oo** vowel sound (that you hear in the words *good* and *book*) is written /ŏŏ/.

Instructor: In this lesson we are going to practice a new sound called the short-**oo** sound. You can hear this sound in these words: *good*, *book*, and *stood*. Let's play a game that will help you hear this sound in the middle of words. Listen to me say this word: *good*. Now you say it.

Child: *good.*

Instructor: There are three sounds in the word *good*. Listen as I separate these sounds for you: /g/, /ŏŏ/, /d/. Now listen as I leave off the first sound: *ood*. Now I want you to try that. Think the sound /g/ but do not say it. Then say the rest of the word out loud.

Child: *ood.*

Instructor: Now let's try that with a different word.

Repeat the same process with the words: *wood*, *book*, *look*, *took*, *wool*. Assist the child as necessary.

Instructor: In this lesson you will read words that contain the **oo** vowel pair. When you see the vowel pair **oo** in *these* words, you say the short-**oo** vowel sound /ŏŏ/. Do you remember saying the words *good*, *cook*, and *book*? That short-**oo** sound is in those words. Let's read this list of words together. First I will read each word. Then you will read each word. Once we are finished going through the list together, you will go back to the beginning and read the list yourself.

wood	good	stood	book	cook
look	hook	took	shook	crook

Instructor: Now you will read a story that uses these words.

I must cook the fish that I did catch on my hook.
I can make it taste good if I add spice and fruit juice.
I look in a book to see which juice to add to my fish.

The last time I made fish, I shook spice on top of it.
I took the fish to the fry pan.
When it was hot and crisp, I ate it.

194

Instructor: There are two words that contain the **oo** vowel pair that do not sound like other similar-looking words. They are not pronounced with the short- or long-**oo** sound. These words are "disobedient words" because they do not follow either pattern. These words are pronounced with a short-**u** vowel sound: /ŭ/! I will read these words to you. Then you will read the words.

blood   flood

Instructor: Now you will read these words in sentences.

The blood in my veins looks blue.

Too much rain will flood the new pool.

Follow-Up:
Take out the magnetic alphabet board. Have the child put an **oo** vowel pair on one side of the board and another **oo** vowel pair on the other side of the board. On the left-hand side of the board, have the child make the word *cool*. On the right-hand side of the board, have the child make the word *wood*. Tell the child that these words are examples of the two different sounds of the **oo** vowel pair. Have him read the words. By removing the consonant tiles and substituting new beginning and ending consonant tiles, have the child make the following sample **oo** words one at a time.

Left side of the board	Right side of the board
cool	wood
roof	good
food	book
moon	cook
smooth	stood
scoop	shook
tooth	wool
spoon	crook

Lesson 114: U Alone as /ŏŏ/
Sight Words: could, would, should

You will need the following: *three index cards and a pen for this lesson. For tomorrow's lesson, you will need twenty-nine index cards, a pen, and clear tape. You may wish to make up the index cards before that lesson.*

Review

Instructor: You already know how to read word with the short-**u** vowel sound. Read these words as a review.

cut   dull   gull   rush

New

Instructor: There are a few words that may look like the words you just read, but are not pronounced the same. In these new words, the vowel **u** stands for the short-**oo** vowel sound. These are "disobedient words" because the single letter **u** does not stand for the short-vowel sound of **u**, it stands for the sound /ŏŏ/. Let's read this list of words together. First I will read each word. Then you will read each word. Once we have finished reading the list together, you will go back to the beginning and read the list by yourself.

put   pull   full   bull   push   bush

Instructor: Now you are ready to read some sentences. Each sentence has a word with a short-**u** vowel sound and a word with a short-**oo** vowel sound. Read the words before you read the sentence.

cut
put

Please put a Band-Aid on my cut.

rush
push

Do not rush and push in line.

dull
pull

Pull the dull brass latch and go in.

gull
full

The gull has a beak full of crab.

196

brush
bush

The cat will brush past the bush.

The following words are very common, but the spelling pattern is rare. I recommend teaching these as sight words.

Instructor: There are three more words that contain the short-**oo** vowel sound. I will write these words on cards for you.

Write each of the following words on an index card.

could   should   would

Read the words to the child. As you read each card, give it to the child. Then have the child read the card and give it back to you. After you have read all three cards, let the child shuffle the cards and read them (do this two more times). Store these cards in the sight word stack.

Instructor: Now you are going to read these words in sentences.

I would read a good book if I could.
I think I should.

Lesson 115: Review of Words with the Short- and Long-OO Vowel Sound

You will need the following: *twenty-nine index cards, a pen, and clear tape.*

Game: The OO Sort and Shuffle

Using fourteen index cards, write one of the following words on each card. Go across. Keep the /ŏŏ/ words in one pile and the /ōō/ words in another pile.

shook	took	crook	wool	stood	book	look
tooth	spoon	cool	roof	moon	soon	stool

Have the child read the words in each group: the short-**oo** vowel sound words and the long-**oo** vowel sound words. Then mix up the cards and have the child sort the cards into the two groups. Read the cards again. If the any of the cards were put into the wrong pile, have the child read the word and then put it the correct pile. Shuffle the cards, and have the child sort the words again.

Game: Scavenger Hunt Cards

Using fifteen index cards, write each of the following phrases in bold print on a card. Keep the cards in order. Have clear tape on hand. Read the beginning of each sentence to the child. When you get to the phrase in bold print, do not read it aloud. Instead, show the child that card. Have him read the phrase to you and then tape the card to a suitable object. When all the cards have been placed on objects, the child should read them again as he collects each one.

Put this card on something **you should clean**.
Put this card on something **you can push**.
Put this card on **a shelf full of books**.
Put this card on something **you could cook**.
Put this card on **a book that looks like it would be good**.
Put this card on something **made of wood**.
Put this card on something that is **as red as blood**.
Put this card on **a piece of fruit**.
Put this card on **a can of soup**.
Put this card on **a thing that is blue**.
Put this card on **a thing you could glue**.
Put this card on something **you drew**.
Put this card on **a thing that you threw**.
Put this card on **a cool tool**.
Put this card on **a smooth bed**.

Lesson 116: The Vowel Pair AW as /ô/

The vowel sound you hear in the words **paw** and **law** is written as this symbol: /ô/. The mark over the **o** is called a circumflex.

Instructor: In this lesson you are going to learn a new sound. This is an "awesome" sound. What would I say if someone told me I was not going to get a birthday present this year? I would sadly say /ô/. This is the same sound that is at the beginning of the word **awesome**. Now you try it. What would you say if I said that you were not going to get a birthday present?

Child: /ô/.

Instructor: Now let's form some words that end in the /ô/ sound. Add a **j** to the front of the /ô/ sound. First think of the sound of the letter **j**: /j/. Then add the /ô/ sound: /jô/. What is the word?

Child: jaw.

Instructor: Now you try it. What is the sound the letter **s** stands for?

Child: /s/.

Instructor: Add that sound to the /ô/ sound. Think of the sound of the letter **s** and add that sound to /ô/.

Child: saw.

Continue to do this exercise with the child, helping him to form the following words: **paw**, **law**.

Instructor: The vowel pair **aw** stands for the /ô/ sound in this list of words below. In most of these words the /ô/ sound is at the end: **jaw**, **paw**, **law**. In some words, the /ô/ is in the middle of the word: **yawn**, **crawl**, **drawn**. First I will read each word to you. Then you will read each word. Once we have finished reading the list together, go back to the beginning and read the list yourself.

It may help to uncover the words sound-by-sound with your finger. Remember to uncover a blend or the vowel pair **aw** as one unit and not as individual letters.

jaw	saw	paw	law	claw
straw	lawn	yawn	drawn	crawl

Instructor: Now you will read a story that uses some of the words you just read.

I saw a huge, wild cat with black spots crawl on my lawn!
It had big teeth in its jaws and long claws on its paws.
I saw the wild cat go to the straw bed.
Would the huge, wild cat try to eat me?
It could, but it should not!
No, the wild cat did yawn and go to sleep on the straw.

Lesson 117: The Vowel Pair AU as /ô/

Don't forget to do the "Two Review and One New" today!

Review

Instructor: Last lesson you learned about an "awesome" sound. What would you say if I said that you were not going to get a birthday present?

Child: /ô/.

New

Instructor: In this lesson you are going to learn a new vowel pair: **au**. When you see the vowels **a** and **u** together, you also say /ô/. Let's read these words. First I will read each word, and you will read it after me. Once we are finished going through the list, you will read it by yourself.

haul   fault   vault   launch   sauce   Paul

Instructor: Do you remember that **s** often sounds like /z/ when it is followed by silent **e** (as in the word *rose*)? This is true for the following words as well. First I will read each word, and you will read it after me. Once we have read the three words, you will read them all yourself.

pause   cause   clause

Instructor: Now you are ready to read a silly story. It is about a Giant Spaghetti Festival. The town has decided to make the world's largest plate of spaghetti. The humongous pile of plain spaghetti has already been dumped at the town center. Now the town is waiting on three trucks: the sauce truck, the cheese truck, and the meat truck. Unfortunately, lots of crazy things happen to the trucks on their way to the festival!

The huge truck will haul a full load of sauce.
The sauce will slosh in the back.
The truck must make a quick stop. Whoops!
A huge glob of sauce hits the side of the hat shop.
The hat shop is quite red!

The truck full of cheese will pause by the pet shop.
The smell of the fresh cheese drifts past the mice in the shop.
The mice squeeze past the slats in the cage. Squeak! Squeak!
The mice chase the cheese truck and try to leap on it.

The meat truck was held up by ice and snow.
The meat froze!
The beef in the truck needs to thaw.
Then the beef and the cheese can be put on the sauce.
It will be a feast!

Lesson 118: A Alone Before L as /ô/
A Alone After W as /ô/

You will need the following: *the magnetic alphabet board.*

Don't forget to do the "Two Review and One New" today!

Instructor: In this lesson you are going to read words in which **a** is the only vowel. In these words, when a single letter **a** is followed by the letter **l** and another consonant, the **a** stands for the /ô/ sound as in *all*, ***ball***, and *salt*. I will read each word to you, and you will read it after me. Once we have finished going through the list together, you will go back to the beginning and read the list yourself.

all	ball	call	fall	hall	mall
tall	wall	small	salt	bald	waltz

Instructor: Now let's read these words in a story.

Joe, the bald man, will step up to the plate.
He is small but strong.
He will hit a wild pitch.
The ball will fly in the sky.

The ball will hit the wall and then fall.
The tall man will make a call and scoop up the ball.
The tall man will drop the ball.
Joe will waltz to the base.
He is safe.

Instructor: Now you are going to read more words with a single **a** that stands for the /ô/ sound. These words do not contain the letter **l**, like the words in the list you just read. However, these words do have another letter in common: The letter **w** comes before the vowel **a**. This tells you that the word contains the /ô/ sound. First I will read each word; then you will read each word. Then you will go back to the beginning and read the list by yourself. Then you will read the words in a story.

wad	wasp	wand	want	wash	watch
swap	swan	swat	swamp		

I want to swat the fly at the swamp.
I will put on bug spray so it will not bite me.
When I get home I must wash off the bug spray with a wad of wet cloth.
I will swap the cloth that smells with a fresh cloth.
Watch me as I toss the old cloth in the sink.
I hope it will be a good shot!

Lesson 119: Review of Words with the /ô/ Sound

Instructor: In this lesson you are going to review words with the /ô/ sound. Read this list of words for me.

Paul	hauls	sauce	pause	swat	wasp
wash	waltz	all	calls	tall	salt
yawns	draw	drawn	straw		

Instructor: Now you are ready to read a story that uses most of the words you just read.

I lie in a deep sleep.
Buzz, buzz, buzz.
I wake up with a jump.
"It is a wasp! It will sting me!" I yelp to Paul.
I jump on the bed and try to swat it.
No, it is not a wasp at all.
It is my clock.
"Go back to bed," Paul yawns.
I sink back in bed and try to sleep.

"You should get up," calls Paul, as he hauls me to my feet.
I brush my teeth and wash my face in a daze.
I pause and sniff.
Do I smell eggs and toast?
I waltz to my seat.
Tall Paul sits on my left.

I look at my blue dish.
Last time I ate, I blew on my hot soup in this dish.
I wish I could eat good fruit on this blue dish, but I like eggs, too.
I shake salt on my eggs.
Paul puts a lot of hot sauce on his.
Paul gulps his cold fruit juice to soothe his throat.
I choose to blow on my spoon full of food to cool it.

Lesson 120: The Vowel Pair OW as /ou/

Review

Instructor: You already know how to read words with the vowel pair **ow** *(Lesson 99)*. You have learned that when you see the vowel pair **ow**, you say the long-**o** vowel sound /ō/. Read the following list of words and the story that follows as a review.

low   blows   snow   show

grow   grown   throw

The truck that blows snow will throw snow on the lawn.
It is quite a show!
We watch the huge wall of snow grow.
The pile of snow is not low.
It has grown to be six feet tall.

New

The vowel sound that you hear in the word **cow** is written /ou/.

Instructor: In this lesson you will read more words with the **ow** vowel pair. In these words, the **ow** stands for a new sound. This is the sound you make when you prick your finger on something sharp: /ou/! Say that sound for me.

Child: /ou/!

Instructor: You can also hear the sound /ou/ in this phrase, "How now, brown cow." Say that with me.

Together: How now, brown cow.

If you are curious about the origin of this phrase, it was once used in speech and diction classes to teach this rounded vowel sound.

Instructor: Now you will read words in which the **ow** vowel pair stands for the sound /ou/. First I will read each word. Then you will read each word. Once we have finished going through the list together, you will go back to the beginning and read the whole list by yourself.

owl   now   how   gown   town   down

clown   frown   growl   brown   crown   crowd

The lesson continues on the following page.

Instructor: Now you will read a story that uses many of the words you just read.

This story contains **ow** words pronounced /ō/ or /ou/. If the child pronounces the word incorrectly, just tell him to try the other **ow** sound.

The king and queen gave a Fall Ball.
On the way to the ball, we saw huge floats with red bows roll by.
How the clown on a float did dance a jig!
The man in the brown suit sold food and drink.

At the ball, the good queen in the blue silk gown did smile at the crowd.
The tall king in the gold crown made a speech.
The band did play a waltz.
The king and queen did dance down the hall.
The small prince slept all the while.
When he is grown, he will go to the ball, too.

Lesson 121: The Vowel Pair OU as /ou/

Don't forget to do the "Two Review and One New" today.

Review

Instructor: You have learned that when you see the vowel pair **ou**, you say the long-**oo** vowel sound /ōo/ *(Lesson 107)*. You have also memorized three words that contain the letters **o** and **u** and have the short-**oo** sound /ŏo/: ***could***, ***should***, and ***would*** *(Lesson 114)*. Read the following list of words and the story that follows as a review.

you   youth   wound   soup

would   should   could

Would it be rude to ask you to move the bed?
It should be in the room and not in the hall.

The youth with the wound on his foot needs to be still.
Could you bring him good, hot soup?

New

Instructor: We learned a new sound in the last lesson. What do you say when you prick your finger on something sharp?

Child: */ou/!*

Instructor: That's right! In the words you are about to read, the **ou** vowel pair stands for the sound /ou/. I will read each word to you, and you will read it after me. Once we have finished reading all the words, you will read all of them by yourself.

out   shout   loud   count

couch   grouch   house   round

ground   sound   south   mouth

Instructor: Now you will read a story that uses many of the words you just read.

The grouch lay on the couch.
A loud sound woke him up.
A big, black rat was out of his hole.
The rat did push a lamp off its stand.
It made a big crash when it hit the ground.
The grouch did leap to his feet and shout, "Out of my house!"
The rat did squint, look him in the eye, and bound out of the house.

Lesson 122: The Vowel Pair OY as /oi/

You will need the following: *a piece of blank paper and drawing supplies for the optional activity.*

Don't forget to do the "Two Review and One New!"

Instructor: In this lesson you are going to learn a new sound: /oi/. You can hear this sound in the word *boy*. I am going to chant a rhyme for you.

When you see a word in bold, clap as you say it, and stress that word. The clapping should occur at a steady tempo.

Instructor: **Roy** the **boy** has a **toy**. Oh **joy**! **Roy** the **boy** has a **toy**. Oh **joy**! Now you try it with me.

Together: **Roy** the **boy** has a **toy**. Oh **joy**! **Roy** the **boy** has a **toy**. Oh **joy**!

Practice this until the child can easily do the chant with the clapping.

Instructor: In this lesson you are going to learn about a new vowel pair: **oy**. When you see the vowels **o** and **y** next to each other, you say /oi/. Let's read this list of words together. First I will read each word. Then you will read each word. Once we have finished going through the list together, you will go back to the beginning and read the list yourself.

Roy   boy   toy   joy   coy   soy

Instructor: Now let's read a story that uses many of the words you just read.

Roy wants a brand new toy.
Roy would like a small tow truck.
He could pull things to the sand box with his truck.
He plans to save his cash so that he can buy the toy.
Roy thinks he would not get it free as a gift.

Now Roy has six bucks.
He goes to the toy shop and buys the truck.
Roy the boy has his toy!

Optional Follow-Up:
Have the child draw a picture of Roy the boy with his toy. At the top of the sheet of paper, write the title for him, "Roy and His Toy."

Lesson 123: The Vowel Pair OI as /oi/

You will need the following: *a piece of aluminum foil and a permanent marker for the optional activity.*

Don't forget to do the "Two Review and One New" today!

Review

Instructor: Let's practice our rhyme with words that contain the /oi/ sound. "Roy the boy has a toy. Oh joy!" Let's clap as we say that twice together.

Together: **Roy** the **boy** has a **toy**. Oh **joy**! **Roy** the **boy** has a **toy**. Oh **joy**!

New

Instructor: In this lesson you are going to learn about another vowel pair that stands for the /oi/ sound. When you see the vowel **o** and **i** side-by-side, you say the sound /oi/. Let's read this list of **oi** words together. First I will read each word. Then you will read each word. Once we have finished going through the list together, you will go back to the beginning and read the list by yourself.

oil	boil	foil	soil	broil	spoil
coin	join	joint	point	moist	oink

Instructor: The following **oi** words end with a silent **e**. Remember, when **c** is followed by **e**, **c** stands for the sound /s/. When the letter **s** is followed by **e**, the **s** stands for the sound /z/.

voice	choice	noise	poise

Instructor: Now you will read a story.

I will pay a coin to buy a small piece of ground steak when I go to town.
I must point to my choice.
I will broil the moist meat on foil so it will not spoil the pan.

I will wash the pan so that it is clean.
I do not want to live like a pig.
Pigs are not clean.
Pigs oink and lie in soil by choice.

Optional Follow-Up:
With a permanent marker, write the **oi** words from this lesson on a piece of foil and have the child read them.

Lesson 124: Review Words with the /ou/ or /oi/ Sound

Instructor: Read these words across from left to right. You have already read them before. Once you have finished reading these words, you will read them in a story.

joy	boys	join	voice	noise
out	round	sound	shout	found
brown	owl	howl	town	down

Instructor: Now you are ready to read a story. I will put a folded piece of paper under the line that you are reading to help you keep your place.

A group of boys went on a hike late in the day.
They saw a cool spring and went to take a drink.
They left the path and got lost in the woods.
They went round and round but could not find the way out.

The sun set in the west, and the sky grew pitch black.
Who! Who! Who!
The bunch of boys did jump at this sound.
Whew!
It was just a brown owl.

Then a noise like a strange howl did reach them.
The boys did join hands and wish to be back in town.
They did shout and scream so that they could be found.
Each did yell at the top of his voice.

Then they found the path.
They ran down the path as fast as they could go.
At last, they came to the town.
They felt such joy when they got out of the woods.

Section 14

OTHER SPELLINGS FOR SHORT-VOWEL SOUNDS

Lesson 125: The Vowel Pair EA as /ĕ/

Review

Instructor: Let's say the names of the five vowels: **a, e, i, o, u**. Say those names with me.

Together: **a, e, i, o, u.**

Instructor: Let's say the short sounds of the vowels: /ă/, /ĕ/, /ĭ/, /ŏ/, /ŭ/. Say those sounds with me.

Together: /ă/, /ĕ/, /ĭ/, /ŏ/, /ŭ/.

Instructor: You already know how to read many words with the vowel pair **ea**. In these three words, the vowel pair **ea** stands for the long-**a** vowel sound *(Lesson 87)*. Read these words to me as a review.

great   steak   break

Instructor: You can also read words in which the vowel pair **ea** stands for the long-**e** vowel sound *(Lesson 90)*. Read these words to me as a review.

meal   pea   beans   leap   scream

flea   please   peach   cream   Bea

Instructor: Now you will read a story that contains the review words you just read.

I sit down to a great meal.
I have steak, peas, and green beans on my plate.
As I lift the spoon to my mouth, I spy a speck with my eye.
"Did that speck just leap?" I ask.
"Eek!" I scream.

A flea is on my pea!
How did I get a flea on my pea?
Could it be that it came off of my dog Bea?
That is so gross!
Take the dog and his fleas out!
May I please have a scoop of peach ice cream to soothe me?

The lesson continues on the following page.

Instructor: In this lesson you will read more words that contain the **ea** vowel pair. In the words you are about to read, the **ea** vowel pair stands for the *short*-**e** vowel sound /ĕ/. Let's read this list of words together. First I will read each word. Then you will read each word. Once we have finished going through the list, you will go back to the beginning and read the whole list by yourself.

dead	head	bread	spread	thread
breath	health	wealth	sweat	meant

Instructor: Now you are ready to read a story.

I will join a health club.
I will run two miles.
I will wipe the sweat off my head and neck.
I will jump rope and get out of breath.
I will swim laps in the pool.
I will have a snack of bread and cheese spread for a break.

Optional Follow-Up:
Read the story above to the child and tell him to act it out (for example, do motions for opening the door to the club, running, swimming, etc…). Then have the child read the story to you or to a sibling for that person to act out.

Lesson 126: The Vowel Pair EA as /ĕ/
Sight Word: said

You will need the following: *one index card and a pen.*

Don't forget to do the "Two Review and One New" today! Be sure to read the two stories in the previous lesson.

Review

Instructor: Do you remember reading the words **wind** (in "the wind blows") and **wind** (in "wind up the string") *(Lesson 96)*? Read these two sentences for me as a review. Read the sentence and think about its meaning. Then you will know if the word is **wind**, "rushing air," or **wind**, "to turn or roll-up."

I will wind up this string so it will stay neat.

Rain and snow can be blown by the wind.

New

Instructor: In this lesson you will read some more words that look exactly alike but have different meanings and pronunciations. We will practice two sets of these words today. I will say each word for you and tell you how the word is used. *Read across from left to right.*

Read each word and use the phrase in parentheses to teach the meaning. When you get to the word *lead* (the metal), show the child a pencil and point out the pencil lead (it is technically graphite inside a pencil, but people still say pencil *lead* because pencils were once filled with lead).

read (I will *read*)   **read** (I have *read*)

lead (*lead* the way)   **lead** (dull, gray *lead*)

Instructor: Now you will read some sentences. Think of the meaning of the sentence, and figure out which way to pronounce the words that look alike.

I must read these two books on my bed.

Last week I read a book on snow and rain.

I am lost. Please lead the way out.

Pipes made of lead can be found in this old house.

The lesson continues on the following page.

211

Instructor: Now you are going to learn a new word by memorizing it. The word *said* rhymes with the words *bread* and *head*. *Said* has the short-**e** vowel sound. I will write this word on a card for you.

said

Write the word on a card. Show it to the child and say the word. Then turn the card over so the word is not visible. Let the child flip the card over, look at the word, and say the word. Then flip the card over again. Repeat this until the child knows the word. Keep this card in the sight word stack.

Instructor: Read the following sentences.

"I have read the tale of a white swan," I said.

You said, "A king of great wealth must have a lot of gold."

"Cut the thread off the coat," he said.

She said, "Spread your bread with jam."

"Broil the cheese toast," you said.

We said, "Let us have ice cream cones."

"That plant is dead," they both said.

Lesson 127: Short Vowel Words that End with a Silent E

Don't forget to do the "Two Review and One New" today!

Review

Instructor: You have read many long-vowel words that end with silent **e**. The presence of a silent **e** usually tells you that the vowel in the word is long. Read these words for me.

plane	pine	those	cute

New

Instructor: There are a few words that look like the words you just read, but are pronounced with a *short*-vowel sound. These are "disobedient words" because they don't follow the normal pattern. These "disobedient words" have two consonants before the final silent **e**. Let's read a list of these words. First I will read each word. Then you will read each word. Once we have finished going through the lists together, you will go back to the beginning and read all of the lists yourself.

twelve	shelve

Instructor: This next list contains words that all end in **se**. These words are even more disobedient because the letter **s** stands for the sound /s/. Normally when the letter **s** is followed by a silent **e**, the letter **s** stands for the sound /z/ *(Lesson 80)*.

rinse	sense	tense	dense

Instructor: The words in this list all end with **ce**. Remember, when the letter **c** comes before the vowels **e**, **i**, or **y**, you say the soft **c** sound: /s/ *(Lesson 77)*.

dance	glance	chance	prance
France	prince	wince	fence

Instructor: The next list of words all end with **ge**. Remember, when the letter **g** comes before the vowels **e**, **i**, or **y**, you usually say the soft **g** sound: /j/ *(Lesson 78)*.

hinge	fringe	twinge	plunge

The lesson continues on the following page.

The prince of France will see a maid fall in the stream.
The prince then will plunge in and try to help.
He will wince when he feels the cold next to his skin.
The stream is twelve feet deep.
This is the last chance to save the maid who did scream!
The prince will find the maid and swim to the banks of the stream.

The maid will rinse the mud off the fringe of the gown.
The prince feels a sense of joy.
The prince will glance at the maid.
"Would you like to dry off and then dance with me at the ball?" the prince asks.
"Thank you. You did save my life," the glad maid said.

Lesson 128: O Alone as /ŭ/

Don't forget to do the "Two Review and One New" today!

Review

Instructor: Let's say the names of the five vowels: **a**, **e**, **i**, **o**, **u**. Say those names with me.

Together: **a**, **e**, **i**, **o**, **u**.

Instructor: Let's say the short sounds of the vowels: /ă/, /ĕ/, /ĭ/, /ŏ/, /ŭ/. Say those sounds with me.

Together: /ă/, /ĕ/, /ĭ/, /ŏ/, /ŭ/.

Instructor: You have read many words with a single **o**. In these words, the letter **o** stands for the short-**o** vowel sound or the long-**o** vowel sound. Read this short story as a review.

An old troll goes on a stroll.
He stops and spots a lot of geese and ducks on the pond.
"Yum! I would like to eat roast duck on a soft roll at lunch."

"I must catch a few ducks," he thinks.
The flocks of ducks and geese spy the old troll.
Most of them fly off to the trees and drop on a branch.
The old troll will not have roast duck this day.

New

Instructor: In this lesson you will read words that also contain a single **o**; but in these words, the single vowel **o** is pronounced with a short-**u** sound: /ŭ/. Let's read this short list of words. First I will read each word. Then you will read each word. Once we have finished going through the list together, you will go back to the beginning and read the whole list yourself.

son	won	ton	from	front	month

Instructor: Now you will read a story using all of the words you just read.

A man and his son will play golf as a team.
They will hike from the club house to the tenth hole.
The man will hit the golf ball off the tee.
Whack!

The golf ball will land in front of the sand trap.
The man and his son like golf.
They won a ton of games this month!

Lesson 129: O Alone as /ŭ/
Sight Words: one, once

You will need the following: *two index cards and a pen. If you do the optional activity, you will need the magnetic alphabet board.*

Don't forget to do the "Two Review and One New" today!

Review

Instructor: Last lesson you read words in which the vowel **o** stood for the short-**u** vowel sound. Read this sentence as a review.

This month I will get my front teeth.

New

Instructor: In this lesson you will read more words in which vowel **o** stands for the short-**u** vowel sound. These words end in a silent **e**, but the **o** in each word is not long. Let's read this list together. First I will read each word. Then you will read each word. Once we have finished reading the list together, you will go back to the beginning and read the list yourself.

done	some	come	dove
love	glove	shove	sponge

Instructor: Now you will learn two sight words. I will write these words on a card for you. Both of these words, *one* and *once*, begin with the letter **o**, although they sound as if they begin with the letter **w**.

one   once

Show the child a card as you say the word on the card. Then turn both cards over so you cannot see the word. Have the child turn over each card, look at the word, and say the word. Repeat this until the child knows both words. Keep these two cards in the sight word stack.

Instructor: Now you are ready to read a story.

My son once ran a long race.
He had to run from town to town.
He had to run up and down some hills.
I did yell and clap when he was done.
I love my son!
I once won one race of my own.
Now we both have won a race!

Optional Follow-Up:
Give the child the necessary letters to form on the magnetic board some of the words from the list in this lesson. Do not form the two sight words. The child should read each word once it is formed.

Lesson 130: Review OU as /o͞o/ and /ou/
The Vowel Pair OU as /ŭ/

Don't forget to do the "Two Review and One New" today!

Review

Instructor: You already know how to read words with the **ou** vowel pair. In some words the **ou** vowel pair stands for the sound /o͞o/ *(Lesson 107)*. Read the following words as a review.

you   group

Instructor: In other words the **ou** vowel pair stands for the sound /ou/ *(Lesson 121)*. Read the following words as a review.

south   count   cloud   round

Instructor: Now you will read some sentences to practice both sounds of the **ou** vowel pair.

Look to the south.
Count the clouds in that group
Do you see the round moon that is next to the clouds?

New

Instructor: There is another sound for which the vowel pair **ou** can stand. In the three words you are about to read, the vowel pair **ou** stands for the short-**u** vowel sound. First I will read each word. Then you will read each word.

Words with this pattern will be covered more extensively once the child is reading words of more than one syllable (example: *country*, *trouble*, *double*).

touch   young   Doug

Instructor: Now you will read these words in a sentence.

Doug, do not touch a young snake on the head.
He may be small, but you should still dread his bite.

Lesson 131: Sight Words: build, built
Review Sight Words

You will need the following: *two index cards, a pen, and the stack of sight word cards.*

Don't forget to do the "Two Review and One New" today!

Review

Instructor: You already know how to read words with the vowel pair **ui** *(Lesson 111)*. Read the following list of words and the sentence as a review.

fruit   juice   bruise

The red fruit juice stain on my leg looks like a bruise.

New

Instructor: Now you will learn two words that look like the words you just read, but the **ui** is pronounced differently. You will memorize these two words. I will write each one on a card for you.

build   built

Show the child a card as you say the word on the card. Then turn both cards over so you cannot see the word. Have the child turn over each card, look at the word, and say the word. Repeat this until the child knows both words. Keep these two cards in the sight word stack.

Instructor: Now you are ready to read a few sentences.

The crew built a huge cruise ship.
A man of great wealth paid to have them build it.

Game: Sight Word Shuffle
Take out the stack of sight words cards and shuffle them. Show the child a word card. If he reads the word correctly, give him the card. If he does not read the word correctly, pronounce the word for him, and put the card back in the stack. Do this until the child has all the cards.

Lesson 132: Y Alone as /i/

Don't forget to do the "Two Review and One New" today!

Review

Instructor: You can already read words in which the vowel **y** stands for the long-**i** vowel sound *(Lesson 94)*. Read the following words and sentences as a review.

why   cry   dry   my   by

Why should you cry when I ask you to dry off?
It is time to come out of the pool!
Stand by my side while I put sun screen on you.

New

Instructor: Now you will read two words in which the letter **y** stands for the short-**i** vowel sound. First I will read each word. Then you will read each word.

The child will read more words with this pattern later in the book (example: **syllable**, **physician**). For now, read these two words, explaining that a myth is a tale or legend.

myth   gym

Instructor: Now let's read some stories.

A gym is a kind of health club.
I like to go to a huge gym.

I will tell you the myth of "How the Dog Lost His Bone."
A dog has a nice, big bone.
He runs home with the bone in his mouth.
But then he comes to a pond.
In the pond he sees a dog with a face just like his and a bone just like his.

He wants the bone that dog has, too!
He howls at the dog with the big bone.
His own bone falls out of his mouth and drops in the pond.
Now the dog has no bone.
He is sad.
He runs home.
The dog has no bone at all.

Lesson 133: Review of Vowel Pairs and Patterns for Short-Vowel Words

Instructor: Let's say the names of the five vowels: **a**, **e**, **i**, **o**, **u**. Say those names with me.

Together: **a**, **e**, **i**, **o**, **u.**

Instructor: Let's say the short sounds of the vowels: /ă/, /ĕ/, /ĭ/, /ŏ/, /ŭ/. Say those sounds with me.

Together: /ă/, /ĕ/, /ĭ/, /ŏ/, /ŭ/.

Instructor: Read this list of words to me. I will help you if you need it. Once you have finished reading the list, you will read these words in a story.

wealth	meant	bread	read	twelve
give	sense	prince	lance	chance
son	won	from	one	once
doves	come	love	young	myths

Instructor: Now you are ready to read a story about a king who decided to test the wisdom of his sons.

I love to read myths.
Once I read of a king who had twelve sons.
The king meant to give his wealth to his sons if they would use good sense.
He gave them a test.
He gave each son a small pile of gold.

One son, Prince Lance, spent his gold on a chance deal.
He lost.
Prince Craig spent all of his wealth on a flock of doves from a man who told him they would lay gold eggs.
Prince Craig did hope he would get rich quick.
Then the doves flew south and did not come back.
The rest of the sons did not use good sense.
They did not do wise things with the gold.

But the young son made a wise choice.
He spent his gold on bread and gave it to those who could not buy food.
He won praise from the king.

Section 15

SILENT LETTERS

Lesson 134: The Silent Letter Pair GH: IGH

Review

Instructor: You already know how to read words in which the single vowel **i** stands for the long-**i** vowel sound *(Lesson 96)*. Read the following words and a sentence as a review.

wild   child   mild

When the wild child took a nap, she was mild.

New

Instructor: In this lesson you will read more words in which the single vowel **i** is long. In these words, the **i** is followed by the letter pair **gh**. The **gh** pair is almost always silent when it follows a vowel. Let's read this list of words together. First I will read each word. Then you will read each word. Once we have finished going through the list together, you will go back to the beginning and read the list by yourself.

high   sigh   night   light

right   sight   tight   might

fight   flight   fright   bright

Instructor: Now you are ready to read these words in a story

Mom said that Maud and I might like to camp in my room.
We set up a tent right next to my bed.
Mom said that this night we could stay up late.
When the moon was high in the sky, the light was so bright that the lake was in sight.

We saw an owl in flight and it gave us a fright.
We gave a sigh and fell deep in sleep.
Maud and I did not wake up till ten the next day.

Lesson 135: The Silent Letter Pair GH: EIGH

Don't forget to do the "Two Review and One New" today!

Review

Instructor: In the last lesson you read words that contained the silent letter pair **gh**. Read this sentence as a review.

The bright light by my bed is on my right.

Instructor: In this lesson you will read more words with the silent **gh** pair. Rather than having just one vowel, these words contain a vowel pair. Read the following words and sentences as a review of the vowel pair **ei**, which stands for the long-**a** vowel sound *(Lesson 87)*.

reins   veil

The bride will flick the reins and set off to be wed.
The veil will trail in the wind.

New

Instructor: Now you are ready to read words that contain both the **ei** vowel pair and the **gh** silent letter pair. First I will read each word. Then you will read each word. Once we have finished going through the list together, you will go back to the beginning and read the list by yourself.

eight   freight   weight   weigh   sleigh

Instructor: Read the following story.

I live in a place that is so cold.
We have no roads, just snow and ice.
I must take a sleigh and load it with lots of freight.
Eight dogs pull the sleigh.

I flick the reins and they pull the weight.
It seems to weigh a ton, but the strong dogs do not mind.

Lesson 136: The Silent Letter Pair GH: AIGH and AUGH

Don't forget to do the "Two Review and One New" today!

Review

Instructor: Read this story as a review of the silent letter pair **gh**.

The gray gulls might fight in flight at night.
One of the eight gulls has a fish in his beak.
The weight of the fish drags him down.
The fish must weigh as much as much as the gull.

Instructor: Read the following words and sentence as a review of the **ai** vowel pair.

chain   train   trails

A chain of smoke trails from the train as it whisks off.

New

Instructor: There is only one common short word that contains both the **ai** vowel pair and the silent letter pair **gh**. First I will read the word. Then you will read the word.

straight

Instructor: Now you will read this word in sentences.

Can you draw a straight line?

When Mom calls, come straight in.

Instructor: You already know how to read words with the **au** vowel pair, which stands for the sound /ô/ *(Lesson 117)*. Read the following words and sentence as a review.

haul   sauce

The huge truck will haul a full load of sauce.

Instructor: Now you are ready to read words that contain both the **au** vowel pair and the **gh** silent letter pair. First I will read each word. Then you will read each word.

caught   taught

Instructor: Now you will read these words in sentences.

My dog caught the ball.
I taught him to play fetch.

Lesson 137: Review the Silent Letter Pair GH: IGH, EIGH, AIGH, and AUGH

You will need the following: *the magnetic alphabet board for the optional activity.*

Instructor: Read these words as a review. Once you are finished, you will read them in a story.

sight	light	right	tight	night
bright	thigh	eight	weigh	weight
caught	taught	straight		

Instructor: Now you will read a story.

I take a trip to catch fish.
The boat sails eight miles out to sea.
Land is still in sight.
The sun is so bright.
I must shield my eyes from the light.

I set the fish bait on my thigh.
I put the bait on the hook.
I wind the line on my pole and cast it out to sea.

I see a splash on my right.
I feel the weight of a huge fish on my tight line.
I reel in the fish.
It must weigh eight pounds!
I have caught a fish!

The man on the boat has taught me a few things.
Put fish straight in a cool place.
We will have a fish fry this night!

Optional Follow-Up:
Take out the magnetic alphabet board. Help the child to form the following words. Always keep **gh** on the board; add and take away letters to form new words.

night	bright	flight	eight	weight
sleigh	caught	taught	straight	

224

Lesson 138: Review the Vowel Pair OU

Instructor: You have learned that when you see the vowel pair **ou**, you say the long-**oo** vowel sound /o͞o/ in the words *group* and *you (Lesson 107)*. The vowel pair **ou** can also stand for the short-**u** vowel sound in the words *touch* and *young (Lesson 130)*. You have also memorized three words that contain the letters **o** and **u** and have the short-**oo** sound /o͝o/: *could*, *should*, and *would (Lesson 114)*. Read the following review words.

touch   you   mouse

Instructor: As you can see, **ou** can stand for different sounds in the words *touch*, *you*, and *mouse*.

Instructor: Remember, if you do not know which sound to say when you see the **ou** vowel pair, you can try each of the different **ou** sounds and see which one makes sense. Read the following sentence.

Touch the young, soft chick.

Instructor: Now let's try something fun. I want you to read that sentence again, except this time I want you to try the different **ou** sounds each time you see the **ou** vowel pair.

Have the child try the **ou** sound in *you*. Then have the child read the sentence again trying the **ou** sound in *ground*.

Touch the young, soft chick.

Instructor: Sentences can sound quite silly, can't they? Now let's read the sentence using the correct sound for the words.

Touch the young, soft chick.

Instructor: Now you are ready to read a story about a clever, little mouse. Remember, if you don't know which of the **ou** sounds to say in a word, try each of them until you find the one that makes sense in that sentence.

A young mouse went on a cheese hunt in the house.
He crept out of his hole in the ground and hid by the couch.
He saw a block of cheese set out by a bowl of soup.
In one jump he was on top of the couch.
In two jumps he was by the cheese.

A loud shout came from the grouch on the couch.
"Do not touch my cheese, you foul mouse!"
The mouse took a quick bite of cheese.
He flew back to his hole in the ground.
The mouse ate his cheese while the grouch ate his soup.

Lesson 139: The Silent Letter Pair GH: OUGH as /o͞o/ or /ou/

Review

Instructor: In the last lesson, you reviewed words with the **ou** vowel pair. In this lesson, you will read more words with that vowel pair. First you will read a few **ou** words as a review.

you   youth   group

New

Instructor: In the words you just read, the **ou** vowel pair stands for the /o͞o/ sound. The **ou** vowel pair stands for the same sound in this next word. In addition, this word has the silent letter pair **gh**.

through

Instructor: Now you will read a couple of short sentences.

The youth strolls through a group of trees.
Then he goes through the gate to the peach tree.

Instructor: Now read this list of words as a review.

out   loud   house

Instructor: In the words you just read, the **ou** vowel pair stands for the /ou/ sound. The **ou** vowel pair stands for the same sound in these words. Remember, **gh** is a silent letter pair.

Explain to the child that a bough is "a branch of a tree" and a drought is "a long period of time without rain."

bough   drought

Instructor: Now you will read a couple of short sentences.

The drought made the bough of the tree dry out.
I count the leaves as they fall to the ground.

Instructor: Now you are going to read a couple of short sentences that that mix up the words you just read. If you don't know which sound to say when you see the **ou** letter pair, try each of the different **ou** sounds until you find the one that makes sense.

The loud group went through the house.
They went out to see the tree boughs fell due to the drought.

Lesson 140: The Silent Letter Pair GH: OUGH as /ȯ/ and /ō/

Do the "Two Review and One New" today.

Review

Instructor: Let's review some **ough** words. You will read each word and the sentence after it.

through   I went through the door.

drought   If we have no rain, we have a drought.

bough   The cat sat on the bough of the tree.

Instructor: In the word *through*, the **ou** sounds like /o͞o/. In the words *drought* and *bough*, the **ou** sounds like /ou/. In this lesson you will read more words with the **ou** vowel pair and the silent letter pair **gh**. These words have different vowel sounds from the words *through* or *drought* and *bough*. Read these next two words. You have read them before.

caught   taught

New

Instructor: Now we will read words that rhyme with *caught* and *taught* but are not spelled the same. These new words have the vowel pair **ou** in them (as well as the silent letter pair **gh**). I will read each word, and you will read it after me. Once we have read all the words, you will read them by yourself.

ought   bought   fought   sought   thought   brought

Instructor: Now you will read a story that uses some of the words you just read.

Mom said that Paul ought to keep his room neat.
Paul thought that a small pet mouse would not cause a mess.
Paul bought a pet mouse and brought it up to his room.
He did not think the mouse would push the wood chips out of its cage.
He was sad when he saw the mess.
Mom said, "Just clean it up."

Instructor: Here are two words that also contain the vowel pair **ou** and the silent letter pair **gh**. These words contain the long-**o** vowel sound and rhyme with the words *go* and *so*. First I will read each word; then you will read each word.

though   dough

Instructor: Now you will read these words in a sentence.

You may eat some raw dough, though I think you should wait.

227

Lesson 141: GH as /f/
Sight Word: laugh

You will need the following: *an index card, a pen, and the sight word cards.*

Remember to do the "Two Review and One New" today.

Instructor: You have now read many words in which **gh** is a silent letter pair. However, in a few words, **gh** is not silent. The letter pair **gh** can stand for a sound—the same sound for which the letter **f** stands: /f/. Long ago, there were many words in which the **gh** was pronounced like an **f**. Today, there are only a few words that are still pronounced this way. In the word you are about to read, the **ou** vowel pair stands for the same sound in the words ***bought*** and ***thought***. I will read the word. Then you will read the word.

cough

Instructor: Now you will read this word in a sentence.

I do not feel well when I cough a lot.

Instructor: In the next two words, the **ou** vowel pair stands for the short-**u** vowel sound (in the words ***touch*** and ***young***). Remember, the **gh** pair stands for the /f/ sound.

rough

tough

Instructor: Now you will read these words in a sentence.

The gruff man was rough and tough.

Instructor: Now you will learn another word in which the **gh** pair stands for the /f/ sound. You will have to memorize this word because it is pronounced in a funny way. I will write this word on a card for you.

laugh

The word *laugh* is a sight word because the vowel pair **au** stands for the short-**a** vowel sound. Write the word on a card and say the word to the child. Have the child learn the word, and then mix it in with ten words from the sight word stack. Practice these word cards with the child. Keep the *laugh* card in the sight word stack.

Lesson 142: Review the GH Letter Pair

Instructor: Read these words across as a review. Once you are finished, you will read them in a story.

high	night	flight	straight
eight	weigh	caught	through
drought	cough	rough	laugh

Instructor: Now you are ready to read a story about a long night flight. I will put a folded piece of paper under the line that you are reading to help you keep your place.

I flew high in a plane at night.
We left at eight so we could weigh my big case on time.
We flew straight to France.
We caught the last flight that night.

We flew through the sky.
When we got to France, I could see dry fields.
I was told that the plants died in a long drought.

Though I had a cough, it was not a rough trip.
When the trip was done, I had to laugh.
I thought the long flight had been quite fun!

Lesson 143: The Silent Letter G Before N

You will need the following: *the magnetic alphabet board.*

Instructor: In this lesson you will learn about another silent letter. When the letter **g** is in front of the letter **n** in a word, the **g** is silent. So when you see the letter **g** before an **n**, you just pronounce the /n/ sound. Let's read the following list of words. First I will read each word. Then you will read each word. Once we have finished going through the list together, you will go back to the beginning and read the list yourself.

sign   reign   gnat   gnaw   gnash   gnome

Instructor: Now you will read these words in a silly story about a make-believe land.

The king and queen reign in this land.
Signs state the laws that the king and queen make.
One law is that a gnome may not gnash his teeth.
The one time he may gnash his teeth is when a gnat gnaws on him.
Gnats will make a gnome itch and gnash his teeth.
Ouch!

Follow-Up:
Take out the magnetic alphabet board. Have the child assemble each word, one at a time, from the word list above. The child should read the completed word. Then have the child remove the **g** and read each word (except the word ***sign***) without the letter **g**. The pronunciation is the same. Then have the child put the letter **g** back in the word and pronounce it.

Lesson 144: The Silent L

Do the "Two Review and One New" today.

Review

Instructor: Read these words as a review.

all   wall   waltz   bald

New

Instructor: When the letter **a** is followed by the letter **l** in the words you just read, the vowel sound is /ô/. In this lesson you will read more words with this vowel sound. However, in these words the letter **l** is silent. Let's read these words together. First I will read each word. Then you will read each word. Once we have finished going through the list together, you will go back to the beginning and read the list yourself.

In some regions, the **l** is pronounced in *calm* and *palm*.

calm   palm   walk   talk   stalk   chalk

Instructor: There are two other words that also contain the vowel **a** and the silent letter **l**. However, in these words the vowel sound is that of a short **a**: /ă/. First I will read each word; then you will read each word.

calf   half

Instructor: Now you will read two words with the long-**o** vowel sound and the silent letter **l**. First I will read each word; then you will read each word.

folk   yolk

Instructor: Now you will read these words in a story.

I will stay at the home of my aunt.
The stalks of wheat wave in the breeze.
I pick a stalk of wheat and put it in the palm of my hand.
I spot a calf in the field as I walk back to the house.

My aunt takes me to the hen house to get eggs.
She will use a half pint of milk and six eggs in a pound cake.
We will talk and laugh.
I love to stay with my aunt.
She is so calm.

Lesson 145: The Silent K Before N

Do the "Two Review and One New" today.

You <u>may</u> need the following: *paper and drawing supplies for the optional activity.*

Instructor: In this lesson you will read words with another silent letter. When the letter **k** comes before the letter **n** in a word, the letter **k** is silent. Let's read a list of these words. First I will read each word. Then you will read each word. Once we have finished going through the list together, you will go back to the beginning and read the whole list yourself.

knot	knob	knock	know	knew
kneel	knead	knit	knife	knight

Instructor: Now you will read a story that uses some of these words.

The right knight for this fight is in sight.
His steel suit is bright in the light.
He is a knight of might.
He kneels on his knees in front of the king.

The king gives the brave knight a gold knife with gems on it as a gift.
The knight will tie the gold knife to his belt with a strong knot.
He sets out to fight the foes.
He knows that he must win this fight.
He needs to keep the king and the queen safe.

Optional Follow-Up:
Have the child read the story one more time. Ask him the questions below. Have the child answer you in complete sentences. For example, an answer to the first question might begin, "He has to fight...." There are no right or wrong answers; this exercise is just for fun!

You may wish to have the child illustrate the story. if so, you write the title for the picture, "The Brave Knight."

Who do you think the knight has to fight?
Will there be dragons or other warriors at this fight?
Will the knight ride a horse or will he walk into battle?
How will the knight win the fight?
How will the king reward the knight?
What will the knight do next: will he settle down and marry a princess or go on another adventure?

Lesson 146: The Silent W Before R

Do the "Two Review and One New" today.

Instructor: In this lesson you will read words with another silent letter. When the letter **w** comes before the letter **r** in a word, the letter **w** is silent. Let's read a list of these words. First I will read each word. Then you will read each word. Once we have finished going through the list together, you will go back to the beginning and read the whole list yourself. Read across from left to right.

wrap	wren	wreck	wrench	wrist
wring	write	wrote	wrong	wreath

Instructor: Now you will read a story that uses some of these words.

I am in my class.
I was told I must write a tale.
This is my tale.

A cute wren sat in a brown straw wreath on the wall.
The cat sprang up to try and wrench the wren off the wreath.
He made a wreck of the wreath.
That was the wrong thing to do!

My wrist is too weak to write much.
I must wrap it in a cloth.
Mom will wring out a hot cloth and put it on my wrist.
Then I will feel like I can write the rest of the tale.

Lesson 147: The Silent W Before H
Review Sight Words

Do the "Two Review and One New" today.

Review

Instructor: Do you remember that the letter pair **wh** stands for the sound that you make when you are trying to blow out a candle *(Lesson 61)*? Let me hear you blow a /hw/ sound.

Child: /hw/

Instructor: You have already read words that begin with the letters **wh**. Read these words as a review.

whip   when   wheel   which   white   whale

New

Instructor: In a few words that begin with the letter pair **wh**, the **w** is silent. I will read these words to you. In each of these words, the **o** stands for the /o͞o/ sound.

who   whom   whose

Instructor: Now I will read another word in which the letter **w** is silent. This word contains the long-**o** vowel sound.

whole

Instructor: Now you will read each word and a sentence that uses that word.

who

Who is in this room?

whom

To whom shall I give this gift?

whose

Whose bed is made up?

whole

May I eat the whole cake?

Game: Sight Word Shuffle
Take out the stack of sight word cards and shuffle them. Show the child a word card. If he reads the word correctly, give him the card. If he does not read the word correctly, pronounce the word for him, and put the card back in the stack. Do this until the child has all the cards.

Lesson 148: Sight Words: what, does

You will need the following: *two index cards and a pen for the lesson. You will need drawing supplies for the optional activity.*

Do the "Two Review and One New" today.

Instructor: I will write two new words on cards for you. You will have to memorize them.

what   does

Practice these two words with the child until he knows them. Add at least eight cards from the sight word stack and shuffle all the cards. Show the child each card. He keeps a card that he reads correctly. If he has trouble, tell him the word, have him pronounce it, and put that card in a separate stack. Once you have gone through all the cards, practice the cards the child missed. Keep the **what** and **does** cards in the sight word stack.

Instructor: Today you are going to read some jokes. All of these jokes contain the words *what* and *does*.

Some of these jokes are puns. Point out to the child the correct spelling of **choo/chew** and **cheep/cheap**.

What does a train do to food?
Chew, chew it.

What does the chick say when it finds a hat on sale?
This is cheap, cheap, cheap!

What does the frog say when he scrubs his car?
Rub it, rub it, rub it.

What does the cat eat for lunch?
Mice cream and cake.

What does the duck say to the clown?
You quack me up!

What does the crab use to call his mom?
His shell phone.

What does a blue hat on the Red Sea look like?
It looks wet.

What does the corn chip say to his pal?
Should we go for a dip?

Optional Follow-Up:
Have the child illustrate one of the jokes. Write the question on the front of the piece of paper and the answer on the back. The child can draw his picture on one or both sides.

Lesson 149: Silent D Before GE

Do the "Two Review and One New" today.

Review

Instructor: Most words that end with silent **e** contain a long-vowel sound. However, there are some words that end with silent **e** but contain a short-vowel sound. Let's review some of these kinds of words. You have read these words before; read them again for me now.

fence   rinse   dance   chance   hinge   plunge

New

Instructor: In this lesson you will read more words that end with silent **e** but still have a short-vowel sound. These new words also contain another silent letter: **d**. When the letter **d** comes before the letters **g** and **e**, the letter **d** becomes silent. Let's read this list of words. First I will read each word. Then you will read each word. Once we have finished going through the list together, you will go back to the beginning and read the list by yourself. Remember, these words all contain short-vowel sounds.

edge   hedge   pledge   ridge   bridge   fridge

judge   fudge   budge   trudge   smudge

Instructor: Now you will read a story that uses some of the words you just read.

I lick a smudge of fudge off the edge of my lip.
I think of a wild wish.
I would like to have a whole lake full of fudge.

A hedge would be on the edge of my fudge lake.
On each bud on this hedge, a mint would grow.
I would suck on a mint as I trudge through the fudge.

If I would like to stay dry, I could walk on the bridge.
The bridge would be made of ice cream and cake.
I would not budge from my lake full of fudge.
This is what I call a sweet dream.

Lesson 150: The Silent Letter B
Sight Word: gone

You will need the following: *one index card and a pen.*

Do the "Two Review and One New" today.

Instructor: In this lesson you will read words in which the letter **b** is silent. First I will read each word, and then you will read it. Once we have read all the words, you will go back and read them by yourself. In these words, the single vowels stand for short-vowel sounds.

lamb   limb   dumb   crumb   thumb   debt

Instructor: In this next word, the **ou** vowel pair stands for the /ou/ sound. I will read this word. Then you will read this word. Remember, the **b** is silent. I *doubt* if you will have any trouble with this!

doubt

Instructor: In these next two words, the vowel sounds are long. I will read each word, and then you will read it.

comb   climb

Instructor: I am going to give a new word on a card to memorize.

gone

Write this word on a card and pronounce the word for the child. Let the child practice saying the word. Keep the card in sight as you read the stories below. Read the stories once normally. Then have the child read the stories again, and tell the him to pick up the card when he sees the word in a sentence. Put the card in the sight word stack at the end of the lesson.

Instructor: Now you are ready to read some stories. To help you keep your place, I will put a folded piece of paper under the line you are reading.

I am glad that the cake is not all gone.
I pledge to eat the last crumb of that cake.
I lick the last crumb off my thumb.
Did you doubt that I would?
Now all the cake is gone.

The cat climbs out on a tree limb.
The cat is too close to the edge of that bough.
Dumb cat! He could fall from the tree.
I call Mom out to help.
By the time she comes out, the cat is gone.
He must have found a way out of the tree.
I doubt if he will climb back up.

Lesson 151: The Silent Letter H

Do the "Two Review and One New" today.

Instructor: In this lesson you will read words with a silent letter **h**. Let's read these words together. There are not very many. First I will read each word. Then you will read each word.

There are very few one-syllable words with the silent letter **h**. More words will be introduced as the child progresses through the book.

Oh   ghost   John

The following is an American folk song. You can find the tune to this song, as well as other traditional favorites, in the book entitled *The Fireside Book of Children's Songs*, edited by Marie Winn with illustrations by Allan Miller and John Alcorn (Simon & Schuster, 1966). When you get to the words **wouldn't** and **chilly**, read those for the child.

Instructor: Now we are going to read the lyrics to a song. There are a couple of words in the song that you do not yet know how to read, so I will read those words when we get to them.

Have you seen the ghost of John?
Long, white bones with the rest all gone,
Oh wouldn't it be chilly with no skin on?

Lesson 152: The Silent Letter U After G

You will need the following for tomorrow's lesson: *twenty-eight index cards and two markers of different colors. You may want to write out the cards before the next lesson.*

Do the "Two Review and One New" today.

Review

Instructor: The letter **g** makes the soft sound /j/ when it comes before the vowels **e**, **i**, or **y**. Listen as I say these words: ***Gene***, ***gel***, ***gym***.

As you say each of the above words, point to it in the sentences below.

Instructor: The letter **g** makes the hard sound /g/ all other times. Listen to these words: ***goes***, ***Gus***, ***gulp***. Now you will read some sentences as a review.

As you say each of the above words, point to it in the sentences below.

Gene likes to draw with gel pens.
The ink goes on with ease.

Gus should not chew gum in gym class.
In one gulp he could choke.

New

Instructor: In the following list of words, the **g** is followed by the vowel **u**. This tells you to say the hard sound of the letter **g**: /g/. In all of these words the letter **u** is silent. The job of the letter **u** is to make sure you say the hard sound of **g**; the letter **u** has no sound of its own. First I will read each word; then you will read each word. Once we have finished going through the list together, you will go back to the beginning and read the whole list yourself.

If your child has any difficulty reading the words, write the words out on a separate sheet of paper. Draw a line through the **u**, crossing it out (but still keeping it visible). Explain that you are crossing out the **u** to make it silent. Then have the child read the word when the silent **u** is not crossed out.

guy   guest   guess   guide   guilt

Instructor: In the following words, both the ending letters are silent: **u** and **e**. First I will read each word; then you will read each word.

Explain to the child that a plague is a terrible thing that causes trouble or destruction (for example, it could be a sickness or a disaster in nature).

plague   league

The lesson continues on the following page.

You have read words in which the vowel **o** stands for the short-**u** vowel sound: /ŭ/. Read these words as a review.

ton   from   month

In this next word, the vowel **o** stands for the short-**u** vowel sound, and the **u** and **e** at the end of the word are both silent.

tongue

Now you are ready to read these words in sentences. Read each word before each sentence.

plague

One of the Ten Plagues was a plague of frogs.
A plague of frogs would drive me mad!

guess

Can you guess which kind of ice cream I like?
Did you guess fudge mint?

league

We have the best team in the league.
I hope we win the last league game.

guide

I will guide you and John through the woods.
What do you think we will see?

guest

The guest will stay the night at the inn.
He will pay his debt when he leaves.

tongue

I can roll my tongue so that it is round.
Can you?
I can catch snow on my tongue.
It is cold!

Lesson 153: Silent Letter Review

You will need the following: *twenty-eight index cards and two markers of different colors.*

Game: *Who* Did *What?*

You will need twenty-eight index cards and two different-colored markers (I will use "red" and "green"—do not use yellow because it is too hard to read). With the red marker, write the following subjects (the *who*) on index cards, one subject per card. With the green marker, write the following predicates (*what* the subject did) on index cards, one predicate per card.

Subject (red)	Predicate (green)
The knight	will save the king and queen from doom.
The palm of my hand	has a smudge of fudge on it.
The calf	will gnaw the stalks of grass.
The egg yolk	will ooze through the cloth.
The drought	will cause all the trees and plants to dry up.
The dough	sticks to the roof of my mouth.
The light brown toad	thought a fly would be nice to eat.
The guest	went on the tall bridge.
The guide	was lost in the hedge.
My tongue	will taste the sweet bun.
His comb	was used to comb the dog.
The crumb on the ground	fed the ants.
The lamb	had snow white wool.
The judge	will cough and speak in a gruff voice.

First, lay the cards out in the order you see above. Set the first pair, "The knight" and "will save the king and queen from doom," in front of the child. Have the child read that sentence. Repeat the same process for the next thirteen sentences. Then shuffle all the cards, keeping the subject cards in one pile and the predicate cards in another. Let the child pick any subject card and pair it with any predicate card. Have fun reading the wacky sentences!

Section 16

R-Changed Vowels

Lesson 154: R-Changed Vowels: AR as /är/

You will need the following: *the magnetic alphabet board.*

The sound taught in this lesson is /är/ in *car*. The mark over the **a** is called an umlaut.

Instructor: When the letter **r** follows a vowel in a short word, it changes the sound of the vowel. We don't call this sound a short or long vowel—we say it is an "r-changed vowel." There are four different **r**-changed vowel sounds: /är/ in *car*, /ôr/ in *door* /âr/ in *hair*, and /ûr/ in *stir*. In this lesson you will read words with the /är/ sound (in *car*, *far*, *yard*). First read these words with the short-**a** vowel sound.

cat	mat	pat	chat
had	ham	ban	tap

Instructor: Let's see what happens to a word when we put the letter **r** after the vowel **a**. This changes the sound of the vowel. I will read each of the following word pairs to you. First I will read the word with the short-vowel sound, and then I will read the word where the **r** follows the **a** and changes the vowel sound. Then you will read each word pair to me. Watch out for that tricky **r**!

The regional pronunciations of **r**-changed vowels vary greatly. If you desire you may use your local pronunciation.

cat	mat	pat	chat
cart	mart	part	chart

had	ham	ban	tap
hard	harm	barn	tarp

Instructor: When the letter **r** follows the vowel **a** in these words, you say the sound /är/ in *car*. Let's read each small list of words together. First I will read each word; then you will read each word. Then you will read the sentences that follow each list by yourself.

tap
tarp

The rain will tap on the roof.
The tarp on the roof keeps the rain out.

mat
mart

He went to the Quick Mart to buy a mat to put on the front steps.

cat   ham
cart   harm

Do not let the cat jump on the cart and harm the ham.

had   Pat
hard   part

Pat had a hard time with that part.

Follow-Up:
Take out the magnetic alphabet board. For each of the word pairs below, assemble the word with the short-**a** vowel sound. The child will read the word. Then have the child insert an **r** to make a new word. The child will read the new word with the **r**-changed vowel sound.

cat   mat   pat   chat
cart   mart   part   chart

had   ham   tap
hard   harm   tarp

Lesson 155: R-Changed Vowels: AR as /är/

Remember to do the "Two Review and One New" today.

Instructor: In the last lesson you learned when the letter **r** follows a vowel, it changes the vowel sound. There are four different **r**-changed vowel sounds: /är/ in *car*, /ôr/ in *door* /âr/ in *hair*, and /ûr/ in *stir*. In this lesson you will read words with the /är/ sound (in *car*, *far*, *yard*). Let's learn a little chant to help us remember those sounds. The first sound is /är/ in car. I will show you a movement to go along with that.

Pretend you are steering a car.

Instructor: Let's try that together. We will both say "/är/ in *car*" and pretend we are driving.

Together (pretending to drive a car):
/är/ in *car*.

Instructor: The second sound is /ôr/ in *door*. I'll show you the movement.

Pretend you are opening a door.

Instructor: Let's say "/ôr/ in *door*" together and pretend to open a door.

Together (pretending to open a door):
/ôr/ in *door*.

Instructor: Let's put both those phrases together. Remember, it's /är/ in *car*, /ôr/ in *door*. Remember to do the movements.

Together: /är/ in *car*, /ôr/ in *door*.

Instructor: The third sound is /âr/ in *hair*. I will show you the movement for that sound.

Pretend you are combing your hair.

Instructor: Let's try that together. We will both say "/âr/ in *hair*" and pretend we are combing our hair.

Together (pretending to comb hair):
/âr/ in *hair*.

Instructor: Let's add those three phrases together: /är/ in *car*, /ôr/ in *door*, /âr/ in *hair*. Remember to do the movements.

Together: /är/ in *car*, /ôr/ in *door*, /âr/ in *hair*.

Instructor: Now we will add the last **r**-changed vowel sound: /ûr/ in *stir*. I will show you the movement for that sound.

Pretend to stir a big pot of soup.

Instructor: Now we will both try it. We'll say "/ûr/ in *stir*" and pretend to stir a big pot of soup.

Together: /ûr/ in *stir*.

Instructor: Now you are ready to put it all together: /är/ in *car*, /ôr/ in *door*, /âr/ in *hair*, and /ûr/ in *stir*. Let both say that with the movements.

Together: /är/ in *car*, /ôr/ in *door*, /âr/ in *hair*, and /ûr/ in *stir*.

Instructor: Last lesson you read some words that contain the sound /är/ in *car*. Read these words again as a review.

cart   part   mart   chart

harm   hard   barn   tarp

Instructor: Now you will read a short list of words and then read those words in a sentence.

Mark
car

Mark will drive his car.

park
March

Mark will drive his car to the park in March.

part
scarf
yarn

Part of the scarf is knit with blue yarn.

Clark
mark
chart

Clark must mark his chart with a straight line.

star
card

In this game you must try to match two stars.
You will lose if you do not pick the right cards.

Lesson 156: R-Changed Vowels: AR as /är/
Sight Word: are

You will need the following: *a blank index card and a pen.*

Review

Instructor: In the last lesson you learned a chant of all the **r**-changed vowel sounds. First I will do the chant and then we will do it together.

The mimed movements are in parentheses. Do not say these out loud.

Instructor: /är/ in *car*,   (steer the car)
/ôr/ in *door*,   (open a door)
/âr/ in *hair*,   (comb your hair)
and /ûr/ in *stir*. (stir the soup)

Instructor: Now let's do that together.

Together: /är/ in *car*,   (steer the car)
/ôr/ in *door*,   (open a door)
/âr/ in *hair*,   (comb your hair)
and /ûr/ in *stir*. (stir the soup)

Instructor: In the last two lessons you read words with the /är/ sound. Read this sentence as a review.

Part of the scarf is knit with blue yarn.

New

Instructor: Now you are going to learn a new word that sounds exactly like the sound /är/. You will memorize this word. I will write this word on a card for you.

are

Hand the card to the child and pronounce the word for him. Have the child read the word three times. Tell him to pick up the card when he reads the word in the story later. When you are finished with this lesson, put the card in the sight word stack.

Instructor: Now you are going to learn three words that also contain the /är/ sound. These words end in a silent **e**. The silent **e** is there to tell you to say the soft sound of the letter **g**.

large   barge   charge

You are almost ready to read a story. First read this list of new /är/ words. I will help you if you need it.

jar	far	farm	bark	dark
yard	hard	harm	charm	charge
large	start	sharp	guard	are

Instructor: Now you are ready to read a story. Remember, when you see the word **are**, pick up the card. To help you keep your place, I will put a folded piece of paper under the line you are reading.

If you find that picking up the **are** card distracts the child from his reading, you may wish to have him read the story twice: once normally, and once picking up the card.

A lot of jobs are done on this farm.
We raise wheat and rye in the large field.
It is a hard task to bring the grain in from the field.
Geese, hens, and ducks are fed with grain.

I will save a jar of wheat to give to my best hen.
Then the dogs start to bark and round up the sheep and lambs.
The dogs will keep a sharp eye on the yard.
They are in charge.
The dogs guard the sheep from harm.

The cats are far up in the hay loft.
They sleep in the day and hunt mice when it is dark.
This farm has charm.

Lesson 157: R-Changed Vowels: OR and ORE as /ôr/

You will need the following: *the magnetic alphabet board for this lesson.*

Do not do the typical "Two Review and One New" today. Have the child read the list of words from the last lesson as a review.

Review

Instructor: Let's begin this lesson with the chant of the **r**-changed vowels. We'll do it together.

The motions are in parentheses. Remind the child of the chant and the motions if necessary.

Together: /är/ in **car**,   (steer the car)
            /ôr/ in **door**,   (open a door)
            /âr/ in **hair**,   (comb your hair)
            and /ûr/ in **stir**.   (stir the soup)

Instructor: Now read the following list of words for me.

pot   spot   shot   cod

foe   toe

New

Instructor: Let's see what happens to a word when we put the letter **r** after the vowel **o**. This changes the sound of the vowel. I will read each of the following word pairs to you. First I will read the short-vowel sound word, and then I will read the word with the **r**-changed vowel sound. Then you will read each word pair to me. Watch out for that tricky **r**!

pot   spot   shot   cod
port   sport   short   cord

Instructor: Now we will see how the letter **r** changes the *long-***o** vowel sound. First I will read each pair of words. Then you will read each pair of words.

Explain to the child that the word *fore* means "in the front." This word can also be a prefix, in *forehead* (which is in the front of your head) and *foreground* (the ground right in front).

foe   toe
fore   tore

Instructor: Let's review some of the words you have read so far in this lesson.

port   short   sport   cord

fore   tore

Instructor: Can you hear the same /ôr/ sound in each of those words? Now you will read these words in
               sentences. Read each pair of practice words before you read the sentence itself.

spot
sport

In this sport, you stand and kick the ball from that spot.

pot
port

The cook made a pot of soup when the ship came to the port.

shot
short

The pain in my arm was short when I got a shot.

toe
tore

The hard rock tore the skin on my toe.

Follow-Up:
Take out the magnetic alphabet board. For each of the word pairs below, assemble the word with the
short-**o** vowel sound. The child will read the word. Then have the child insert an **r** to make a new word.
The child will read the new word with the **r**-changed vowel sound.

pot   shot   spot   cod
port   short   sport   cord

foe   toe
fore   tore

Lesson 158: R-Changed Vowels: OR and ORE as /ôr/

Remember to do the "Two Review and One New" today.

Instructor: Let's begin this lesson with the chant of the **r**-changed vowels. We'll do it together.

The motions are in parentheses. Remind the child of the chant and the motions if necessary.

Together: /är/ in *car*,   (steer the car)
/ôr/ in *door*,   (open a door)
/âr/ in *hair*,   (comb your hair)
and /ûr/ in *stir*. (stir the soup)

Instructor: Last lesson you read words with the /ôr/ sound. Read these words as a review.

port	short	cord	sport	tore	fore

Instructor: Let's read this list of new words together. First I will read each word. Then you will read each word. Then you will go back to the beginning of the list and read it by yourself.

or	cord	corn	morn	horn	worn
torn	pork	forks	short	snorts	lords
north	more	store	swore	shore	York

Instructor: Now let's read a story that uses the words you just read. If you need help staying on a line, use a folded sheet of paper to help you keep your place.

The Duke of York and one of his lords take a short trip on a ship.
They push off the shore late in the morn.
They swore they would eat lunch at noon or one.
The duke and the lord eat pork and corn with gold forks.
Then the man on guard sounds the horn.
A storm has come.

The winds blow hard from the north and the east.
The worn sails of the ships may be torn by the harsh gusts.
The crew winds the cord to tie up the loose sails.
They store the goods on deck in a safe place.

They ride out the storm with its wild winds and huge waves.
The duke snorts, "No storm will sink this ship!"
"We will head back to port and sail no more for the day."

Lesson 159: R-Changed Vowels: OUR as /ôr/

Review

Instructor: Let's begin this lesson with the chant of the **r**-changed vowels. We'll do it together.

Together: /är/ in *car*,   (steer the car)
             /ôr/ in *door*,   (open a door)
             /âr/ in *hair*,   (comb your hair)
             and /ûr/ in *stir*.   (stir the soup)

Instructor: In the last lesson you read words with the sound /ôr/ in *door*. Read the following words to me as a review.

for   sport   storm   more   sore   horse

New

Instructor: The next list of words may look a little different from the list we just read, but they are pronounced the same way. These words have the vowel pair **ou** before the **r**, but they are still pronounced /ôr/ in *door*. Let's read this list together. First I will read each word. Then you will read each word. Once we have finished going through the list together, you will go back to the beginning and read the list yourself.

pour   your   four   fourth   course   court

Instructor: Let's read these words in some sentences.

The king and his court sit down for a meal.
Each lord in the court brings four guests.
A large roast is the fourth course.
The king pours sauce on his meat.

The king tells the man on his right, "Eat more. Your plate is not full."
When the meal is done, the men sit and snore.

Lesson 160: R-Changed Vowels: OAR and OOR as /ôr/

Remember to do the "Two Review and One New" today.

Review

Instructor: Let's begin this lesson with the chant of the **r**-changed vowels. We'll do it together.

Together: /är/ in **car**,   (steer the car)
 /ôr/ in **door**,   (open a door)
 /âr/ in **hair**,   (comb your hair)
 and /ûr/ in **stir**. (stir the soup)

Instructor: Let's review some words with the sound /ôr/ in **door**. Read this list.

born   fork   tore   chore   four   course

New

Instructor: In this lesson you will read more words with the sound /ôr/ in **door**. When the letter **r** follows the vowel team **oa**, the vowel sound is changed to /ôr/ in **door**. Let's read this list together. First I will read each word. Then you will read each word. Once we have finished going through the list together, you will go back to the beginning and read the list yourself.

Explain to the child that the word **hoard** means "to gather something and store it in a safe place" (example: "*hoard* food for the long winter").

oar   roar   soar   boar   board   hoard

hoarse   coarse

Instructor: Now you will read these words in a story.

The huge wild boar shakes the ground when he stomps.
He snorts and paws the coarse grass.
He would roar if he could.
The wild boar is hoarse from his grunts.

Instructor: When the letter **r** follows the **oo** vowel pair, it stands for the sound /ôr/ in **door**. Let's read the following two words. First I will read each word. Then you will read each word.

door   poor   floor

Instructor: Now you will read a sentence that uses some of those words.

I will cross the porch floor and close the screen door.

Lesson 161: R-Changed Vowels: WAR as /wôr/

Remember to do the "Two Review and One New" today.

Review

Instructor: Let's begin this lesson with the chant of the **r**-changed vowels. I want you to try the chant by yourself. Remember to do the movements, too!

Remind the child of the chant if necessary.

Child: /är/ *in* **car,**   (steer the car)
/ôr/ *in* **door,**   (open a door)
/âr/ *in* **hair,**   (comb your hair)
and /ûr/ *in* **stir.**   (stir the soup)

Instructor: You have already read words in which the letter **w** comes before the vowel **a**. This tells you that the word contains the /ô/ sound instead of the short-**a** vowel sound. Read this list of words as a review.

walk   wash   watch   want

New

Instructor: In the next short list of words, the letter **r** also changes the sound of the vowel. The vowel sound in these words is closest to the sound /ôr/ in **door**. I will read each word to you. Then you will read each word to me. Once we have gone through the list together, you will read the five words by yourself.

The following words have a slight regional variation in pronunciation. These words are fairly common and recognizable, so the child should have little problem identifying them when reading.

war   warm   swarm   warn   wart

Instructor: Now let's read some of these words in a sentence.

I warn you that on a warm day you may see a swarm of bugs.

Lesson 162: R-Changed Vowels: Review /ôr/ Words

Remember to do the "Two Review and One New" today.

Instructor: Let's read a list of review words. These words all contain the sound /ôr/ in **door**.

door	four	more	morn	lord
cord	forth	snort	short	horse
roar	coarse	warn	warts	

Instructor: Now let's read a story that uses these words. If you need help keeping your place, put a folded sheet of paper under the line you are reading.

One morn the horse of the rich lord ate his coarse grain in his pen.
He bent his head to drink from the huge tub when he saw a sight.
"I have four small warts on my nose!" he thought.

"What if I get more than four?
I am a fine horse.
I have a short cord of red silk to bind the braids of my mane."
The horse let out a snort.

When the lord came forth to the pen, the horse ran in the barn.
"The lord should not see me with these warts.
They could leave a scar or a mark.
Why are they not sore?"

The lord went through the door of the barn.
The horse hid his head in the hay.
"Come, horse," he said.
The shy horse kept his head in the hay.

"I warn you. Look at me," the lord said with a roar.
The lord let out a loud laugh.
"You have four oats stuck to your nose!"
The vain horse let out a glad neigh.

Lesson 163: R-Changed Vowels: ARE as /âr/

You will need the following: *the magnetic alphabet board.*

Instructor: You already know how to read words with the /är/ sound in *car*. Read these words as a review.

far	bar	car	scar	star

New

Instructor: When you add a silent **e** to the ends of those words, the vowel sound changes to the sound /âr/ in *hair*. Let's read the following word pairs. First I will read the word with the sound /âr/ in *car*, and then I will read the word and show you how the silent **e** changes the vowel sound to /âr/ in *hair*. Then you will read that same word pair to me. Once we have finished going through the list together, you will go back to the beginning and read all the pairs yourself.

far	bar	car	scar	star
fare	bare	care	scare	stare

Instructor: Now you will read these words in sentences. Before you read each sentence, read the practice words.

far
fare

Mom will give you fare to go far on the train.

car
care

Take care to get on the right train car.

star
stare

At night I like to stare at a bright star and make a wish.

bar
bare

I grip the bar of soap with my bare hands.

Follow-Up:
Take out the magnetic alphabet board and use it to form the word pairs in this lesson. One at a time, form each upper word. Let the child read the word. Have the child add the **e** and read the new word.

Lesson 164: R-Changed Vowels: ARE as /âr/

Review

Instructor: Let's begin this lesson with the chant of the **r**-changed vowels. I want you to try the chant by yourself. Remember to do the movements, too!

Remind the child of the chant if necessary.

Child: /är/ *in* **car,**   (steer the car)
/ôr/ *in* **door,**   (open a door)
/âr/ *in* **hair,**   (comb your hair)
and /ûr/ *in* **stir.**   (stir the soup)

Instructor: Last lesson you read words with the sound /âr/ in **hair**. Read these words as a review.

care   bare   scare   stare

New

Instructor: Now you are going to read a list of new words with the sound /âr/ in **hair**. Then you will read these words in a story.

rare   glare   share   square

Instructor: Now you are ready to read these words in a story.

I got a rare fish for a gift.
He swims in a square tank.
He glares at me through the glass walls of the tank.
He does not blink when he stares.

I share the care of the rare fish with my mom.
I need to net the rare fish when I have to clean the tank.
I dare not touch the rare fish with a bare hand.
It could get sick.

Lesson 165: R-Changed Vowels: AIR as /âr/

Remember to do the "Two Review and One New" today.

Review

Instructor: Let's begin this lesson with the chant of the **r**-changed vowels. I want you to try the chant by yourself. Remember to do the movements, too!

Remind the child of the chant if necessary.

Child:
/är/ in **car,**	(steer the car)
/ôr/ in **door,**	(open a door)
/âr/ in **hair,**	(comb your hair)
and /ûr/ *in* **stir.**	(stir the soup)

Instructor: Last lesson you read words with the sound /âr/ in **hair**. Read these words as a review.

rare   dare   share   square

Instructor: You already know how to read words with the vowel pair **ai**. **Ai** stands for the long-**a** sound. Read these words to me.

pain   stain

New

Instructor: When the letter **r** follows the vowel team **ai**, the vowel sound changes to sound /âr/ in **hair**. Let's read this list of words together. I will read a pair of words to you. The first word in each pair contains the letters **air** which stand for the sound /âr/ in **hair**. The second word in each pair contains the letters **are** which also stand for the sound /âr/ in **hair**. Then you will read that same pair to me. Notice that though the words in each pair are spelled differently and have different meanings, they are pronounced the same.

hair	fair	pair	stair
hare	fare	pare	stare

Instructor: Now you will read these words in sentences. Read the practice words before you read each sentence.

Explain that a hare is a small, furry animal that is like a rabbit except it is larger and has longer legs and ears.

hare
hair

The hare has fur, not hair.

257

fare
fair

The fare for the ride was a fair price.

pare
pair

Pare the pair of plums with a knife.

stare
stair

I will stare at the wee babe as he crawls up one stair at a time.

Lesson 166: R-Changed Vowels: EAR as /âr/

Remember to do the "Two Review and One New" today.

Review

Instructor: Let's begin this lesson with the chant of the **r**-changed vowels. I want you to try the chant by yourself. Remember to do the movements, too!

Remind the child of the chant if necessary.

Child:
/är/ *in* **car**,   (steer the car)
/ôr/ *in* **door**,   (open a door)
/âr/ *in* **hair**,   (comb your hair)
and /ûr/ *in* **stir**. (stir the soup)

Instructor: Last lesson you read words with the sound /âr/ in **hair**. Read these words as a review.

hair   fair   pair   stair

Instructor: Read this short story as a review.

I share in the care of a pair of white mice.
That is the fair thing to do.
My sis and I try not to scare them.
We speak to them in sweet, soft tones.

Instructor: You already know how to read words in which the vowel pair **ea** stands for the long-**a** vowel sound. Read these words as a review.

great   steak   break

New

Instructor: When the letter **r** follows the vowel team **ea**, the vowel sound changes to sound /âr/ in **hair**. Let's read this list of words together. First I will read each word. Then you will read each word.

bear   pear   tear ("rip")   wear

Instructor: Now you will read sentences that use some of these words.

The young child eats a pear for lunch.
He will wear a bib with a bear on it.
The bib will catch the juice that he spills.

Lesson 167: R-Changed Vowels: Review /âr/ Words

Instructor: Let's begin this lesson with the chant of the **r**-changed vowels. I want you to try the chant by yourself. Remember to do the movements, too!

Remind the child of the chant if necessary.

Child: */är/ in* **car,**   (steer the car)
           /ôr/ in **door,**   (open a door)
           /âr/ in **hair,**   (comb your hair)
           and /ûr/ in **stir.** (stir the soup)

Instructor: In the past few lessons, you have been reading words with the sound /âr/ in **hair**. Let's review these words. Read the following list to me. Read across.

bare	stare	glare	spare	dare	share
fair	hair	stair	wear	tear	swear

Instructor: Now you will read a story that uses these words.

The maid with the fair hair comes down the stairs.
She wears no hat.
The head of the fair maid is bare.
She sits in a chair.

The wife of the duke comes in the room.
She stares and glares at the maid with the bare head.
The maid pipes up with a mild voice, "I could not wear a hat."
"My spare hat had a tear," the maid swears.
"I dare not wear it."

The wife of the duke smiles and speaks to the maid.
"I will go get my spare hat and share it with you."
"Thank you so much," breathes the maid with fair hair.

Lesson 168: R-Changed Vowels: ER as /ûr/

Review

Instructor: Let's begin this lesson with the chant of the **r**-changed vowels. You will do it by yourself. Remember to do the movements, too!

Child: /är/ *in* **car**, (steer the car)
/ôr/ *in* **door**, (open a door)
/âr/ *in* **hair**, (comb your hair)
and /ûr/ *in* **stir**. (stir the soup)

New

Instructor: In this lesson we will read words with the sound /ûr/ in **stir**. The vowels **e**, **i**, and **u** can all stand for this sound when they are followed by the letter **r**. The letter **r** *changes* the sound of a vowel! I am going to teach you a little chant to help you remember that the vowel sounds of **e**, **i**, and **u** are changed when the vowel is followed by the letter **r**.

Point to **er**, **ir**, and **ur** as you spell it and then pronounce it. Say the chant slowly.

er   ir   ur

Instructor: **er** /ûr/, **ir** /ûr/, **ur** /ûr/.

Instructor: Now I am going to say that again. This time, I want you to point to each vowel above as I say it.

Instructor: **er** /ûr/, **ir** /ûr/, **ur** /ûr/. Now I want you to say the chant with me. You will point to the letter pairs above as we say each one.

Together: **er** /ûr/, **ir** /ûr/, **ur** /ûr/.

Instructor: Now let's read a list of **er** words that stand for the sound /ûr/ in **stir**. First I will read each word. Then you will read each word. Once we have finished going through the list together, you will go back to the beginning and read the words yourself.

The letters **er** are most commonly found at the ends of words (for example: **brother**, **tiger**). The child will read more of these words later in the book. Also, remind the child that the word **herb** begins with a silent letter **h**. Read across.

her	herd	verb	herb
jerk	clerk	term	germ
pert	perch	fern	stern
Vern	Bert	Sherl	

The lesson continues on the following page.

The stern clerk sold Sherl a small green fern.
She brought the fern to Vern who was sick from a germ.
When Vern saw her with the fern, his face lit up with a smile.
He said in a pert way, "Put the fern by the herb plants!
Thank you, Sherl."

Instructor: There are some **er** words that end with a silent **e**. They still contain the sound /ûr/ in *stir*.
First I will read each word. Then you will read that same word. Once we have finished going
through the whole list together, you will go back to the beginning and read the list by
yourself.

nerve   serve   swerve   verse

verge   merge

Instructor: Now you will read a sentence that uses some of the words you just read.

He had the nerve to swerve when he was on the verge of a wreck.

Lesson 169: R-Changed Vowels: IR as /ûr/

Remember to do the "Two Review and One New" today.

Review

Instructor: Let's begin by saying the chant we learned last lesson. I will point to each of the vowels as we say the chant together.

Point to **er**, **ir**, and **ur** as you spell it and then pronounce it. Say the chant slowly.

er   ir   ur

Together: **er** /ûr/, **ir** /ûr/, **ur** /ûr/.

Instructor: Let's do that two more times.

Together (two times):
             er /ûr/, **ir** /ûr/, **ur** /ûr/.

Instructor: Last lesson you read **er** words with the sound /ûr/ in *stir*. Read these words as a review.

her   term   verse   serve

New

Instructor: Now you are going to read **ir** words with the sound /ûr/ in *stir*. First I will read each word. Then you will read each word. Once we have finished going through the list together, you will read it by yourself. I will put a piece of folded paper under the line that you are reading to help you keep your place. Read across.

sir	stir	fir	firm
first	girl	dirt	bird
birth	third	thirst	swirl
twirl	whirl	shirt	skirt
squirt	squirm	chirp	Kirk

Instructor: Now you are ready to read these words in a story.

The small girl goes out to the yard in her new shirt and skirt.
She is in the first grade.
She twirls in her full skirt.
The skirt whirls and swirls.
The third time she twirls a bird chirps in the tree.
This is so much fun!

Lesson 170: R-Changed Vowels: WOR as /wûr/

Remember to do the "Two Review and One New" today.

Review

Instructor: Let's begin by saying the chant we learned. I will point to the vowels as we say the chant together.

Point to **er**, **ir**, and **ur** as you spell it and then pronounce it. Say the chant slowly.

er   ir   ur

Together: **er** /ûr/, **ir** /ûr/, **ur** /ûr/.

Instructor: Let's do that one more time. This time you will point to each vowel when we say it.

Together: **er** /ûr/, **ir** /ûr/, **ur** /ûr/.

Instructor: Last lesson you read **ir** words with the sound /ûr/ in *stir*. Read these words as a review.

first   stir   bird   third

New

Instructor: Now you are going to read **ur** words with the sound /ûr/ in *stir*. First I will read each word. Then you will read each word. Once we have finished going through the list together, you will read it by yourself.

fur   curb   curl   hurt

turn   burn   churn   surf

burst   purr   blurt   church

Instructor: These **ur** words end with a silent letter **e**. This does not affect the **r**-changed vowel sound.

curve   purse   nurse   urge

Instructor: Now you are ready to read a story.

Do you see the young cat with the white fur?
He sits on the curb by the church.
He has a hurt paw.
I have an urge to turn and help him.
I will take him to the vet and a nurse will fix his paw.
I will stroke his soft fur, speak soft words, and hear him purr.
He will curl up on my lap and sleep.

Lesson 171: R-Changed Vowels: WOR as /ûr/

You will need the following: *paper and drawing supplies for the optional activity.*

Remember to do the "Two Review and One New" today.

Review

Instructor: Read this list of words as a review. They contain the sound /ôr/ in **door** *(Lesson 161)*.

war   warm   warn   wart

New

Instructor: Remember, the letter **w** often changes the pronunciation of a word. The words in this next list contain the letters **or**, but because these words also begin with the letter **w**, the **or** is pronounced /ûr/ in **stir**. I will read each word to you. Then you will read each word to me. Once we have gone through the list together, you will read the five words by yourself.

worm   work   word   world

worst   worse

Instructor: Now you will read a sentence that uses some of those words.

The worst worm in the world is the one in your soup.

Optional Follow-Up:
Write the sentence from this lesson on the top of a piece of paper. Have the child draw a picture of someone looking at a worm in his or her soup.

Lesson 172: R-Changed Vowels: EAR as /ûr/

Remember to do the "Two Review and One New" today.

Review

Instructor: In the last lesson you read words with **wor** and the sound /ûr/ in *stir*. Read the following words to me as a review.

worm   word   work   world

Instructor: You already know how to read words with the vowel pair **ea**. The vowel pair **ea** can stand for the long-**a** vowel sound *(Lesson 87)*, the long-**e** vowel sound *(Lesson 90)*, or the short-**e** vowel sound *(Lesson 126)*. Read the following words to me as a review.

great   break   eat   seat

lean   dream   head   breath

Instructor: You can also read words with the letters **ear** in them. In these words, **ear** stands for the sound /âr/ in *hair* *(Lesson 166)*. Read the following words to me.

bear   wear   tear

New

Instructor: This next list of words also contains **ear**. In these words, ear stands for the sound /ûr/ in *stir*. I will read each word to you. Then you will read each word to me. Once we have finished going through the list together, go back to the beginning and read the list yourself.

earn   earth   learn   yearn

heard   pearl   search

Instructor: Now you will read some of those words in a story.

I heard there is a pearl of great price.
It is in a deep crack in the earth.
I yearn to search the world for it.
I will learn how to find it.

Lesson 173: Sight Words: where, there, were

You will need the following: *three index cards and a pen.*

Remember to do the "Two Review and One New" today.

Review

Instructor: You know how to read words with all the **r**-changed vowel sounds. Let's do the chant of the **r**-changed vowels together. Remember to do the movements, too!

Together: /är/ in **car**,   (steer the car)
/ôr/ in **door**,   (open a door)
/âr/ in **hair**,   (comb your hair)
and /ûr/ in **stir**.   (stir the soup)

New

Instructor: In this lesson you will learn a new word. You will memorize it. I will write this word on a card for you.

there

Say the word to the child and hand him the card. Have the child practice saying the word and pointing to the word on the card.

Instructor: Now you are going to read some knock-knock jokes. When you read the word **there**, I want you to pick up the card.

If necessary, explain to the child that he must *spell out* the word **who** in the last line of the third joke.

Knock! Knock!
Who is there?
Boo.
Boo who?
Do not cry! It is I!

Knock! Knock!
Who is there?
Hatch.
Hatch who?
I did not mean to make you sneeze!

The lesson continues on the following page.

Knock! Knock!
Who is there?
Spell.
Spell who?
W-H-O. That is how you spell who.

Instructor: Now you will learn two more words. I will write these words on cards for you.

where   **were**

Say each word and pass the cards to the child. Ask the child to say the word on each card as he passes it back to you. Add the **there** card. Put all three cards face down; shuffle. Ask the child to pick up a card and read it aloud. If he reads the word correctly, he keeps the card. If he reads it incorrectly, put it back on the table face down. Repeat this practice until the child is comfortable with the words. Keep the three cards in the sight word stack (you will also use these same three cards in the next lesson).

Instructor: Now you will read some questions about the places you have been. After you have read the question, tell me your answer.

After the child reads the question, he should answer himself, "I was…"

Where were you last night?

Where were you born?

Where were you when you ate your best meal?

Where were you when you felt glad?

Where were you when you did hard work?

Lesson 174: Sight Words: their, here

You will need the following: *two index cards, a pen, and the **there**, **where**, and **were** cards.*

Remember to do the "Two Review and One New" today.

Instructor: In this lesson you will read two new words. I will write these words on cards for you.

their   here

Say each word and pass the cards to the child. Ask the child to say the word on each card as he passes it back to you. Add the three cards from the last lesson: **there**, **where**, and **were**. Put all five cards face down; shuffle. Ask the child to pick up a card and read it aloud. If he reads the word correctly, he keeps the card. If he reads it incorrectly, put it back on the table face down. Repeat this practice until the child is comfortable with the words. After this lesson, all of these cards will go in the sight word stack.

Instructor: Now you will read a story.

Will you help me bring a treat to the kids?
Here are three bowls of ice cream.
Do not put their bowls there on the stove.
Put them here on the tray.
I will lift the tray and you will hand their bowls to them.

In the next story, there are two characters. You will read the first sentence and the child will respond by reading the indented sentence. Continue this dialogue to the end. Then switch characters and read the story again.

Where are you? I thought you were there.

I am here.

I do not see you there.

Look here.

Where?

Here in the play tent.

Why are you in there?

I found a game that they left. Their game is still here.

May I come in there?

Yes! You may play their game with me.

Lesson 175: R-Changed Vowels: Slightly-Changed Vowel Sounds

Remember to do the "Two Review and One New" today.

Instructor: Read these words as a review.

peep   steep   cheep

Instructor: There are some words in which the vowel sound is changed *just slightly* by the letter **r**. The words in the next list contain the vowel pair **ee** and end with the letter **r**. First I will read each word; then you will read each word.

peer   deer   steer   sneer

cheer   sheer

Instructor: Now you will read a sentence.

I will peer at the deer on the steep hill.

Instructor: Now read these words as a review.

team   speak   neat

Instructor: The words in the next list also contain the vowel pair **ea**. The vowel sound in these words is just slightly changed by the letter **r**. First I will read each word; then you will read each word.

rear   fear   near   year

tear   smear   clear   spear

Instructor: Now you will read these words in a story.

A car sped by the girl.
A splash of mud made a brown smear on her new dress.
A tear fell down her cheek.
I fear the girl was too near the road.

Instructor: Now read these words as a review.

cube   cute

Instructor: The next two words also contain the long-**u** vowel sound. The vowel sound is slightly changed by the letter **r**. First I will read each word; then you will read each word.

cure   pure

Instructor: Now you will read these words in a story.

The nurse in the pure white coat will help to cure you.
She will give you a pill and a clear drink.
Do not fear!
She will cheer you up.

Instructor: Read these words as a review.

out   sound   house

Instructor: These next words also contain the **ou** vowel pair. The vowel sound is slightly changed by the letter **r**. First I will read each word; then you will read each word.

our   hour (silent **h**)   sour   scour

flour

Instructor: Now you will read these words in a story.

We will make a sour cream cake.
We mix the eggs, flour, and sour cream in a large bowl.
Now our stove has flour on it.
We will scour it clean.
We will each eat a thick slice of cake in one hour.

Instructor: Read these words as a review.

wipe   time   fine

Instructor: These next words also contain the long-**i** vowel sound. The vowel sound is slightly changed by the letter **r**. First I will read each word; then you will read each word.

Explain to the child that a *shire* is like a county. The word *dire* means "very great."

wire   tire   fire   dire

spire   shire

Instructor: You will read these words in a sentence.

The dire fire in the church spire will tire the men who fight it.

Lesson 176: R-Changed Vowels Review

Instructor: Read this list of words as a review. Then you will read a story.

bird	third	dirt	chirp	squirm	worm
yard	warm	porch	perch	hear	

Instructor: Now you will read a story that uses these words. This is a story about a bird that spies a worm.

The bird will perch and chirp on the edge of the porch.
He will spy a worm in the warm dirt of the yard.
He will fly to the spot and yank at the worm.
The worm will squirm and come out on the third tug.
Then the bird will hear a cat and drop the worm.

Instructor: Now read this list of review words.

poor	soar	glare	stare	air	ferns
bird	first	wire	perch	near	course

Instructor: Now you will read these words in a story about a cat that pursues the bird.

The cat will creep near the bird and crouch down in the ferns.
The cat will stare and glare at the bird.
The bird will turn and fly off to a wire.
The cat will watch the bird soar in the air.
Poor cat!
That bird will not be the first course of his meal.
Then the cat will hear a dog.
The cat will scat.

Lesson 177: R-Changed Vowels Review

Instructor: Read the following list of review words. Then you will read the words in a story.

sharp	bark	large	charge	stores	snort
tear ("rip")	church	steer	clear	hear	pure

Instructor: Now you will read these words in a story about a dog that chases the cat.

A large dog will spot the pure white cat.
He will snort and let out a sharp bark.
He will charge at the cat.
The cat will howl in fear and tear down the street.
The cat will steer clear of the cars and the stores as she sprints.
The dog will chase the cat past the church.
Then the dog will hear the man.
The chase will end.

Instructor: Read this next list of review words.

are	dart	sport	your	hoarse	poor
care	fair	warn	nerve	twirl	turn
heard	where	were	here	near	our

Instructor: Now you will read a story that uses the words you just read. This story is about a man and his dog.

The man will call to the dog, "Come here now!
Where were you?"
The dog will turn and come near the man with a hurt look on his face.
The man will say, "You have nerve to dart off from me."
The man will sigh, pat the dog on the head, and twirl his fur.

"I heard your bark.
We do not chase our friends.
The cat is our friend.
I do not care if you thought it was fun.
You are too huge.
It is not fair to chase the cat for sport.
You may bark till you are hoarse, but you may not chase the poor cat."

Section 17

SIMPLE TWO-SYLLABLE WORDS

Lesson 178: Compound Words

You will need the following: *the magnetic alphabet board for the optional activity.*

Review

Instructor: Up until now, you have been reading short words with one vowel sound. These are words of one *syllable*. A syllable is a part of a word containing one vowel sound. Read these words.

air   plane   base   ball

New

Instructor: Now look at these two-syllable words as I read them.

I am using compound words to introduce the child to the concept of syllables because it is clear and easy to see the parts of the words.

airplane   baseball

Instructor: Now I will read those two syllable words again and clap on each syllable.

Read the words from the list above. Clap on **air**, **plane** and **base**, **ball**.

Instructor: These two syllable words are made up of words you already know like **air** and **plane**. When you put these words together, a larger, two-syllable word is formed: **airplane**. Read each pair of one-syllable words, and then read the two-syllable word that is formed when the smaller words are combined.

| air plane | base ball | her self | your self | out side |
| airplane | baseball | herself | yourself | outside |

Go back through the list and clap as you say each syllable. Then go through the list a second time, having the child join you in saying the words and clapping as he says each syllable.

Instructor: Now read some sentences to me.

Come see for yourself.
There is an airplane outside!
The man flew on an airplane to go to a baseball game.

Optional Follow-Up:
The child should form each of the one-syllable words on the board, side-by-side (but not touching). The child should read each word once it is formed. Then the instructor should slide the words together and ask the child to read the compound word. Do this for any of the compound words from this lesson that your child had difficulty reading.

Lesson 179: Compound Words

Remember to do the "Two Review and One New" today.

Instructor: In this lesson you will read more two-syllable words that are made from two smaller words put together. I will read each pair of words for you. Then you will read each pair of words to me. Once we have finished going through all the pairs of words together, you will go back to the beginning and read them by yourself.

up stairs	bath room	tooth paste	tooth brush	in to
upstairs	bathroom	toothpaste	toothbrush	into

bed room	night light	can not	with out	night shirt
bedroom	nightlight	cannot	without	nightshirt

Instructor: Now you will read these words in a story.

If the child has difficulty reading the compound word, cover up the second half of the compound word with your finger and let the child see the word parts separately.

Dad tells me I have to go to bed.
I march upstairs to the bathroom.
I put toothpaste on my toothbrush and clean my teeth.

I go into my bedroom and flick on my nightlight.
I cannot sleep without its small, warm glow.
I change into my nightshirt and climb into bed.
I touch my soft bear and tuck him in.
As I curl up in bed, I hope for sweet dreams this night.

Lesson 180: Compound Words

Instructor: This lesson you will read more two-syllable words. First I will read each word pair, and then you will read it after me. Then you will read those words in a three-part story.

birth day	bed room	down stairs	bath room
birthday	bedroom	downstairs	bathroom

snow storm	out side
snowstorm	outside

This day is my birthday.
I leave the bedroom and head downstairs to dress in the bathroom.
There is a snowstorm outside.
I can see a pile of snow on the hedge.

in doors	sun light	mail man	foot ball
indoors	sunlight	mailman	football

fire works
fireworks

It is hard to stay indoors.
The snow stops and I see sunlight.
The mailman comes with a card for me.
It is from Aunt Sue.
It says, "You may go to the football game and fireworks with us."

base ball	flash light	wrist watch	some where
baseball	flashlight	wristwatch	somewhere

suit case	pea nut	can not
suitcase	peanut	cannot

I like both football and baseball.
I look for my flashlight and wristwatch.
They are somewhere in my room.
I find them near my suitcase.
I take my coins so that I can buy some peanuts.
I cannot wait to watch the game with my aunt.

Lesson 181: The Schwa

You will need the following: *a children's dictionary if you do the optional activity.*

Instructor: For the past few lessons you have been reading two-syllable words that are formed when two small words are put together: *airplane, snowstorm*. However, not all two-syllable words are like this. Listen as I say these words. I will point to each word as I say it. Follow along with your eyes.

brother	teacher	Friday	Thursday	Tuesday	photo
suggest	about	among	again	divide	because

Instructor: When you read a two-syllable word, one syllable is spoken with more force than the other. This syllable is called the *accented* syllable. Listen as I say this list of words again. These words have been divided into syllables

Read the list below, overemphasizing the accented syllable which is in bold. Point out to the child that the word *again* contains the vowel pair **ai** which stands for the short-e vowel sound (like the word **said**).

broth-er	**teach**-er	**Fri**-day	**Thurs**-day	**Tues**-day	**pho**-to
sug-**gest**	a-**bout**	a-**mong**	a-**gain**	di-**vide**	be-**cause**

Instructor: Sometimes we can hardly hear the vowel in a syllable that is not accented. Listen as I read the following words. Pay attention to the unaccented syllable. It will sound much quieter than the accented syllable. I will point to each softer, unaccented syllable when I read it.

Overemphasize the accented syllable (in bold print). Point to the unaccented syllable (in regular print) when you say it. These words all contain the schwa sound (similar to the /ŭ/ on the unaccented syllable). This is the same sound at the beginning and end of the word **America**.

so-fa	**so**-da	**lem**-on	**ex**-tra	**chi**-na	**ba**-con

Instructor: In words of more than one syllable, often the unaccented vowel sound barely even makes a sound. This is the same sound that you hear in the beginning and end of the word *America*. Any of the vowels in an unaccented syllable may be pronounced with a schwa. This sound is similar to a quiet short-**u** vowel sound: /ŭ/. This sound has a funny name; it is called a *schwa*. The schwa sound is represented by a funny symbol in a dictionary. The symbol is an upside-down and backwards **e**. It looks like this:

ə

The lesson contines on the following page.

Instructor: Now we will read the words together. Remember, these words all contain the schwa sound on the unaccented syllable. Any vowel can stand for the schwa sound. I will read each word; then you will read each word.

so-fa   so-da   lem-on   ex-tra   chi-na   ba-con

For beginning readers, as long as they get the meaning from the word, it is not critical whether they pronounce a vowel with a schwa or with another vowel sound. For example, they may say /ă/ for the first syllable in **away**. Just say the word correctly to the child and have him pronounce it after you.

Instructor: Now I am going to teach you a rule that will help you sound out words of more than one syllable. When words are divided into syllables and the beginning syllable ends in a vowel, the vowel in that syllable is usually long. *So-fa* and *so-da* both have the long-**o** sound because the first syllable ends with the vowel **o**.

Point to **sofa** and **soda** in the row at the top of the page and have the child repeat those words after you.

Instructor: If the syllable ends in a consonant, the vowel in that syllable is usually short. **Lem**-*on* has the short-**e** sound because the first syllable in **lemon**, *lem*, ends with the consonant **m**.

Point to **lemon** in the row at the top of the page and have the child repeat the word after you.

Instructor: When the last syllable of the word ends in a vowel, that vowel often pronounced with a schwa. *Sofa*, *soda*, *extra*, and *china* all end with the schwa sound.

Point to **sofa, soda, extra,** and **china** in the row at the top of the page and have the child repeat those words after you.

Optional Follow-Up:
If the child is old enough and you want to build his dictionary skills, explore the use of the schwa in a children's dictionary. Look up each word in the row at the top of the page, and point to its phonetic spelling in the dictionary. Point out the schwa. Be aware that some dictionaries do not use the schwa for all of the words; sometimes the vowel is omitted altogether in phonetic markings.

Lesson 182: The LE Ending

Do the "Two Review and One New" today.

Instructor: In this lesson you are going to read words that all end with the letter **l** next to the silent letter **e**. Listen as I read you a few of these words. These words have the schwa sound in the last syllable. I will point to each word as I read it.

apple   circle   middle

Instructor: Now we are going to read a list of two-syllable words together. We will read a word divided into syllables; then we will read the same word under it that is not divided into syllables. First I will read both versions of each word. Then you will read both versions of that same word. Once we have finished going through the words together, you will go back to the beginning of the list and read them yourself.

The following words all end with a similar sound pattern. By reading words that all end in a similar way, the child gains confidence because the words are familiar. He begins to see that reading two-syllable words is not that difficult.

ap-ple	bot-tle	cir-cle	jin-gle	mid-dle	pur-ple
apple	bottle	circle	jingle	middle	purple

puz-zle	lit-tle	scram-ble	snug-gle	tur-tle	un-cle
puzzle	little	scramble	snuggle	turtle	uncle

Instructor: Now you will read a story that uses some of these words.

The little girl snuggles in the middle of her purple crib.
She sucks on a bottle of apple juice.
Her uncle will sing a jingle to lull her to sleep.

When she wakes, he will scramble an egg for her.
Then he will help her with her turtle puzzle.

Lesson 183: The ER Ending

Instructor: You already know how to read words with the letters **er** in them *(Lesson 168)*. Remember, when the letter **r** follows the letter **e**, it changes the sound of the vowel to /ûr/ in *stir*. Read the following words as a review.

her   fern   serve   verse

New

Instructor: In this lesson you will read two-syllable words that all *end* with the letters **e** and **r**. We will read a word divided into syllables; then we will read the word under it that is not divided into syllables. First I will read both versions of each word. Then you will read both versions of that same word. Once we have finished going through the list together, you will go back to the beginning and read the list yourself.

| crack-er | fing-er | moth-er | broth-er | of-fer | num-ber |
| cracker | finger | mother | brother | offer | number |

| pa-per | sis-ter | sum-mer | win-ter | cen-ter | let-ter |
| paper | sister | summer | winter | center | letter |

Instructor: The following two words contain the vowel sound /ô/ in **all**. These words also end with **er**. First I will read each word; then you will read that same word after me.

| fa-ther | wa-ter |
| father | water |

Instructor: Now you will read a story that uses some of the words you just read.

I will offer the purple bird a cracker.
It will nibble and tickle my finger.
The bird can talk and squawk a number of words.

It will walk up my arm where it will perch on my head.
Mother, Father, Sister, and Brother all chuckle at me and my bird.

Lesson 184: The ING Ending

Do the "Two Review and One New" today.

Review

Instructor: Let's begin this lesson by practicing more two-syllable words. Read these words to me.

out-side	to-night	wrist-watch	lit-tle	mid-dle
outside	tonight	wristwatch	little	middle

Instructor: Do you remember a chant you learned a long time ago? It went like this: /ăng/, /ĭng/, /ŏng/, /ŭng/ *(Lesson 54)*. Say that with me three times.

Together (three times):
  /ăng/, /ĭng/, /ŏng/, /ŭng/.

Instructor: Read these words as a review.

sing	wing	thing	bring	swing

New

Instructor: Let's read a list of two-syllable words that end with **ing**. We will read a word divided into syllables; then we will read the same word under it that is not divided into syllables. First I will read both versions of each word. Then you will read both versions of that same word. Once we have read the whole list together, you will read the entire list yourself.

go-ing	yearn-ing	shoot-ing	watch-ing	blink-ing
going	yearning	shooting	watching	blinking

light-ing	wait-ing	look-ing	check-ing	point-ing
lighting	waiting	looking	checking	pointing

Instructor: Now you will read a story that uses the words you just read.

I am going outside tonight, yearning to view a shooting star.
I set out a sheet and start watching the sky.
There are lots of little stars blinking and lighting the dark sky.
I am waiting quite a long time.
I am looking at the sky and then checking the time on my wristwatch.

I snuggle in the middle of my sheet.
I am fighting the urge to sleep.
Wait, what is that light?
I am pointing at the sky with my finger.
That is my shooting star.

Lesson 185: Practice with Two-Syllable Words

Do the "Two Review and One New" today.

Instructor: In this lesson you will be reading more two-syllable words. We will read each short list of words. First I will read each word; then you will read that same word. Then you will read the sentence that uses those words. Then we will move on to each of the next short lists of words and the sentences that go with that list. I will put a folded piece of paper under the line that you are reading.

pho-to	dol-phin	a-gain	to-day
photo	dolphin	again	today

I took a photo of a dolphin again today.

prac-tice	trum-pet	Mon-day	Tues-day	Thurs-day
practice	trumpet	Monday	Tuesday	Thursday

I practice my trumpet on Monday, Tuesday, and Thursday.

broth-er	sis-ter	birth-days	A-pril	Au-gust
brother	sister	birthdays	April	August

My birthday is in April.
The brother and sister have birthdays in August.

res-cue	val-ue
rescue	value

Will you please rescue my cat from that tree?
He is of great value to me.

to-night
tonight

Star light, star bright,
First star I see tonight.
Wish I may, wish I might
Have the wish I wish tonight.

Lesson 186: Practice with Two-Syllable Words

Review

Instructor: Read these words as a review. They all contain the ou vowel pair and the silent letter pair gh.

though   thought   through

Instructor: Now read this new word. It is pronounced /thûr-ō/. I will read the word; then you will read the word.

thor-ough
thorough

Instructor: Now read these words in a very short story.

Though I thought I did a thorough job in my room, I was not through yet. There was still dust under my bed.

New

Instructor: In this lesson you will be reading more two-syllable words followed by sentences that use these words. I will read each word; then you will read that same word. Then you will read the sentences that use those words. Then we will move on to the next list of words and the sentences that use those words.

| thir-teen | four-teen | fif-teen | lit-tle |
| thirteen | fourteen | fifteen | little |

| neph-ew | six-teen | nine-teen | col-lege |
| nephew | sixteen | nineteen | college |

When I am twelve or thirteen years old, I get to stay up late.
When I am fourteen or fifteen years old, I can watch my little nephew.
When I am sixteen years old, I can drive a car.
When I am nineteen, I might go to college.

| Fri-day | thou-sand | feath-ers | yel-low |
| Friday | thousand | feathers | yellow |

| al-though | hon-est | eigh-teen | |
| although | honest | eighteen | |

One Friday I saw a thousand birds on a walk.
Their feathers were yellow, and they were in a flock.
Although, to be honest, how could that be true?
It was not a thousand; it was eighteen that flew!

Section 18

OTHER LETTER PATTERNS AND SILENT LETTERS

Lesson 187: OU as Short-U

Review

Instructor: Let's practice more two-syllable words. Read these words to me.

| won-der | gar-den | el-der | al-ways | sur-prise |
| wonder | garden | elder | always | surprise |

Instructor: Read these words as a review.

touch   young   rough   tough

New

Instructor: The words you just read all have the **ou** vowel pair that stands for the short-**u** vowel sound. Here are some two-syllable words that also contain this vowel pair. First I will read each word. Then you will read each word. Once we have finished going through the list together, you will go back to the beginning and read the list yourself.

| cou-ple | cou-sin | dou-ble | trou-ble | young-er |
| couple | cousin | double | trouble | younger |

| jeal-ous | joy-ous | fa-mous | south-ern | e-nough |
| jealous | joyous | famous | southern | enough |

Instructor: Now you are ready to read a story.

I have a couple of young cousins.
They seem to cause double the trouble.
I wonder where they could be.
I heard that they plan to search the garden for snakes.
The younger is famous for his tricks.
The elder always adds to the pranks.
I hope they will not surprise me with a snake!

Lesson 188: OR as /är/
S as /sh/

Do the "Two Review and One New" today.

Review

Instructor: You already know how to read words with the letters **or** in them *(Lesson 157)*. Remember, when the letter **r** follows the letter **o**, it changes the sound of the vowel to /ôr/ in *door*. Read the following words as a review.

porch   sport   fork

New

Instructor: The words you just read all contain the sound /ôr/ in *door*. Let's read some more **or** words together. These words are not pronounced with the regular **or** sound. They are "disobedient words" because they do not follow the regular pattern. Instead of having the sound /ôr/ in *door*, these words all contain the sound /är/ in *car*: ***forest, foreign, orange***. First I will read each word. Then you will read each word. Once we have finished going through the list together, you will read the list by yourself.

Regional pronunciations of these words vary widely.

for-est	for-eign	or-ange	bor-row	sor-row
forest	foreign	orange	borrow	sorrow

Instructor: Now you will read a story that uses these words.

A whole forest of orange trees has been cut down.
The forest is in a foreign land.
I felt great sorrow when I heard the news.

Instructor: The English language has "borrowed" many words from other languages. As a result, some words do not follow regular English rules of pronunciation. The words in this lesson come from the French language. In these words, the letter **s** sounds like /sh/. I will read each word to you. Then you will read each word to me. Once we have finished reading the list together, you will go back to the beginning and read all five words by yourself.

sure	sug-ar	is-sue	tis-sue	pres-sure
	sugar	issue	tissue	pressure

Instructor: Now you will read some of these words in sentences.

Do not make an issue of it.
A sugar spill will come clean when you wipe it with a tissue.
I am sure of it.

Lesson 189: CH as /k/
Sight Word: choir

You will need the following: *an index card and a pen.*

Do the "Two Review and One New" today.

Review

Instructor: Let's begin this lesson by practicing more two-syllable words. Read these words to me.

ser-vice	weath-er	can-dles	win-dows	Bi-ble
service	weather	candles	windows	Bible

Instructor: Read these review words to me. They all contain the letter pair **ch** which stands for the sound /ch/ in *choo-choo*.

church	chant	child	chap-ter	chap-el
			chapter	chapel

New

Instructor: In the last lesson, I told you that the English language "borrowed" many words from other languages. The words you will read today are taken from the Greek and Latin languages. In these words, the **ch** does not stand for its usual sound of /ch/ in *choo-choo*. Instead, it stands for the hard sound /k/ as in the word *chorus*. Let's practice these words together. First I will read each word; then you will read each word. Once we have finished going through the list together, you will go back to the beginning and read the list yourself.

Pronounce **Christmas** as /krist-məs/, which is an acceptable alternate pronunciation to /kris-məs/. Words with a silent letter **t** will be covered in Lesson 191.

chord	Chris	Christ	school	ache
Christ-mas	chor-us	chem-ist	ech-o	Stom-ach
Christmas	chorus	chemist	echo	stomach

Instructor: Now you are going to learn a new word. You will have to memorize it. I will write this word on a card for you.

choir

Write the word on a card. Say the word and point to the card. Hand the card to the child. Have the child point to the card and say the word and hand the card back to you. Do this until the child knows the word.

Instructor: Now you are ready to read a story.

We gather tonight for a church service.
The weather is crisp and cold.

Candles line the windows of the chapel.
It is Christmas Eve, the night before Christ was born.

The leader of the choir sings a chant.
The choir will echo him after a loud chord.

My teacher from school chose a chapter from the Bible to read.
We all sang the chorus of a Christmas carol about the Christ child and peace on earth.

Lesson 190: The Soft Sound of the SC Blend

Remember to do the "Two Review and One New" today.

Review

Instructor: Let's begin this lesson by practicing more two-syllable words. Read these words to me.

| les-son | flow-er | pet-als | col-lect | sun-light |
| lesson | flower | petals | collect | sunlight |

Instructor: Now read these review words.

cent   cell   mice   race

Instructor: Remember, the letter **c** makes the soft sound when it is followed by the vowel **e**, **i**, or **y**. The letter **c** makes the hard sound all other times *(Lesson 77)*. Read these review words with the hard sound of **c**.

scale   scarf   scare   scrub   scream

New

Instructor: Now you will read more words that begin with the letter blend **sc**. Notice that in these words, the **c** makes the soft sound because it is followed by the vowel **e**, **i**, or **y**. The soft sound of **c** sounds just like the sound of the letter **s**: /s/. So these words all begin with this /s/ sound. Let's read this list together. First I will read each word. Then you will read each word after me. Once we have finished going through the whole list together, you will go back to the beginning and read the list by yourself.

| scene | scent | sci-ence | scis-sors | scep-ter |
| | | science | scissors | scepter |

Instructor: Now you are ready to read a story.

For our science lesson, we will snip flower petals with scissors.
We will collect them and lay them out to dry in the sunlight.
Then we will mix all the petals in a bowl and sniff their scent.
The smell is sweet!

Lesson 191: Silent W After S
Silent T After S
Silent M Before N

Review

Instructor: Let's begin this lesson by practicing more two-syllable words. Read these words to me.

prin-cess	res-cue	es-cape	drag-on	fright-ens
princess	rescue	escape	dragon	frightens

Instructor: You have already read words with a silent letter **w** *(Lessons 146 and 147)*. Read these words as a review.

wrist   wring   write   who   whole

New

Instructor: In the words you just read, **w** is silent before the letters **r** and **h**. In this lesson you will read words in which the **w** is silent when it comes *after* the letter **s**. First I will read each word. Then you will read each word after me. Then you will read both words by yourself—there are only two of them!

sword   an-swer
               answer

Instructor: Now you will read these words in a story.

Did I not tell you before?
Do not swing that plastic sword inside the house.
Put it down, and answer the phone.

Instructor: You already know how to read many words with silent letters. In this lesson you will also read words with a silent letter **t** at the beginning of the second syllable. Let's read this list of words together. First I will read each word. Then you will read each word after me. Once we have finished going through the list together, you will go back to the beginning and read the list yourself.

lis-ten	fas-ten	chris-ten	cas-tle	rus-tle
listen	fasten	christen	castle	rustle

nes-tle	wres-tle	this-tle	whistle
nestle	wrestle	thistle	whistle

Instructor: Now you will read a story that uses many of the words you just read.

The princess listens for the whistle of the knight outside the castle.
That is his signal that he has come to rescue her.
She hopes the dragon will not see them escape.
She hears a rustle and a knock beneath her window.
The knight and his horse stand beside the thistles.
The dragon hears the noise of the whistle.
The knight frightens the dragon with his sword.
The dragon flees to the other side of the world.
The princess and knight ride off into the sunset.

Instructor: Now you will read words that contain a silent letter **n**. First I will read each word. Then you will read each word after me. Once we have finished going through the list together, you will go back to the beginning and read the list yourself.

hymn	col-umn	sol-emn	con-demn	au-tumn
	column	solemn	condemn	autumn

Instructor: Now you will read a sentence that uses some of the words you just read.

We sing hymns of thanks in the autumn.

Lesson 192: TI as /sh/

You will need the following: *a pencil and paper.*

Instructor: In this lesson you will learn about three new letter pairs that need special attention: **ti**, **ci**, and **si**. These are tricky letter pairs, because each of them can stand for the /sh/. I am going to teach you a little chant to help you remember. Watch as I point to each of the letter pairs below.

As you spell aloud each letter pair, point to it below.

Instructor: **ti** /sh/, **ci** /sh/, **si** /sh/

ti   ci   si

Instructor: Now let's say that together as I point to each letter pair.

Together: **ti** /sh/, **ci** /sh/, **si** /sh/

Instructor: Now let's add something to make this fun. As we say the chant together, put your finger to your lips every time you say /sh/, as if you are telling yourself to be quiet. I will still point to each letter pair in the list above.

Together (putting finger to lips):
    ti /sh/, **ci** /sh/, **si** /sh/

Instructor: Now you will do the chant several times by yourself. The first time you will say the chant in a loud voice. The next time you will say the chant you will say it a little quieter. Then the next time you say the chant you will say it quieter still. Keep saying the chant until you are using just a whisper. I will continue to point to the letter pairs as you say them.

Let the child say the chant around four times (or whatever it takes to get him to whisper it). Repeat this exercise one more time if the child is enjoying it.

Child (getting quieter and quieter):
    ti /sh/, **ci** /sh/, **si** /sh/…

Instructor: Now I am going to write out some words with the letter pair **ti** in them. In these words, the **ti** stands for the sound /sh/. After I write each word, I want you to draw a circle around the letter pair **ti** and say /sh/. Then I will pronounce the word for you.

Write out the four words from the list below (do not divide the word into syllables).

Instructor: Now you are ready to read these words. First I will read each word, and you will read it after me. Once we have read all the words together, you will go back to the beginning and read all the words yourself. Then you will read some of the words in a sentence.

pa-tient	par-tial	cau-tious	quo-tient
patient	partial	cautious	quotient

The cautious doctor listens as the patient complains of an ache.

Lesson 193: CI as /sh/
SI as /sh/

You will need the following: *the magnetic alphabet board.*

Do the "Two Review and One New" today.

Review

Instructor: Let's begin this lesson by practicing more two-syllable words. Read these words to me.

fla-vors	pump-kin	sug-ar	dou-ble
flavors	pumpkin	sugar	double

Instructor: Say the chant of the letter pairs like you did last lesson while you point to the letter pairs below. Remember to say the chant softer each time until you are whispering.

Child (four times, getting quieter each time):
    ti /sh/, **ci** /sh/, **si** /sh/…

ti   ci   si

New

Take out the magnetic alphabet board.

Instructor: In this lesson you will read words with the letter pair **ci** which stands for the sound /sh/. I will form a word on the magnetic alphabet board. Then I will pronounce the word. Then I want you to push the letter pair **ci** above the word. As you move it, say the sound the **ci** stands for: /sh/. Then put the **ci** back inside the word, and pronounce the whole word.

Form each of the four words below, one at a time, on the magnetic alphabet board.

Instructor: Now I will read each word, and then you will read it after me. Once we have read all the words, you will go back to the beginning and read them yourself. Then you will read a story that uses some of these words.

spe-cial	so-cial	gla-cial	an-cient
special	social	glacial	ancient

Ralph and I went to an ice cream social.
Special flavors were glacial mint, pumpkin swirl, and fudge ripple.
I ate glacial mint on a sugar cone until my mouth was numb.

Instructor: We will read two words with the letter pair **si** which stands for the sound /sh/. I will read each word; then you will read each word. You will read more words with this pattern later.

mis-sion	ten-sion
mission	tension

The child will read more words with **si** when he gets to the **sion** ending (like *admission* and *permission*).

Lesson 194: S as /zh/
Sight Word: people

You will need the following: *an index card and a pen.*

Review

Instructor: Read these two-syllable words to me.

vis-it	be-cause	al-ways	some-thing
visit	because	always	something

Instructor: You have already read these words in which the **s** stands for the sound /sh/. Read them to me.

sure   sugar   tissue

New

Instructor: The letter **s** stands for the /sh/ sound in all the words you just read. When you add a voice to this /sh/ sound, you get the sound /zh/ (in ***measure***). Notice that in all these words, the letter **u** follows the letter **s**. Let's read a list of words in which the **s** stands for the voiced /zh/ sound. First I will read each word. Then you will read each word after me. Once we have finished going through the list together, you will go back to the beginning and read the three words by yourself.

mea-sure	trea-sure	plea-sure
measure	treasure	pleasure

Instructor: Now you are ready to read a sentence that uses these words.

I cannot measure the pleasure I felt when I found the treasure.

Instructor: Now you are going to learn a new word. I will write this word on a card for you.

people

Write the word on a card. Point to the word and pronounce it. Have the child point to the word card and say the word three times. Once you have finished with the card, put it in your sight word stack.

Instructor: Now you will read this word in a sentence.

People like to visit the zoo all year because there is always something to see.

Lesson 195: Review Two-Syllable Words

Instructor: Let's begin this lesson by practicing two-syllable words. Once you have finished reading this list, you will read these words in a story.

ar-rives	moth-er	fath-er	pa-tient	gi-ant
arrives	mother	father	patient	giant
an-cient	mea-sure	sol-emn	people	young-er
ancient	measure	solemn		younger
be-lieve	be-cause	nes-tles	lis-ten	an-swers
believe	because	nestles	listen	answers

Instructor: Now you are ready to read a story about a family that visits the zoo.

There are some additional two-syllable words found in the story that were not in the list above. If your child has difficulty reading some of the words, assist him.

When spring arrives, Mother, Father, Sister, Brother, and I go to the zoo.
We learn a lot about living things.
Science is quite fun when you can learn outside at the zoo.
We go in time to watch the lizards crawl out into the sunshine.
We are patient and wait to see what reptile will come out next.

A giant sea turtle lumbers out to a rock.
He looks like some ancient monster!
I wish we could measure this turtle because he looks eight feet long!
He casts a solemn glance at the crowd of people.
My younger brother Dwight cannot believe what he sees.

We walk to the snake cage.
We are sure that the snake cannot get out.
At first, we are not able to see the snake because he nestles under a huge pile of leaves.
But when we listen, we hear the leaves rustle.

We ask mother if we may get something to eat.
She answers that we may.

Lesson 196: Review Two-Syllable Words

Read the story from last lesson to the child before you begin today's lesson.

Instructor: Let's begin by practicing some two-syllable words. Once you have finished reading the words from this list, you will read these words in a story.

Tues-day	Au-gust	gla-cial	Chris-ta	or-ange
Tuesday	August	glacial	Christa	orange
wrist-watch	wa-ter	pen-guins	cir-cle	cou-ple
wristwatch	water	penguins	circle	couple
sto-machs	scene	be-fore	an-nounce	a-gainst
stomachs		before	announce	against

Instructor: Now you will read these words in a story.

There are some additional two-syllable words found in the story that were not in the list above. If your child has difficulty reading some of the words, assist him.

Mom, Dad, Sister, Brother, and I go to the zoo on a Tuesday in August.
Since it is such a hot summer day, we decide to visit the Glacial Park.
My mom buys Christa, Dwight, and I orange sodas.

I check my wristwatch and announce that it is time for the show.
The scent of fish is in the air.
A couple of penguins swim around the tank in a circle.
The penguins waddle up to the slide and scoot down on their stomachs.
What a scene!

Then the dolphins come in and jump through single and double hoops.
Then the seal arrives and does lots of tricks.
Did you know a seal can balance a ball on the tip of its nose?
After the seals leave, the giant whale swims in the tank.
He throws himself into the air and comes down with a splash.
The splash of water soaks me to the bone.

I say to my father, "I ache to see the polar bear before we go."
I press my face against the glass of his tank.
Now my day is perfect.

Section 19

POSSESSIVE WORDS AND CONTRACTIONS

Lesson 197: Possessive Words

Review

Instructor: Read these two-syllable words to me.

eigh-teen	Da-vid	mar-bles	par-ents	pho-to
eighteen	David	marbles	parents	photo

al-bum	cous-in	down-stairs	chil-dren	scis-sors
album	cousin	downstairs	children	scissors

New

Instructor: In this lesson you will learn a mark of punctuation. It is called the *apostrophe*. This is what it looks like in a word. I will point to it in the word **Pat's**.

Pat's bike

Instructor: Today we are going to talk about one use of the apostrophe. In the example above, the apostrophe tell you that the bike belongs to Pat. Pat owns the bike. To show that someone or something owns the word that it follows, you add an apostrophe and the letter **s**. Sometimes the apostrophe comes before the letter **s**, and sometimes it comes after the **s**. You still pronounce it the same way. So you can follow along, I will point to each word as I read the following sentences.

The boy owns a shirt.
This is the boy's shirt.

All the boys own shirts.
These are the boys' shirts.

Instructor: The apostrophe has no sound of its own. It is a punctuation mark that shows that the boy or boys own shirts. Now you will read some sentences with apostrophes.

Those are David's eighteen marbles.

That is my parents' photo album.

My cousin's house has an upstairs and a downstairs.

These are the children's scissors.

Lesson 198: Contractions
Sight Word: been

Instructor: In this lesson you are going to learn another use for the apostrophe. The apostrophe is used in *contractions*. The word **contract** means "to draw together or shorten." So, a contraction occurs when two words are drawn together and shortened by dropping some letters. Every contraction has an apostrophe in it. The apostrophe tells us where the letters were dropped to form the contraction. The apostrophe does not change the way you read the word. Let's read some contractions. Look at the first group of words. First you will read the two words that will be drawn together. Then I will point to the two words with different print that show the letters to be dropped. I will not pronounce the dropped letters as I read the remaining letters. Then I will read the contraction. You will repeat the contraction after me. We will do this for all the groups of words.

Slide a finger or pointer under each word as you read it.

it is	it has	I am	I have
it is	it has	I am	I have
it's	it's	I'm	I've
I will	I would	you are	you have
I will	I would	you are	you have
I'll	I'd	you're	you've
you will	you would	he is	he has
you will	you would	he is	he has
you'll	you'd	he's	he's
he will	he would	she is	she has
he will	he would	she is	she has
he'll	he'd	she's	she's
she will	she would	let us	
she will	she would	let us	
she'll	she'd	let's	

Instructor: Before you read some sentences, I am going to teach you a new word. I will write this word on a card for you.

been

Point to the card and pronounce the word. Have the child say the word three times as he points to the card. Keep this word card in your sight word stack.

Instructor: Now you will read a story that contains contractions.

It's cold outside.
It's been a long time since summer.
I'm sure I should wear a coat outside.
I've been inside all day.

I'll go out and play.
I'd like to find a friend with whom to play.
You're my best friend.
You've been my friend my whole life.
You'll have fun with me.
You'd like the cold, I'm sure.

He's on the hill.
He's got a sled.
He'll share it with us.
He'd be glad to play with us.

His sister is with him.
She's younger than he is.
She's been out all day.
She'll like to sled with us.
She'd make a fuss if we did not let her ride.
Let's share with her and have fun!

Lesson 199: Contractions

Do the "Two Review and One New" today.

Instructor: In this lesson we will read some more contractions. Look at the first group of words. First you will read the two words that will be drawn together. Then I will point to the two words with different print that show the letters to be dropped. I will not pronounce the dropped letters as I read the remaining letters. Then I will read the contraction. You will repeat the contraction after me. We will do this for all the groups of words.

Slide a finger or pointer under each word as you read it.

we are	we have	we will	we would
we are	we have	we will	we would
we're	we've	we'll	we'd

they are	they have	they will	they would
they are	they have	they will	they would
they're	they've	they'll	they'd

is not	are not	was not	were not
is not	are not	was not	were not
isn't	aren't	wasn't	weren't

has not	have not	cannot	does not
has not	have not	cannot	does not
hasn't	haven't	can't	doesn't

should not	would not	could not
should not	would not	could not
shouldn't	wouldn't	couldn't

Instructor: I will read the next two contractions to you. Then I want you to read them to me.

do not	will not
don't	won't

Instructor: Now let's read a story that uses contractions.

299

When you get to the word *heights*, tell the child the word. It is irregular in its pronunciation.

We're off from school today.
We've taken the bus to the center of town.
We'll watch a hotel being built all morning.
We'd like to get quite close to the workers.
They're high up on steel scaffolds.
They've no fear of heights.
They'll work hard until lunch break.
They'd like to take an hour to eat.

Isn't it fun to watch the workers?
Aren't they brave?
Wasn't the man at the top afraid?
Weren't the other men afraid too?
There hasn't been a cloud in the sky today.
I'm glad.
The workers can't work in the rain.

My little brother didn't know that.
He doesn't know as much as I know.
It shouldn't be long until lunch.
I wouldn't mind standing here all day.
I couldn't think of a thing I'd rather do.
Don't you want to see this as well?
Won't you come with us next time?

Section 20

OTHER SPELLINGS FOR THE LONG-E SOUND

Lesson 200: Y as Long E
Sight Word: busy

You will need the following: *an index card and a pen.*

Instructor: Listen to the last sound in these words as I read them to you.

puppy   candy   baby

Y at the end of a two-syllable word is pronounced by some as a short-**i** and by others as a long-**e**. Even dictionaries differ in their preferred pronunciation of this pattern. (For example you may say either /sĭt-ĭ/ or /sĭt-ē/ for the word *city*.)

Instructor: **Y** at the end of these words stands for the long-**e** vowel sound. I will read the words below, and you will read them after me. Then you will read the sentence by yourself.

frisk-y	pup-py	mud-dy	sli-my
frisky	puppy	muddy	slimy

The frisky puppy has fur that is muddy and slimy.

Mom-my	fus-sy	baby	jolly
Mommy	fussy	baby	jolly

Mommy will make the fussy baby jolly.

gloom-y	twen-ty	ver-y	ug-ly
gloomy	twenty	very	ugly

real-ly	dirt-y
really	dirty

One gloomy day, twenty very ugly snakes were in the really dirty water.

Instructor: Now I am going to teach you a new word. I will write this word on a card for you. Say the word five times and then read it in the sentence below.

busy

Keep this word in the sight word stack.

The busy bee will fly from flower to flower and then go back to its hive.

Lesson 201: EY as Long E

Do the "Two Review and One New" today.

Instructor: Now you will read a word in which the **or** stands for the sound /är/ in *car* and the **y** at the end of the word stands for the long-**e** vowel sound. I will read the word; then you will read the word.

sor-ry
sorry

Instructor: Let's practice one more word; then you will read a sentence. This word has the normal **or** pronunciation: /ôr/ in *door*.

stor-y
story

I am sorry that I was too busy to read your story.

Instructor: In this lesson you will read words that end with the vowel pair **ey**. These words are pronounced just like words that end with the single vowel **y** in *story*. First I will read each word. Then you will read each word after me. Once we have finished going through the list together, you will go back to the beginning and read the list yourself.

Again, dictionaries differ in the correct pronunciation. It is equally acceptable to say the short-**i** vowel sound or the long-**e** vowel sound on the second syllable.

key	mon-key	don-key	mon-ey
	monkey	donkey	money
val-ley	tur-key	chim-ney	hon-ey
valley	turkey	chimney	honey
hock-ey	pars-ley		
hockey	parsley		

Instructor: Now you will read a story that uses these words.

I will visit a country farm on the edge of a valley.
Cows and a donkey graze outside in the field.
Fifteen chickens and one busy turkey peck at worms on the parsley.
The main house is white with a sturdy brick chimney in its center.
The lady who owns the farm asks me in for tea and a pastry.
I dip my finger into a jar of very sticky honey.
How sweet it is to be on this farm!

Lesson 202: IE as Long E

Do the "Two Review and One New" today.

Instructor: In this lesson you will read words that end with the vowel pair **ie**. These words are pronounced just like words that end with the single vowel **y** in *story* or the vowel pair **ey** in *monkey*. First I will read each word. Then you will read each word after me. Once we have finished going through the list together, you will go back to the beginning and read the list yourself.

Again, dictionaries differ in the correct pronunciation. It is equally acceptable to say the short-**i** vowel sound or the long-**e** vowel sound.

brown-ie	mov-ie	cook-ie	prai-rie	ee-rie
brownie	movie	cookie	prairie	eerie
ge-nie	col-lie	Ka-tie	Liz-zie	Las-sie
genie	collie	Katie	Lizzie	Lassie

Instructor: Now you are ready to read a story.

I went to Katie's house to watch a movie.
Katie's movie was about life on the prairie.
Scary storms blow through the prairie.
The black clouds that form just before the storm are eerie.

In the story, there is a girl by the name of Lizzie.
She has a collie with a rough, brown coat.
Lizzie's collie knows that a storm is coming.
Lizzie's collie warns Lizzie's mother about the storm.

The collie's barks are sharp and loud.
Lizzie, her mother, and the collie go to their storm shelter.
After the storm is over, Lizzie's mother gives the collie a treat.
Lizzie eats a brownie and a cookie.

Section 21

PLURAL AND HYPHENATED WORDS

Lesson 203: Two-Syllable Plural Words That End in ES

Don't forget to do the "Two Review and One New!"

Instructor: Do you remember that singular means "one thing" and plural means "more than one" *(Lesson 49)*? There are some plural naming words that end with **es** and not just an **s**. These plural naming words have to be pronounced with two syllables. I will read you this list of two-syllable plural words. I will also tap my pencil eraser on each syllable. Once I am through, you will read all the words in the list by yourself. I will help you if you need it.

| dress-es | box-es | fox-es | lunch-es | ditch-es |
| dresses | boxes | foxes | lunches | ditches |

| branch-es | bush-es | quiz-zes | roach-es | dish-es |
| branches | bushes | quizzes | roaches | dishes |

Instructor: Now you will read some sentences that have both singular and plural words in them.

I own a white dress.
My other dresses are blue and yellow.

When we move, I will pack my own box.
Many boxes will be put on the moving truck.

One little fox was playing alone.
The other foxes were chasing mice.

There is a ditch on each side of the highway.
Both ditches are full of water.

Instructor: Lots of two-syllable words that are *not* plural naming words *(nouns)* also end with **es**. Let's read some of these action words *(verbs)* that end with **es**. First I will read a word. Then we will read a word together. Then you will read the word by yourself.

| rush-es | squish-es | catch-es | fix-es | munch-es |
| rushes | squishes | catches | fixes | munches |

Instructor: Now you will read these words in a story about creepy, crawling roaches.

Our basement is crawling with roaches.
They live in damp, dark corners and come out at night.
We call a man who catches and kills bad bugs.
A roach rushes by him.
He squishes it with his boot.
He fixes many traps and sets them around our basement.
He tells us that when a roach munches on the poison bait, it will die.
I will sleep better tonight knowing roaches will **not** crawl in my bed!

Lesson 204: Plural Words That End in IES

You will need the following: *the magnetic alphabet board.*

Remember to do the "Two Review and One New" today.

Instructor: Look at these two singular words. I will read them to you

fly   puppy

Instructor: Both of these words end in **y**. Now look at the plural word beneath each singular word. I will read each pair of words to you.

Point to the **y** and the **ies** as you read these words.

fly   puppy
flies   puppies

Instructor: Did you notice that the **y** changed to an **i** when **es** was added to make each plural word? The plural naming words *(nouns)* end in **ies**. This doesn't change the vowel sounds in the words, it just changes the way the words look. Let's read the pairs of words below. First I will read the singular naming word that ends in **y**. Then I will read the plural naming word that ends in **ies**. Then you will read that same pair of words back to me.

Point to the **y** and the **ies** as you read the words.

fly	sky	pup-py	bun-ny	ba-by
flies	skies	puppy	bunny	baby
		puppies	bunnies	babies

ru-by	la-dy	du-ty	cit-y
ruby	lady	duty	city
rubies	ladies	duties	cities

Instructor: Now read the following sentences with plural naming words that end in **ies**.

I have one bunny. Sally has three bunnies.

The white puppy plays with the other puppies in the yard.

One fly buzzes past the other flies.

Follow-Up:
Assemble the word *fly* on the board. Have the child read the word, then remove the letter **y** and replace it with **ies**. Have the child then read the plural word. Repeat this exercise with the list of words above.

Lesson 205: Plural Words That End in VES

You will need the following: *the magnetic alphabet board.*

Remember to do the "Two Review and One New" today.

Instructor: Look at these three pairs of words. The singular word is written first, and the plural word is written beneath it. When a singular word ends in the letter **f**, the **f** changes to **v** when the word is made plural by adding **s** or **es**. I will read each pair of words to you.

Point to the **f** and the **v** in each pair of words as you read them.

leaf	scarf	life
leaves	scarves	lives

Instructor: Let's read more singular and plural words that follow this pattern. First I will read each pair of words. Then you will read that same pair of words back to me.

Point to the **f** and the **v** in each pair of words as you read them.

leaf	calf	scarf	loaf	shelf
leaves	calves	scarves	loaves	shelves

wolf	yourself	knife	wife	life
wolves	yourselves	knives	wives	lives

Form the word *leaf* on the magnetic alphabet board. Have the child read the word. Then have him remove the letter **f** and replace it with the letters **ves**. Have the child read the new word. Repeat this process for the rest of the words on the list below. When you get to the words *knife*, *wife*, and *life*, explain to the child that you change the **f** to **v** and add **s** to form the plural word.

Instructor: Now you will read sentences with some of the pairs of words from this lesson.

One leaf falls on the tall pile of leaves.

One calf roams in the meadow with the other calves.

One loaf is enough for you.
It would be greedy to eat five loaves.

Put all of the knives in the knife drawer.

The wives want to make a cookbook.
Each wife will write down how to make her special dish.

Seat belts save lives.
Buckle up to keep your life safe.

Lesson 206: Hyphenated Words

Do the "Two Review and One New" today.

Review

Instructor: Let's begin this lesson by practicing some numbers with more than one syllable. Read these words to me.

twen-ty	thir-ty	for-ty	fif-ty	six-ty
twenty	thirty	forty	fifty	sixty
sev-en-ty	eigh-ty	nine-ty	Grand-pa	o-bey
seventy	eighty	ninety	Grandpa	obey

New

Instructor: We have been looking at words that been divided into syllables with a hyphen. Some words are *always* written with a hyphen, not just when they are divided into syllables. Read these words to me.

good-bye	left-hand	one-half	grown-up	one-way
first-class	ice-skate	baby-sit	brand-new	well-known

Instructor: Many numbers are also always written with a hyphen. Read these words to me.

twenty-one   thirty-two   forty-three   eighty-four   ninety-eight

Instructor: Now you will read a story that uses some of the words you just read.

Mommy will ask a grown-up to baby-sit this weekend.
My Grandpa is a first-class sitter.
I always obey him.

Grandpa is well-known for his skill on the ice rink.
We all love to ice-skate.
He bought me brand-new skates.

He acts so young, though he is sixty-six.
I am sorry when he has to say good-bye.

308

Section 22

THREE-SYLLABLE WORDS

Lesson 207: Three-Syllable Words

Instructor: I will read some *three*-syllable words to you. I will tap my pencil on each syllable.

Tap your pencil on the syllables as you say **af-ter-noon**, **ta-ble-cloth**, and **hon-ey-bee**.

afternoon   tablecloth   honeybee

Instructor: The three-syllable words I just read are made up of smaller words you already know how to read. You can already read the words **after** and **noon**. When you put these words together, a larger, three-syllable word is formed: **afternoon**. Now you will try reading words like this. First you will read the one- and two-syllable words that make up the larger, three-syllable word. Then you will read the new three-syllable word.

vol-ley ball   an-y where   gin-ger bread
volleyball   anywhere   gingerbread

Instructor: Now you will read three-syllable words that are not made up of two smaller words put together. I will read each word in a group. Then you will read each word after me. Once we have finished reading all the words in a group, you will read the sentences by yourself. We will do this for each group of words and sentences.

Sep-tem-ber   Oc-to-ber   No-vem-ber   De-cem-ber
September   October   November   December

The weather is cool in September and October.
It is cooler in November and December.

Have the child sound out the word **Wednesday**, pronouncing all the letters ("Wed-nes-day"), but then tell him that the first **d** is silent, making the word sound like it has two syllables instead of three: /wĕnz-dā/. Even though **Wednesday** is a two-syllable word in America, it is included in this section so that the child will learn to spell it correctly.

Wed-nes-day   Sat-ur-day
Wednesday   Saturday

The days of the week are Sunday, Monday, Tuesday, Wednesday, Thursday, Friday, and Saturday.

The lesson continues on the following page.

| syn-a-gogue | his-to-ry | to-mor-row | u-su-al |
| synagogue | history | tomorrow | usual |

In the synagogue one learns the history of the Jewish people.
Tomorrow he will go to his usual class there.

| phy-si-cian | tel-e-phone | phar-ma-cy | med-i-cine |
| physician | telephone | pharmacy | medicine |

The physician will tell the pharmacy over the telephone what medicine I need.

| Grand-moth-er | com-pu-ter | li-bra-ry | yes-ter-day |
| Grandmother | computer | library | yesterday |

| al-pha-bet | syl-la-bles |
| alphabet | syllables |

Grandmother helps me search for library books on the computer.
Yesterday I found an alphabet book that divides words into syllables.

| Dan-i-el | choc-o-late | dis-gust-ing |
| Daniel | chocolate | disgusting |

Daniel enjoys his hot chocolate.
It makes him feel joyful.
If I put an oyster in his moist, hot drink, it would taste disgusting.

| con-tin-ue | bar-be-cue |
| continue | barbecue |

Continue to barbecue that beef until it is tender.

Lesson 208: Three-Syllable Words

Instructor: In the last lesson you read three-syllable words. Let's read some more three-syllable words together. First I will read each word. Then you will read each word after me. Once we have finished going through the entire list together, you will go back to the beginning and read the list by yourself.

to-mor-row	hol-i-day	grand-fa-ther	bi-cy-cles	li-bra-ry
tomorrow	holiday	grandfather	bicycles	library
chem-is-try	pho-to-graphs	com-pu-ter	his-to-ry	to-geth-er
chemistry	photographs	computer	history	together
gro-cer-y	de-li-cious	cin-na-mon	choc-o-late	
grocery	delicious	cinnamon	chocolate	

Instructor: Now you will read those words in a story.

Tomorrow is a holiday.
Grandfather and I will ride our bicycles to the library.

Grandfather will look at books on chemistry.
I like to look at books with photographs.
I also like to use the computer at the library.
I will check out some books for my history lessons.

After the library, my grandfather and I will go together to the grocery store.
There we will buy delicious chocolate and cinnamon doughnuts.
Then we will go home.
What a pleasant day!

Lesson 209: Y Alone as /ī/ in Multi-Syllable Words

Review

Instructor: You already know how to read one-syllable words that end with the letter **y** and the long-**i** vowel sound *(Lesson 94)*. Read these words as a review.

by	my	fry	fly
cry	sky	why	shy

New

Instructor: Now we will read two-syllable and three-syllable words that end with the letter **y** and the long-**i** vowel sound. First I will read each word. Then you will read each word after me. Once we have finished going through the list together, you will go back to the beginning and read the list yourself.

Ju-ly	re-ply	sup-ply	ap-ply	mul-ti-ply
July	reply	supply	apply	multiply
sat-is-fy	lul-la-by	oc-cu-py	mag-ni-fy	sim-pli-fy
satisfy	lullaby	occupy	magnify	simplify

Instructor: Now you will read a short story that uses some of these words.

I will hum a sweet lullaby to satisfy the crying baby.
I will apply cream to the baby's skin to soothe him.
Then I will supply toys to interest and occupy him.

Lesson 210: OUR as /ûr/

Do the "Two Review and One New" today.

Review

Instructor: Let's begin this lesson by practicing some two-syllable and three-syllable words. Read these
words to me.

al-ways always	dan-ger danger	prac-tice practice	im-por-tant important
char-ac-ter character	com-plain complain	what-ev-er whatever	health-y healthy

---

New

Instructor: In these words that come from the French language, the **our** is pronounced /ûr/ as in *stir*.
Let's read this list of words together. First I will read each word. Then you will read each
word. Once we have finished going through the list together, you will go back to the
beginning and read the list yourself.

jour-ney journey	cour-age courage	cour-te-sy courtesy	tour-na-ment tournament
nour-ish nourish	jour-nal journal	en-cour-age encourage	cour-te-ous courteous

Instructor: Now you will read "The Knight's Code of Conduct." You will read many of the words from
the list above in this story.

A knight has a code of conduct.
The knight's code states that he should always be courteous.
He should show great courage in the face of danger.
He must practice his skills in tournaments.
Endurance on a long journey is important.

A knight should keep a journal of his brave and kind deeds.
This will encourage others to be of good character.
A knight should never complain.
He should eat whatever will nourish the body and keep him healthy.
As a courtesy, he must freely help those in need.

Lesson 211: D and DI as /j/

Instructor: In words of more than one syllable, the letter **d** before the letter **u** often stands for the /j/ sound. Do you recall that the English language has "borrowed" words from other languages? All of the words in this lesson come from Latin. So remember, when you see the letter **d** in these words, you say the sound /j/.

ed-u-cate	sched-ule	grad-u-ate	grad-u-al	pro-ce-dure
educate	schedule	graduate	gradual	procedure

Instructor: The letters **di** stand for the /j/ sound in these words.

The letter **i** has no vowel sound in these words.

sol-dier	cor-dial
soldier	cordial

Instructor: Now you will read those words in a story.

My teacher will help to educate me.
It is a gradual process.
Her procedure is to have me follow a schedule.

She likes to encourage me to work hard like a soldier.
We are always cordial to one another.
I look forward to the day that I will graduate.

314

Section 23

ENDINGS, SUFFIXES, AND PREFIXES

Lesson 212: The Endings ER and EST

Do the "Two Review and One New" today.

Instructor: In this lesson we will add **er** and **est** to ends of words. First I will read each short list of words. Then you will read each short list of words to me. Then you will read the sentences using those words. We will do this for each group of words and sentences.

quick   quick-er   quick-est

A car is quick.
A train is quicker.
An airplane is the quickest.

small   small-er   small-est

A beetle is a small bug.
An ant is a smaller bug.
A gnat is the smallest bug of all.

qui-et   qui-et-er   qui-et-est

A soft voice is quiet.
A whisper is quieter
A hush is the quietest.

nice   ni-cer   ni-cest

A wave is nice.
A handshake is nicer.
A hug is the nicest of all.

hap-py   hap-pi-er   hap-pi-est

I am happy when I do a puzzle.
I am happier when I read a book.
I am the happiest when I play in the park.

Lesson 213: The Endings LY, LIER, and LIEST
Review Sight Words

Remember to do the "Two Review and One New" today.

You will need the following: *the stack of sight word cards.*

Instructor: In this lesson we will add **ly** and **lier** and **liest** endings to words. First I will read each short list of words. Then you will read each short list of words to me. Then you will read the sentences using those words. We will do this for each group of words and sentences.

live-ly   live-li-er   live-li-est

A skip is lively.
A waltz is livelier than a skip.
A square dance is the liveliest dance of all.

kind-ly   kind-li-er   kind-li-est

She acts kindly.
Her mother acts kindlier than she.
Her grandmother acts the kindliest of all three.

cost-ly   cost-li-er   cost-li-est

A ruby is a costly red gem.
A lovely green emerald is costlier than a ruby.
A clear, sparkling diamond is the costliest gem of all.

love-ly   love-li-er   love-li-est

A yellow rose is lovely.
A pink rose is lovelier than a yellow rose.
A red rose is the loveliest of all.

Game: Sight Word Shuffle
Take out the stack of sight word cards and shuffle them. Show the child a word card. If he reads the word correctly, give him the card. If he does not read the word correctly, pronounce the word for him, and put the card back in the stack. Do this until the child has all the cards.

Lesson 214: The ED Ending

Do the "Two Review and One New" today.

Instructor: There are many words that end with **ed**. The ending **ed** can be pronounced three different ways: as /ĕd/ (as in *counted*), as /d/ (as in *phoned*), and as /t/ (as in *wished*). In this lesson you will first read words in which the **ed** ending sounds like /ĕd/ (as in *counted*). Let's read a list of words together. I will read each word to you. Then you will read each word to me. Once we have finished going through the list together, you will go back to the beginning and read the list yourself.

Don't worry about teaching verb tenses right now—you are teaching the child to read!

ex-plod-ed	e-rup-ted	shred-ded	squirt-ed	gra-ted	de-ci-ded
exploded	erupted	shredded	squirted	grated	decided

Instructor: Now you will read a story that uses these words.

I decided to fix a giant salad for my friends.
I grated the cheddar cheese and shredded the lettuce.
I squirted some dressing on it.
The dressing exploded out of the bottle.
We all erupted into giggles.

Instructor: Let's read a list of words together in which the **ed** ending sounds like /d/ (as in *phoned*). First I will read each word to you. Then you will read each word to me. Once we have finished going through the list together, you will go back to the beginning and read the list yourself.

spilled	screamed	groaned	frowned	shrugged	hap-pened
					happened

Instructor: Now you will read those words in a story.

When I spilled my milk, I screamed and groaned.
"What happened?" Dad called from the other room.
I frowned.
"I filled my glass with milk and it spilled."
Dad shrugged. "Just clean it up!"

The lesson continues on the following page.

Instructor: Let's read a list of words together in which the **ed** ending sounds like /t/ (as in ***wished***). First I will read each word to you. Then you will read each word to me. Once we have finished going through the list together, you will go back to the beginning and read the list yourself.

watched   picked   jumped   squished   fixed   es-caped

escaped

Instructor: Now you will read a story that uses the words you just read.

Melinda watched her three little puppies.
Claude and Herbert jumped on top of little Clifford.
He escaped to the edge of the box and was not squished.
Melinda picked him up and rocked him in her arms.
Clifford soon slept.

Lesson 215: Practice Reading Four-Syllable Words

Instructor: In this lesson you will read words with two, three, and four syllables. First I will read each word in the short list. Then you will read that same word after me. Once we have finished going through all the words in that list, you will read the sentence that follows the list by yourself. We will do this for each short list of words. I will put a folded piece of paper under the line you are reading.

There are several different ways to pronounce the word *February*. If you have no preference, teach the child the pronunciation that he can read phonetically: /fĕb-rə-âr-ē/. This will also help him to spell the word correctly later on.

| Jan-u-ar-y | Feb-ru-ar-y | ev-er-y-thing | cov-ered |
| January | February | everything | covered |

In January and February, everything is covered in snow.

| fa-vor-ite | sub-jects | ge-og-ra-phy | a-rith-me-tic |
| favorite | subjects | geography | arithmetic |

My favorite school subjects are geography and arithmetic.

| par-tic-u-lar | cat-er-pil-lar | u-su-al-ly | nib-bles |
| particular | caterpillar | usually | nibbles |

This particular caterpillar usually nibbles on leaves.

| am-phib-i-ans | wa-ter | some-times | a-quar-i-um |
| amphibians | water | sometimes | aquarium |

Frogs are amphibians who live in both the land and water.
Sometimes I let my frog take a swim in the aquarium.

| moth-er | par-a-graph | his-tor-i-cal | e-vent |
| mother | paragraph | historical | event |

My mother said I should read the paragraph about this historical event.

| el-e-va-tor | sym-pho-ny | e-mer-gen-cy | but-ton |
| elevator | symphony | emergency | button |

I rode on an elevator when I went to the symphony.
There was an emergency button on the wall of the elevator.

Lesson 216: The Endings TION and SION

The purpose of introducing prefixes and suffixes at this time is for the child to learn to recognize and pronounce them. It is not necessary to stop and discuss meanings.

Do the "Two Review and One New" today.

___

Review

Instructor: Do you remember this chant: **ti** /sh/, **ci** /sh/, **si** /sh/? Say that for me. Remember to say it with a loud voice and then get quieter each time until you are whispering.

Let the child look at the letter pairs below as he spells the two letters and then says the sound.

Child (getting quieter each time):
   ti /sh/, **ci** /sh/, **si** /sh/...

ti   ci   si

Instructor: When you see the letter pair **ti**, you say /sh/. Read these words to me as a review.

| pa-tient | par-tial | cau-tious | quo-tient |
| patient | partial | cautious | quotient |

___

New

Instructor: In this lesson you will read more words in which the **ti** letter pair stands for the sound /sh/. These words all end with **tion**. **Tion** is pronounced /shən/. Let's read a list of words together. First I will read each word. Then you will read each word after me. Once we have finished going through the list together, you will go back to the beginning and read the list yourself.

| na-tion | sec-tion | ac-tion | va-ca-tion |
| nation | section | action | vacation |

| ed-u-ca-tion | ad-di-tion | sub-trac-tion | di-rec-tion |
| education | addition | subtraction | direction |

Instructor: Now you will read two words in which the sound of the **ti** is slightly changed. The letter pair **ti** stands for the sound /ch/ in the following two words. I will read each word; then you will read each word.

| ques-tion | sug-ges-tion |
| question | suggestion |

Instructor: Now you will read sentences that use some of the words from this lesson.

I have a question about my education during vacation.
Will I do addition and subtraction?

There are two slightly different ways to pronounce the suffix **sion**: /shən/ (as in *mission*) and /zhən/ (as in *vision*). Words that have a consonant before the **s** in **sion** are pronounced as /shən/ (as in *expansion*) while words that have a vowel before the letter **s** in **sion** are pronounced as /zhən/ (as in *exclusion*). It is not necessary to explain this to the child. Just pronounce the words naturally.

Instructor: Do you remember the chant from the beginning of the lesson: **ti** /sh/, **ci** /sh/, **si** /sh/? Now you will read words in which the **si** letter pair stands for the sound /sh/. When you see the letter pair **si**, you say /sh/. The words in this lesson all end with **sion**. **Sion** is pronounced /shən/. Let's read a list of words together. First I will read each word. Then you will read each word after me. Once we have finished going through the list together, you will go back to the beginning and read the list yourself.

mis-sion	im-pres-sion	ad-mis-sion	ex-pan-sion
mission	impression	admission	expansion
ex-ten-sion	ex-pres-sion	per-mis-sion	in-ter-mis-sion
extension	expression	permission	intermission

Instructor: Now you will read a sentence that uses some of the words you just read.

If you pay the admission, you have permission to visit backstage at intermission.

Instructor: The following words also end in **sion**. However, in these words **sion** is pronounced /zhən/ like in *vision*.

vi-sion	di-vi-sion	ex-plo-sion	tel-e-vi-sion
vision	division	explosion	television

Instructor: Now you will read a sentence that uses some of the words you just read.

I watched a television show about volcanoes.
There was an explosion of dust, steam, and red-hot lava!

Lesson 217: The Ending TURE: TU as /ch/
                The Endings IBLE and ABLE
                Sight Word: only

You will need the following: *one index card and a pen.*

Do the "Two Review and One New" today.

Instructor: In this lesson you will read words that all end with **ture**. When you see **ture** at the end of a word, you say /chər/. Let's read a list of these words. First I will read each word. Then you will read each word after me. Once we are finished going through the list together, you will go back to the beginning and read the list yourself.

mix-ture	crea-ture	fea-ture	fur-ni-ture
mixture	creature	feature	furniture
fu-ture	mois-ture	na-ture	pic-ture
future	moisture	nature	picture

Instructor: Now you will read some sentences.

The artist paints pictures of creatures in nature.

In the future I would like new furniture in my room.

Instructor: There are two more endings you will read today: **ible** and **able**. Both of these endings are pronounced with a schwa sound: /ə-bəl/. Let's read the following list of words. First I will read each word. Then you will read each word after me. Once we have finished going through the list together, you will go back to the beginning and read the list yourself.

When a child is beginning to read multi-syllable words, it is acceptable to let him say the short or long sound of the vowel when sounding out the word that contains a schwa sound. You should quickly pronounce the word after him using the schwa sound. (This is also a helpful technique to use later when the child is learning to spell.)

in-vis-i-ble	re-ver-si-ble	di-vis-i-ble	im-pos-si-ble
invisible	reversible	divisible	impossible
val-u-a-ble	mis-er-a-ble	wash-a-ble	break-a-ble
valuable	miserable	washable	breakable

Instructor: Before you read a story, you will learn a new word. I will write this word on a card for you.

only

Write the word on an index card, give the card to the child, and pronounce the word. Have the child hide the card behind his back, bring it forward, and read it. Do this three times. Keep this card in the sight word stack.

Instructor: Now you are ready to read a story.

My neighbor Taylor came over to play.
He brought a pen that his brother had given to him.
We sat down at the only table in the living room.

I asked to see the pen, and I broke it by mistake.
The pen squirted ink all over my grandmother's valuable tablecloth!
We thought it would be impossible to remove.
We wondered if the tablecloth was washable or reversible.
We were miserable thinking about the stain on Grandmother's only tablecloth.

Then the blue ink stain started to fade away.
The stain was soon invisible.
Taylor's brother had given him a pen with disappearing ink!
Taylor and I laughed with relief.

Lesson 218: More Common Endings

Do the "Two Review and One New" today.

This lesson contains words with other common endings. Many of these endings are pronounced with the schwa sound. Model the correct pronunciation for the child and have him repeat it after you. Then have the child read the words in each short list and the sentence that follows those words. Assist him as necessary.

NESS

hap-pi-ness   wil-der-ness
happiness   wilderness

I am filled with happiness when I am in the wilderness.

LESS

noise-less   end-less
noiseless   endless

The noiseless mouse creeps around the kitchen on its endless hunt for cheese.

MENT

base-ment   as-sign-ment
basement   assignment

My work assignment was to clean the basement.

HOOD

child-hood   neigh-bor-hood
childhood   neighborhood

I spent my childhood in this lovely neighborhood.

FUL

thank-ful   de-light-ful   won-der-ful
thankful   delightful   wonderful

I am thankful for the delightful and wonderful music of the choir.

IST

fi-nal-ist   art-ist
finalist   artist

Marco was a finalist in the contest for Best Artist.

TIVE

at-ten-tive   de-tec-tive   talk-a-tive
attentive   detective   talkative

The detective was attentive to the talkative witness in court.

SIVE

im-pres-sive   ex-pen-sive
impressive   expensive

The impressive sports car was really expensive.

IZE

mem-or-ize   rec-og-nize
memorize   recognize

I will memorize certain words so that I will recognize them when I read.

ANCE

im-port-ance   ap-pear-ance
importance   appearance

My parents teach me about the importance of a neat appearance.

ENCE

con-fi-dence   in-de-pen-dence
confidence   independence

I have confidence that my cousins will visit on Independence Day.

Lesson 219: Prefixes

This lesson contains words with common prefixes. Have the child read the words and then read the sentence that uses those words. Assist him as necessary.

UN

un-wrap   un-known
unwrap   unknown

Do not unwrap the unknown present until Christmas Day.

IM

im-pos-si-ble   im-pa-tient   im-po-lite
impossible   impatient   impolite

It is impossible to believe that my son was impatient and impolite.

IN

in-cor-rect   in-ex-pen-sive
incorrect   inexpensive

The spelling of that word is incorrect.

I saved my allowance for an inexpensive toy.

IL

il-le-gal   il-leg-i-ble
illegal   illegible

Driving on the wrong side of the road is illegal.

Illegible handwriting is impossible to read.

IR

ir-reg-u-lar   ir-re-spon-si-ble
irregular   irresponsible

Even though our schedule is irregular, it would be irresponsible not to do my work now.

NON

non-stop   non-sense
nonstop   nonsense

I do not like nonstop nonsense.

DIS

dis-ap-proved   dis-hon-est   dis-o-beyed
disapproved   dishonest   disobeyed

My mother disapproved of the dishonest, young child who disobeyed.

DE

de-ice   de-frost
deice   defrost

The airport crew worked to deice the wings and defrost the windshield of the plane.

ANTI

an-ti-freeze   an-ti-sep-tic
antifreeze   antiseptic

Pour antifreeze into the car's radiator so that the engine will not freeze in the wintertime.

My mother dabbed antiseptic on my wound to clean it.

MIS

mis-un-der-stood mis-spelled
misunderstood   misspelled

I misunderstood the meaning of the word because it was misspelled.

Lesson 220: Prefixes

This lesson contains more words with common prefixes. Have the child read the words and then read the sentences that use those words. Assist him as necessary.

RE

re-match   re-fill   re-cy-cle
rematch   refill   recycle

Emily and Phyllis went to watch the rematch at the ball park.
Emily bought a lemon and lime soda.
She drank it fast and got a refill.
Then she put the empty cup in the recycle bin.

EN

en-fold-ed   en-cir-cled   en-a-ble   en-joy
enfolded   encircled   enable   enjoy

I went to the store to pick out a new winter coat.
I tried on a thick, furry coat and felt enfolded in warmth.
I bought a matching cap that encircled my head.
This coat will enable me to enjoy the cold weather.

SUPER

su-per-he-ro   su-per-mar-ket
superhero   supermarket

I saw a picture of a superhero on a cereal box at the supermarket.

SUB

sub-ma-rine   sub-way
submarine   subway

The submarine travels underwater.

The subway travels underground.

TRANS

trans-plant   trans-form
transplant   transform

When we transplant the rose bushes, it will transform the look of our yard.

INTER

in-ter-act   in-ter-net
interact   internet

My brother can interact with other college students on the internet.

MID

mid-day   mid-night
midday   midnight

The clock displays "12:00" at midday and at midnight.

OVER

o-ver-charged   o-ver-due   o-ver-sight
overcharged   overdue   oversight

I was overcharged for the books that were overdue.
The librarian said it was an oversight.

UNDER

un-der-neath   un-der-wear
underneath   underwear

The long underwear underneath my sweater kept me warm in frigid weather.

PRE

pre-view   pre-cau-tion
preview   precaution

As a precaution, my mother and father preview any movies I might see.

The lesson continues on the following page.

FORE

fore-thought   fore-cast
forethought   forecast

We put a lot of forethought into planning a trip.

We always watch the weather forecast.

SEMI

se-mi-fi-nal   se-mi-cir-cle
semifinal   semicircle

The winners of the semifinal stood in a semicircle for the picture.

UNI

u-ni-cy-cle
unicycle

A unicycle is a cycle with only one wheel.

BI

bi-cy-cle
bicycle

A bicycle is a cycle with two wheels.

TRI

tri-cy-cle   tri-an-gle
tricycle   triangle

A tricycle is a cycle with three wheels.

A triangle has three angles and three sides.

Section 24

MORE LETTER PATTERNS

Lesson 221: The Letter X as /z/
Silent P before S

Review

Instructor: Let's practice reading some words that you will soon read in sentences. Read these words to me.

man-u-fac-tures   sa-cred   writ-ten   po-em
manufactures   sacred   written   poem

prac-ti-ces   spe-cial   pa-tients   be-ha-vior
practices   special   patients   behavior

New

Instructor: In this lesson you will read words that begin with the letter **x**. In these words, the beginning **x** stands for the sound /z/. I will read each of these two words, and you will read them after me. Then you will read the sentences that contain these words.

xy-lo-phone   Xe-rox
xylophone   Xerox

The toddler likes to bang away on a toy xylophone.

Xerox is the name of a company that manufactures copying products.

Instructor: You already know how to read words with silent letters. Now you will read words with a silent **p**. When the letter **p** comes before the letter **s** in these words, the **p** is silent. Let's read these words together. I will read each word; then you will read it after me. Once we have read all the words, you will go back the beginning and read the words by yourself.

psalm   psy-chol-o-gy   psy-chi-a-try   psy-chi-a-trist
                    psychology   psychiatry   psychiatrist

A psalm is a sacred song or poem.
Many of the Psalms in the Bible were written by King David.

Doctor Franklin practices psychiatry.
As a psychiatrist he sees a special group of patients.
They see him about problems with their mind, feelings, or behavior.

Lesson 222: The Letter Pair CH as /sh/

Do the "Two Review and One New" today.

Review

Instructor: Read the following words to me. You will later read these words in a story.

The words in this lesson are predominantly of French origin. In the words *restaurant* (in this list) and *Chicago* (in a later list), the single vowel **a** stands for the /ô/ sound. Model the correct pronunciation for child.

par-ti-ci-pate	sci-ence	res-tau-rant	crys-tal	de-li-cious
participate	science	restaurant	crystal	delicious

Instructor: You have already read two different sounds of **ch** *(Lessons 57 and 189)*. Read these words.

char-act-er	me-chan-ic	stom-ach	chair	cheer-ful-ness
character	mechanic	stomach		cheerfulness

New

Instructor: The letter pair **ch** can stand for a third sound. In the following words borrowed from the French language, the letter pair **ch** stands for the sound /sh/ (as in "/sh/, don't wake the baby!"). I will read each word; then you will read it after me. Once we have finished going through the list together, you will go back to the beginning and read the list by yourself.

chef	cha-rade	chan-de-lier	chap-e-rone	Chi-ca-go
	charade	chandelier	chaperone	Chicago

Mich-i-gan	schwa	pis-tach-i-o	par-a-chute	mus-tache
Michigan		pistachio	parachute	mustache

Instructor: In this next word, the letter **i** stands for the long-**e** vowel sound. The **ch** still stands for the /sh/ sound. I will read the word; then you will read the word and a story that uses many of the words from this lesson.

ma-chine
machine

I went to Chicago with my family to participate in the science fair.
After the fair we went to a fancy restaurant to celebrate.
The restaurant had a sparkling crystal chandelier on the ceiling.
The waiter with the thin mustache told us about the special dishes.
The chef's famous dish is fish encrusted with pistachio nuts.
The dinner was delicious.
Afterward, we watched the waiter make coffee in a giant espresso machine.

Lesson 223: The Vowel Pair EU as Long U

Do the "Two Review and One New" today.

Review

Instructor: Let's begin this lesson by practicing some words you will later read in sentences. Read these words to me.

quar-rel	moun-tains	gov-ern-ment	mil-i-ta-ry
quarrel	mountains	government	military

New

Instructor: In this lesson you will read words that come from the French language. These words contain the vowel pair **eu** which stands for the long-**u** vowel sound. Let's read the following list of words together. First I will read each word. Then you will read each word after me. Once we have finished going through the list together, you will go back to the beginning and read the list yourself.

In the word *grandeur*, the **d** is pronounced /j/.

feud	feud-al	neu-tral	Eu-rope
	feudal	neutral	Europe
Eu-gene	ma-neu-ver	lieu-ten-ant	gran-deur
Eugene	maneuver	lieutenant	grandeur

Instructor: Now you will read some sentences.

A feud is a quarrel between families.

The lieutenant and his troops maneuver through the grandeur of the mountains.

Eugene took a trip to Europe to study the feudal system of government. In the feudal system, lords gave people land in return for their military service.

Lesson 224: The Letter Pair QU as /k/

Do the "Two Review and One New" today.

Instructor: You will begin the lesson by reading words to me.

Mus-lim	wor-ship	pier-ces	wrig-gling	crea-tures
Muslim	worship	pierces	wriggling	creatures

Instructor: Now you will read words that come from the French language. In these words, the letters **qu** stand for the sound /k/. First I will read each word, and you will read each word after me. Once we have read all the words, you will read the list yourself.

plaque	clique	mosque	opaque	pic-tur-esque
				picturesque

gro-tesque	et-i-quette	tur-quoise	con-quer
grotesque	etiquette	turquoise	conquer

Instructor: In the next words, **qu** still stands for the sound /k/. However, these words also contain a letter **i** that sounds like the long-**e** vowel sound: /ē/. Let's read this list of words together. First I will read each word. Then you will read each word after me. Once we have finished going through the list together, you will go back to the beginning and read the list yourself.

pique	u-nique	mos-qui-to	an-tique	tech-nique
	unique	mosquito	antique	technique

Instructor: Now you will read sentences and a story that use many of the words you just read.

A mosque is a Muslim place of worship.

It is not good etiquette to form a clique of friends.

The water in the picturesque mountain lake appears opaque and turquoise.

Would it pique your interest to know that only female mosquitoes bite?
Male mosquitoes suck on plant juice, but females suck on blood.
I know it sounds grotesque!
The female mosquito has a unique technique of sucking blood.
She pierces your skin with a long hollow tube in her beak.
She sucks blood to help her eggs mature.
These eggs hatch into tiny, wriggling creatures that turn into mosquitoes.

Lesson 225: The Vowel Pairs IO, IA, IE as /yə/

You will need the following for tomorrow's lesson: *twenty index cards and two markers of different colors. You may want to write out the index cards in advance of the next lesson.*

Do the "Two Review and One New" today.

Instructor: There is a group of words that contain the special vowel pairs **io**, **ia**, and **ie** that do not act like any other vowel pairs we have studied. In these words, **io**, **ia**, and **ie** are pronounced /yə/ (as in *onion*). Let's read a list of these words together. First I will read each word. Then you will read each word after me. Once we have finished going through the list together, you will go back to the beginning and read the list yourself.

on-ion	o-pin-ion	mil-lion	com-pan-ion	con-ve-nient
onion	opinion	million	companion	convenient

com-mu-nion	bril-liant	Cal-i-forn-ia	Vir-gin-ia	Aus-tra-lia
communion	brilliant	California	Virginia	Australia

Instructor: In the following words, the **io**, **ia**, and **ie** are slightly modified by the letter **r**. I will read each word. Then you will read that same word to me. Once we are finished going through the list together, you will read this list by yourself.

pe-cu-liar	fa-mil-iar	ju-nior	be-hav-ior	Xa-vier
peculiar	familiar	junior	behavior	Xavier

Instructor: Now you will read some of these words in a story.

Junior and Xavier entered an onion contest in California.
They brought the onion they had grown in Junior's garden.
There seemed to be millions of onions at the contest.
People came all the way from Pennsylvania and West Virginia, even though it was not convenient.

Prizes were given for the biggest onion, the juiciest onion, and the most peculiar onion.
Junior and his companion had the most peculiar onion in the opinion of the brilliant judges.

Lesson 226: Review the Letter Patterns from Lessons 221-225

You will need the following: *twenty index cards and two markers of different colors.*

Don't forget to do the "Two Review and One New" today.

Game: *Who* Did *What*?
You will need 20 index cards and two different-colored markers (I will use "red" and "green"—do not use yellow because it is too hard to read). With the red marker, write the following subjects (the *who*) on index cards, one subject per card. With the green marker, write the following predicates (*what* the subject did) on index cards, one predicate per card.

Subject (red)	Predicate (green)
The brilliant chef	whipped up pistachio ice cream.
The lieutenant from Virginia	forgot good etiquette when he burped.
The man with the oily mustache	brushed the plaque from his teeth.
This xylophone	is a delicate and beautiful antique.
The chandelier	hung from the ceiling.
The turquoise parachute	floated underneath the clouds.
The convenient Xerox machine	sputters and hums when working.
The psychologist	helped Eugene conquer his fear of spiders.
This peculiar type of mosquito	has bitten many people in Europe.
Lake Michigan	is full of fish.

First, lay the cards out in the order you see above. Set the first pair, "The brilliant chef" and "whipped up pistachio ice cream," in front of the child. Have the child read that sentence. Repeat the same process for the next nine sentences. Then shuffle all the cards, keeping the subject cards in one pile and the predicate cards in another. Let the child pick any subject card and pair it with any predicate card. Have fun reading the wacky sentences!

Section 25

THE FINAL SECTION

Lesson 227: Homonyms, Homophones, and Homographs

The goal of this lesson is to introduce homonyms, homophones, and homographs so that the child is able to understand what he is reading. He does not need to memorize all the "homo" terms.

Instructor: In this lesson you are going to learn about *homonyms*. Homonyms are words that are spelled and pronounced alike but have different meanings. I will read you a sentence with a pair of homonyms in it.

I **can** eat tuna fish from a **can**.

Instructor: The first *can* means "able to" (in "I *can* eat"). The second *can* means "a metal container." The words *can* and *can* are spelled the same way, pronounced the same way, but they have different meanings. *Can* and *can* are homonyms. You are going to read six more sentences with homonyms that are spelled the same way, pronounced the same way, but have different meanings.

After the child has read each sentence, ask him to identify the homonyms. Discuss the meanings of each of the words with the child. Here is a key to help you if you have trouble defining a word.

light: not heavy   *light*: not dark
bear: endure; stand   *bear*: a fuzzy animal
pen: writing instrument   *pen*: fenced enclosure
fair: reasonable   *fair*: exhibition; carnival
bank: place of business that takes care of money   *bank*: a ridge of earth
rose: got up; moved upward   *rose*: scented flower

I saw a light feather float in a ray of light.

I can't bear to be chased by a bear.

I dropped my pen in the muddy pen.

I paid a fair price to enter the fair.

The bank where I keep my money sits on the edge of a steep bank.

The woman rose to receive a beautiful red rose.

Instructor: Now you will learn a new term: *homophones*. Homophones are words that sound alike, but have different spellings and different meanings. I will read you a sentence with homophones in it.

The lesson continues on the following page.

I **ate** a breakfast of **eight** tiny pancakes.

Instructor: The words *ate* and *eight* sound the same but have different spellings and meanings. They are homophones. There are many homophones in the English language; you will read a few now.

After the child has read each sentence, have him identify the homophones.

The blue balloon blew through the air.

From here you can hear the wind whistle through the trees.

It is not right to write on furniture.

There will be no peace in this house if you eat that last piece of cake.

I ate a pear while I walked around in my pair of new shoes.

He threw the ball through the hoop.

Instructor: *Homographs* are words that are spelled alike but are pronounced differently and have different meanings. I will read you a sentence with homographs.

Rebecca shed a **tear** when she found a **tear** in her dress.

Instructor: *Tear* and *tear* are spelled the same way, but are pronounced differently and have different meanings. *Tear* and *tear* are homographs. Now you will read some sentences with homographs.

After the child has read each sentence, ask him to identify the homographs. Discuss the meanings of each word with the child. If you need help, use this key.

wound: to twist around	*wound*: gash or injury
desert: to leave or abandon	*desert*: dry place
object: to oppose or protest	*object*: something that can be seen
present: in attendance	*present*: to give or hand over
bow: lean forward	*bow*: loops of ribbon

The doctor wound a bandage over my fresh wound.

Please do not desert me in the desert with no water.

I object to your setting that wet object on my bed.

We all need to be present when we present Joseph with his farewell gift.

The gentleman will bow to the lady with the beautiful yellow bow in her hair.

Lesson 228: Exercise Your Reading Muscles (Reading Multi-Syllable Words)

Instructor: In this lesson we are going to look at some gigantic words that are really easy to read if you divide them up into little syllables. I want you to try to read these words syllable-by-syllable on your own. I will help you if you need it. Then you will read the words in a sentence.

If the child seems to struggle or become discouraged, pronounce the word for him as you run your finger under each syllable. You also may want to do this lesson over two days. Whether you do the lesson in one day, or two, encourage a mood of excited discovery—the child *can* figure out long words!

e-lec-tri-fy-ing pos-si-bil-i-ty
electrifying possibility
An electrifying possibility is that men may live on the moon.

ex-as-per-at-ing mis-un-der-stand-ing
exasperating misunderstanding
The exasperating misunderstanding about the trip made him cry.

ex-hil-a-rat-ing en-ter-tain-ment
exhilarating entertainment
A roller coaster is exhilarating entertainment.

par-tic-u-lar cal-cu-la-tor
particular calculator
This particular calculator belongs to my sister.

rep-e-ti-tious in-for-ma-tion
repetitious information
I do not need all of that repetitious information in order to plan my trip.

un-be-liev-a-ble co-op-er-a-tion
unbelievable cooperation
The unbelievable cooperation between the teams made the work easier.

un-for-get-ta-ble de-ter-mi-na-tion
unforgettable determination
The woman showed unforgettable determination in the dog sled race.

en-vi-ron-men-tal e-mer-gen-cy
environmental emergency
An oil spill in the sea is an environmental emergency.

ha-bit-u-al-ly pro-cras-ti-nat-ing
habitually procrastinating
The lazy student is habitually procrastinating.

man-u-fac-tur-ing re-frig-er-a-tors
manufacturing refrigerators
The company is busy manufacturing refrigerators.

ac-ci-den-tal-ly pho-to-cop-y-ing
accidentally photocopying
The man is accidentally photocopying too many pages.

or-di-nar-i-ly in-tim-i-dat-ing
ordinarily intimidating
Huge wild animals are ordinarily intimidating.

un-for-tu-nate-ly in-ex-pe-ri-enced
unfortunately inexperienced
The cook was unfortunately inexperienced.

tem-po-rar-i-ly ar-gu-men-ta-tive
temporarily argumentative
The toddler was temporarily argumentative.

el-e-men-ta-ry mul-ti-pli-ca-tion
elementary multiplication
Soon I will learn elementary multiplication.

mo-men-tar-i-ly mag-ni-fy-ing
momentarily magnifying
I am momentarily magnifying the leaf with this magnifying glass.

Lesson 229: Exercise Your Reading Muscles (Reading Multi-Syllable Words)

Instructor: In this lesson we are going to look at more gigantic words that are really easy to read syllable-by-syllable. I want you to try to read these words on your own.

If the child seems to struggle or become discouraged, pronounce the word for him as you run your finger under each syllable. You also may want to do this lesson over two days.

un-in-ter-est-ed hip-po-pot-a-mus
uninterested hippopotamus
The uninterested hippopotamus ignored the birds on his back.

un-be-liev-a-ble i-mag-i-na-tion
unbelievable imagination
My little brother has an unbelievable imagination.

un-com-fort-a-ble ac-com-mo-da-tions
uncomfortable accommodations
I do not want to go to a hotel with uncomfortable accommodations.

un-ac-cept-a-ble caf-e-te-ri-a
unacceptable cafeteria
The unacceptable cafeteria was swarming with bugs.

pre-cip-i-ta-tion e-vap-o-rat-ed
precipitation evaporated
The precipitation evaporated before it hit the ground.

au-to-mat-i-cal-ly com-pli-men-ta-ry
automatically complimentary
A large drink is automatically complimentary when you buy popcorn.

un-der-stand-a-bly in-ap-pro-pri-ate
understandably inappropriate
Kicking a stranger is understandably inappropriate.

in-tel-lec-tu-al math-e-ma-ti-cian
intellectual mathematician
The intellectual mathematician solved the problem quickly.

The lesson continues on the following page.

con-sid-er-a-ble con-tam-i-na-tion

considerable contamination
The considerable contamination of the water made it unsafe to drink.

rec-re-a-tion-al or-gan-i-za-tion
recreational organization
The recreational organization sold hot dogs at the game.

un-mis-tak-a-ble op-por-tu-ni-ty
unmistakable opportunity
Playing with your sister is an unmistakable opportunity to show
kindness.

com-mu-ni-ty par-tic-i-pa-tion
community participation
Keeping the streets clean takes community participation.

char-ac-ter-is-tic an-tic-i-pa-tion
characteristic anticipation
I waited for our vacation with characteristic anticipation.

dra-mat-i-cal-ly ex-ag-ger-at-ed
dramatically exaggerated
He dramatically exaggerated the size of the fish he caught.

sup-ple-men-ta-ry vo-cab-u-lar-y
supplementary vocabulary
These supplementary vocabulary words are fun!

ab-bre-vi-at-ed in-tro-duc-tion
abbreviated introduction
The abbreviated introduction is ten pages shorter than the original.

pa-thet-i-cal-ly ir-re-spon-si-ble
pathetically irresponsible
It is pathetically irresponsible to leave tools out in the rain.

Lesson 230: Exercise Your Reading Muscles (Reading Multi-Syllable Words)

Instructor: In this lesson you will read some very large words. I want you to try to read each group of words on your own. Then you will read those words in a story.

If the child seems to struggle or become discouraged, pronounce the word for him as you run your finger under each syllable. You can always divide this lesson over two days if the child becomes tired or has trouble.

en-cy-clo-pe-di-a
encyclopedia

vet-er-i-nar-i-an
veterinarian

de-pend-a-bil-i-ty
dependability

in-di-vid-u-al-i-ty
individuality

au-to-bi-og-ra-phy
autobiography

I read in the encyclopedia about a famous veterinarian.
The veterinarian was known for his dependability and his individuality.
Later I checked out his autobiography from the library.

ar-che-o-log-i-cal
archeological

o-ver-pop-u-la-ted
overpopulated

un-co-op-er-a-tive
uncooperative

The archeological site was overpopulated with uncooperative, curious people.

pa-le-on-tol-o-gist
paleontologist

un-i-den-ti-fi-a-ble
unidentifiable

en-thu-si-as-ti-cal-ly
enthusiastically

Brach-i-o-sau-rus
Brachiosaurus

Gi-gan-to-sau-rus
Gigantosaurus

The paleontologist found a cave full of bones that were unidentifiable.
He enthusiastically brought them out to examine.
He hoped the bones were from a Brachiosaurus or a Gigantosaurus.

The lesson continues on the following page.

ex-tra-ter-res-tri-al
extraterrestrial

in-ter-plan-e-tar-y
interplanetary

un-in-hab-it-a-ble
uninhabitable

ra-di-o-ac-tiv-i-ty
radioactivity

im-pos-si-bil-i-ty
impossibility

tel-e-com-mu-ni-ca-tion
telecommunication

in-vis-i-bil-i-ty
invisibility

im-prac-ti-cal-i-ty
impracticality

un-sat-is-fac-to-ry
unsatisfactory

su-pe-ri-or-it-y
superiority

au-to-mat-i-cal-ly
automatically

The extraterrestrial creature wanted to do some interplanetary space travel.
The first planet he saw was uninhabitable.
The radioactivity level was so high his telecommunication system wouldn't work.
Staying on that planet was an impossibility.

The second planet he visited was surrounded with an invisibility shield.
He liked that planet a lot, but the impracticality of staying there was that no one could ever see you.
Since the invisible planet was also unsatisfactory, the extraterrestrial realized his home planet's superiority over other planets.
He set the controls of his space craft to take him home automatically.

Lesson 231: The Final Lesson: Reading a Really Long and Silly Word

Instructor: This is the final lesson in this book. You are now a super reader! In fact, you are such a super reader you can now read a fourteen syllable word! This word does not mean anything; it is just a fun word from a song.

su-per-cal-i-fra-gi-lis-tic-ex-pi-al-i-do-cious

supercalifragilisticexpialidocious

PART 2

INFORMATION FOR THE ORDINARY PARENT

PRE-READING :
PREPARING A YOUNG CHILD TO BE A READER

"Reading readiness" is not something that just happens. You prepare a child for reading by engaging in four elements of reading instruction. You should:

- Have the child frequently hear adult spoken language.
- Read aloud to the child.
- Teach the child to recognize the alphabet letters.
- Teach the child the sounds these letters represent.

Have the child frequently hear adult spoken language

A child first learns to understand language by being talked to and sung to when you feed, bathe, dress, and play with him. This constant, pleasant chatter lays the foundation for his language development. As you go about your daily activities, use adult language to talk to your child about what you are doing. Look for opportunities for your child to hear you *repeat the same things over and over*—nursery rhymes, poetry, songs, simple stories, Bible verses, catechism, etc.… Children love the repetition. At first babies learn just to understand what you are saying, but with continued repetition, they learn to say words. A child who is just beginning to talk hears a word hundreds of times before it becomes part of his active vocabulary. If he hears a variety of words, he is better able to express his thoughts. This is language development at its best. Additional tips are given below:

- When a child speaks to you in incomplete sentences or uses incorrect grammar, repeat what he has just said using correct grammar in a complete sentence. Say this with the vocal inflection of a question. The child will often correct himself and repeat what you have said. For example:

    Child: Train go fast.
    Parent: The train goes fast?
    Child: Yes, the train goes fast.

    Some children will naturally repeat the corrected phrase after you because they want to please and get it right. If the child will not repeat after you, continue to engage in this ear training. Meanwhile, try to discern if you are dealing with an issue of understanding or an issue of disobedience.

- When you are reading aloud to a child, have the child repeat long or unusual words found in stories (such as *rhinoceros*). Repeat them over and over—have fun with it.
- Start a story for the child (example: "One day I was walking down the road and I saw…"). The child finishes the sentence with whatever strikes his imagination. Continue to prompt the child's imagination with phrases like "and then…" "until he saw a…" and "suddenly, a giant…."
- Play games in which the child thinks of rhyming words. In the beginning, you may have to supply the rhymes for the child to repeat. The more you play these games with the child, the better his rhyming skills become. For example:
    1. Say to the child, "I am going on a trip and I am going to take a *hat* and a…" The child supplies a rhyming word for *hat* (example: *cat, bat,* or *rat*).
    2. Say to the child, "Did you ever see a *pig* …." The child makes up an ending that gives an action that rhymes with *pig* (example: "dance a *jig*?" or "try on a *wig*?").

3. Play "Milly-mee, Mally-mee, Moo[1]." To start the game chant with the child: "Milly-mee, mally-mee, moo; a giant cow sat on you. Milly-mee, mally-mee, mus; a giant cow sat on us." Then prompt the child with "Milly-mee, mally-mee, **mog**; a giant cow sat on a…." The child will supply the rhyming word to **mog** (ex. *frog, dog, hog,* or *log*). Repeat this with other rhyming words, including:

    Milly-mee, mally-mee, **mug**; a giant cow sat on a (*rug, bug, jug*).
    Milly-mee, mally-mee, **man**; a giant cow sat on a (*van, fan, man, can*).
    Milly-mee, mally-mee, **mop**; a giant cow sat on a (*top, mop, shop*).

- Play games in which the child thinks of words that begin with the same sound. At first you may have to coach the child. Walk around the house and find words that start with the same sound (regardless of letter). For example:

    Soap, sink, sofa, cereal, socks.
    Table, toy, truck, tool, television.
    Dish, dog, door, desk, deck, dime.
    Book, basket, ball, bag, bed, box.

- Play games in which the child practices hearing the individual sounds in words. For example, to play "Smush the Sounds," start with the word *pat*. Say the separate sounds of the word *pat*: /p/, /ă/, /t/. Increase the speed at which you say the sounds until you gradually blend the sounds to make the real word. The goal is for the child to guess the word as early as possible. Here are some other words you can use for this game:

sat	bed	fit	fox	gum
cat	red	zip	mop	hug
van	ten	wig	job	nut
can	pet	kid	log	rub
tap	met	lip	sob	cup

Read aloud to the child

Literacy starts *before* formal schooling. Prepare your child for reading instruction by reading *to* him as much as possible. Let the child sit in your lap or snuggle next to you. Start bedtime preparations early so you have time to read before saying good-night. Read on rainy days. Read to a sick child. Read after lunch before rest time. Help your child associate reading with pleasure.

- Read rhymes, especially traditional nursery rhymes. Rhymes help children listen for individual sounds in words. Read books with lots of repetition. In picture books, point to objects as you name them.
- When you begin to read to your child, run your finger under the words as you read. This lets him know that:
    1. We read books right-side up.
    2. We read *printed words* and not just pictures.
    3. We turn pages right to left as we go through a book.
    4. We read sentences from left to right.
- Reading aloud to a child develops his vocabulary. Exposure to language in books is also important because the language is more complex and more formal than in conversation. The child then hears a better-organized sentence and paragraph structure than he hears in conversational dialogue. When you read aloud to a child, the child becomes familiar with words, language patterns, and the structure of stories. He also acquires background knowledge that will aid him when he actually starts to read.
- Make sure your child has a quiet afternoon rest time. Never let the toddler know that giving up the afternoon nap is an option. Even if your child doesn't sleep, the quiet time refreshes him and gives

---

[1] This exercise is based on the poem "Willoughby Wallaby Woo" by Dennis Lee from *Alligator Pie* (MacMillan Company of Canada, 1974).

you a much-needed uninterrupted time to relax or finish tasks. You should plan to keep this period of the child's day just for rest, looking at books, and eventually reading. This habit of quiet rest for the child is a forerunner of the habit of quiet afternoon reading. Here are some ideas for the child's rest time:

1. Read a few books to the young child in his crib at the beginning of naptime and bedtime. You will find that in order to delay your leaving, he will ask for more. Then leave the books in the crib or bed so that the child may look at the pictures of things about which you have just read.

2. Give the child books in the crib. Start with plastic and cloth, move on to board books, and finally transition to paper books (once you have taught him not to tear pages). Don't worry if you lose a few pages to the toddler who thinks he is a puppy and chews on them!

3. During rest time, let the child listen to classic books on tape. Most public libraries have shelves of books on tape in the children's sections. Children can listen to and enjoy books that are far, far above their vocabulary level. In one year, my three-year-old and five-year-old grandchildren listened to all of Rudyard Kipling's *Just So Stories* and the original *Jungle Book*, Edith Nesbit's series *The Railway Children,* C.S. Lewis's *The Chronicles of Narnia*, J. M. Barrie's *Peter Pan*, E. B. White's *Charlotte's Web* and *The Trumpet of the Swan*, Frances Hodgson Burnette's *A Little Princess*, the unabridged *A Christmas Carol* by Charles Dickens, and the Bible.

4. Get a baby-proof tape recorder. Make your own tapes as you read, sing, talk, tell stories, and recite poems. At times, record your reading to your child along with his comments. He can listen to these tapes during his quiet time or when you are busy.

- Talk with the child about the books you read together. This expands oral vocabulary, background knowledge, and communication skills.

Teach the child to recognize the alphabet letters

Before a child can learn to read, he must learn his letters. Children can learn to name and recognize their letters very early. When you hold up a cookie and the child can say, "cookie," he is ready for you to show him a three-dimensional wooden or plastic **A** and learn its name. Let the child play with each three-dimensional letter, to feel it as well as see it. When he knows "little **a**" you can hold up "big **A**," and then "little **b**" and "big **B**."

Systematically teach the child to recognize and name the big (also called *capital* or *uppercase*) and little (also called *lowercase*) form of each letter. Teach the big and little letters together. Here are some activities that will help your child learn the names and shapes of the letters:

- Frequently sing and then say the alphabet until the child can say the alphabet in order. You can record yourself singing or saying the alphabet song and play it often for your young child.
- Put an alphabet chart (with both big and little letters) where the child can see it.
- Play naming the letters with a wooden alphabet puzzle, saying the letter as the child puts it into place.
- Have the child play with magnetic plastic letters on the refrigerator while you are working in the kitchen.
- Read alphabet books—the same ones over and over to make alphabet sounds second nature. Favorites of my children and grandchildren have been *Dr. Seuss's A B C* and *Curious George Learns the Alphabet,* by H. A. Rey.
- Have the child find certain letters when a lot of letters are laid out. Start with a small group of letters and gradually increase the number until all twenty-six letters are laid out.
- Have the child match big and little three-dimensional letters.
- Have the child practice putting the alphabet in sequence, and naming the letters as he puts them in sequence.

- Help the child trace the letters in corn meal or grits in a cookie sheet with sides. If sand is available outside, draw the letters with a finger or a stick. In the beginning, guide his hand to form the letters.
- Help the child to form letters out of clay. This helps the child see the letters in three dimensions. Many children see letters this way before they can visualize them flat on paper.
- Put letters on 3 x 5 cards (one letter to a card). Show the child each card and have him name the letter. If the child says the right letter name, he gets the card. If he misses it, the card goes on the bottom of the pile. Start with two or three cards, and then work up to the whole alphabet. When the very young child is learning the letters, you should teach them in alphabetical order.
- Put paper letters of the alphabet under a clear plastic tablecloth in the kitchen. When you are working in the kitchen, have your child identify as many letters as he can. Start with a few letters, and add others one at a time.
- Help the child find letters in magazines and advertisements. Clip them out and paste them into a notebook. There should be twenty-six pages in the notebook, one for each letter of the alphabet. Each page will have one letter of the alphabet written at the top—the big and little letters written side-by-side. Write on the cover "My Alphabet Book" and let the child draw or glue pictures on it.
- Make your child aware of letters all around him—at home, at the grocery, on boxes, on signs, and on books and magazines. **M** (M & M's and McDonald's) and **z** (on a pizza box) are the first letters many children learn.
- Play with alphabet blocks.
- Play "Feed the Hungry Animal": Make a "bunny box" (or kitty, or puppy, or lion) that likes to eat letters! Cover a shoebox and its top separately with plain brown or white paper. On the end of the lid, draw eyes and paste on ears. Put the lid back on the box and then draw a nose, whiskers and a mouth large enough to "eat" letters. Cut out the mouth so the child can push letters into the mouth. Print letters on pieces of paper small enough to fit through the mouth of the animal. Put these in a container (bag, envelope, or box). *The game:* When a child first begins to play this game, put only a few letters in the container to insure success. Take out a letter from the container. If the child reads the letter correctly, he gets to "feed" the animal. If he doesn't read it correctly, it goes back into the container with the other letters to be fed later. Once these letters have been mastered, add two or three new letters to the container. The hungry animal box can be used later with words printed on pieces of paper.

Teach the child the sounds these letters represent

The words we speak are made up of *individual speech sounds*. Written words are made up of letters that are symbols for these sounds. Your ultimate goal is for the child to see printed letters and say the sounds they represent. Lessons 1-26 teach this systematically, but it is easier and more enjoyable for the child if he is familiar with this skill before he begins formal lessons. Here are some activities that will help him learn:

- Run your finger under the print as you read and sing nursery rhymes from books.
- When you are out shopping, point out and read the print on products and signs.
- Point to the vowels **a, e, i, o, u** and then teach the child that these letters are called *vowels* and that all other letters are called *consonants*. Practice saying the names of the vowels.
- Chant the *sounds* of the short vowels in order. At first, let him chant with you. When he can do this easily, have the child say them alone. Do this chant daily until he learns the sounds; then review them about once a week thereafter. The sounds of the short vowels are the sounds of:
  a in *apple*.
  e in *elephant*.
  i in *igloo*.
  o in *octopus*.
  u in *umbrella*.

- To help children hear the difference between the sounds of the vowels (especially **e** and **i**), demonstrate and exaggerate the movements of the mouth. The mouth is open for all the vowels but the shape of the mouth is different. Let the child look at himself in a mirror as he exaggerates saying the vowels.
- To help the child learn the sounds of consonants, let the child look in the mirror as he practices saying each sound. As you model each consonant sound for the child, show him that:
  1. The consonant sound is produced with your voice (*voiced*) or with just air (*unvoiced*).
  2. The sound or flow of air is stopped by the lips or tongue (against the teeth, roof of the mouth, or throat).
- Lay out three letter tiles (or plastic or paper letters) in random order that spell a three-letter word. Say the word very slowly, letter-sound by letter-sound, (example: /k/, /ă/, /t/), and have the child find each individual sound as you say it. Give him any help he needs. After he can successfully do this activity with three letter tiles, put out a variety of letters, some of which are not in the word you say. If he picks up a letter that is *not* in the word you say, tell him, "You picked up the letter **l**, but that letter is not in this word. Listen again: /k/, /ă/, /t/." When all the letters in the word are laid out in order, have the child run his finger under the letters as you blend the sounds together into the whole word. Use words from the lists in Lessons 27 through 43.
- Review the short sounds of the five vowels before you play this game. Put letters on 3 x 5 cards (one letter to a card). Show the child each card and have him say the sound that letter represents. If the child says the right sound, he gets the card. If he misses it, the card goes on the bottom of the pile. Start with two or three cards, and then work up to the whole alphabet.

MANAGING THE READING SESSION

Have the lesson in the same place everyday. The child's mind is more ready to work when the body is in the work place. I tried to tutor phonics on a sofa. I learned that the sofa is a wonderful place for pleasure reading but not for the intensive teaching of new material. Look for the quietest place your house has to offer. Be sure the child's chair is comfortable and that his feet can touch the floor. Make sure that there is sufficient light, but it should not glare off the paper or shine directly into the child's eyes.

Minimize distractions. Don't try to teach a difficult concept when the other children in the family are at play time. They should be occupied with assignments or chores that can be carried out without interrupting you or distracting your student. Store your lesson materials together so you do not have to interrupt the flow of the lesson to stop and get anything. Remove toys and games from the child's line of sight. Take the phone off the hook or have an answering machine. Turn off the television and the stereo. Don't sit where a child can look out a window; this may draw his attention away from the lesson. One student I tutored had to sit facing a blank wall to stay focused on the lesson.

Even with minimal distractions, expect the ability to concentrate to be uneven, or possibly sporadic. A typical case was my grandson Daniel. Some days his throat was "too dry" to read. (I gave him a drink of water.) Often he said he was hungry. (If it was not close to meal time, I learned to give him a snack before we started.) He wiggled. He talked about unrelated topics. Some days he seemed unable to concentrate. But I patiently and consistently kept working on the lessons with him until he became a competent reader. Don't be discouraged with a child's lack of focus—patiently keep moving forward.

Choose a time to teach reading when the child is alert. Children have difficulty tackling unfamiliar material when tired. Late afternoon and bedtime are not productive times to tackle new, difficult material. You should strive to have the reading lesson at the same time each day.

Try to eliminate excuses not to work on the lesson. Make sure the child has just gone to the bathroom and had a drink of water. Be aware of low blood sugar. If a child is consistently cranky and uncooperative at one time of day (mid-morning, mid-afternoon, or just before lunch or dinner), make sure the child is not hungry. I have learned that a high protein breakfast makes reading instruction easier in the morning. An afternoon snack might also speed up a reading lesson.

Don't allow the child to interrupt you when you are going through an explanation. Otherwise, you may never finish explaining the lesson to him. Teach the child that you will hold up a finger or a hand as a sign that you will listen later to what he has to say. Finish your explanation, and then keep your promise to listen to his question or comment.

Be in charge. When you are teaching, you should be in control. You do not have to be unpleasant. During the reading session, *you* direct the lesson, and you require the child to follow *your* directions. You know how to read, and the child does not. You see ahead to future consequences; the child may not. I met one mother who allowed her child to decide when and what he wanted to learn. The child made immature choices that led him to be woefully behind in his academics. She told me, "I let him decide for himself, and I am so sorry. Now he is fifteen, and all he wants to do is stay in his room and play videogames."

Don't ask, "Do you want to read now?" unless the alternative is truly awful. Reading instruction should be as matter-of-fact as brushing teeth—it is part of the day. Most five-year-olds are capable of learning to read, which doesn't mean they will choose to read instead of play. A child who squirms, complains, or protests isn't necessarily demonstrating "reading unreadiness;" he is simply being a child.

Don't give in to bad attitudes—arguing, laziness, or whining. A child will often try all of these tactics to avoid hard, mental work. Pleasantly, firmly, and consistently move forward in your instruction and review. Small successes and genuine praise will motivate any child.

Some children need to be challenged. They want encouragement to put forth effort. One mother wrote me about her eight-year-old son, Zachary. One morning, during his lessons, he collapsed into tears and said, "You and Daddy have such different thoughts about me. He tells me to study hard and be smart. You think I am stupid." In her letter, the mother said, "Now, I am nowhere near a perfect mom, but even on my worst days I have never considered calling my child stupid."

She talked to Zachary to find out what he meant. He said, "If you thought I was smart you would give me lots of work to do. But you make things easy on me, so you think I am stupid." Few children are excited about doing hard work, but they do realize that they are capable if given the proper instruction and motivation. Children do not respect a parent who is intimidated by their resistance. You will not lose a child's affection if you challenge him. To the contrary, if you are firm, patient, persistent, and encouraging, you will be surprised by the child's pleasure in his accomplishments.

Reading instruction does not need to be "fun." Children need to be taught that everything in life is not entertainment. The work the child puts into learning to read will lead the child to much *greater* joy when the child can read. If a child is trained early that some of life is work, then as an adult he will not be hindered by the idea that everything has to be enjoyable all of the time. An adult does not always have a choice whether or not to work and neither should a child. We discipline ourselves to work because it is necessary either for immediate needs or to achieve future goals. Even if you like working on a task, discipline is still required at times to finish it. Work is a fact of life.

Be sensitive to a child's pace of learning. Although you should be a firm, patient teacher who challenges the child, you should also remain sensitive to the level of a child's frustration. I have observed over the years that when tears of frustration begin, learning ceases.

I have recently experienced this first-hand. Learning to use the computer as a mature adult gave me fresh insight into the value of a patient instructor. I had been happy for most of my life with a good electric typewriter. It met my needs until I began to write *The Well-Trained Mind.* Then it became necessary for me to get a computer. I had to use a word-processing program, navigate web sites, and communicate via e-mail.

My husband had been using the computer for many years, and he volunteered to teach me. Everything about the computer was so new to me and so different from my trusty typewriter. My husband would give me instructions, but since the skills were so new, I would often forget them. One day, he said in exasperation, "I just *told* you how to do that!" My eyes welled up with tears. My husband threw up his hands. "If you're going to cry, I can't help you." All learning immediately ceased. I couldn't think. I couldn't remember what he had taught me while I was upset.

It came as a revelation to me that learning to read can make a child feel similarly overwhelmed. Don't express frustration to your child over his pace of learning. Your impatience will only hinder his progress.

Every child's pace is different. Learning to read is a skill, and mastering skills takes practice. Do some form of reading each day. Some very verbal children learn to read rather quickly, but it is common for a child to need two or three years of instruction to become a good reader.

When a child is working hard, but still struggling, it is encouraging for you to do some of the reading, moving your pencil or finger for him to follow along as you read. Alternating lines, or sounding out a word with the child helps keep him moving forward. Acknowledge to the child that you know it is hard and you are proud he is doing so well.

ENCOURAGING A CHILD TO BE A READER

Read to the child—lots, even when you think he is too old for this. Read aloud after dinner with parents and children taking turns. One literate family continued to read aloud together through high school and even when the children returned home from college for holidays. It is a wonderful tradition.

Engage the child's imagination by reading to him with expression and talking to him about what you read. Use words and phrases from the book in this conversation (example: "What did the man bring with him when he 'ascended the rugged, barren mountain'?").

Read to your children at odd moments of waiting (the doctor's office, waiting for food at a restaurant). Have an older child read to a younger child at any time.

Read books yourself and let your children see that you love to read.

Visit the library often—once a week, if possible. Get each child his own library card.

Choose a book on your child's reading level that you think will interest him. Read it aloud until you get to an interesting place in the plot, and then give him the book to finish by himself.

At some time during the day (an hour of afternoon rest time or at bedtime), make reading the only activity allowed. Provide the child with easy books or picture books that are favorites. Some children will look at books and begin to read out of sheer boredom, if there is no alternative activity available. Often they will discover that reading is a pleasurable way to pass time and discover information.

Severely limit television, videos, and videogames. They require little thinking on the part of the child. Television, videos, and movies impose another person's imagination on your child. He is never free again to imagine his own scene when the words are read. One of my grandchildren burst into tears when watching a video of a favorite book. "That's not the way it is in my mind," he cried. Let a child's imagination develop by providing a peaceful and quiet environment where reading can be done with minimal distraction.

Keep books around the house. Keep a stack of books in the child's bedroom. Buy books, visit bookstores, and give special books for presents. Children need to be provided with many opportunities to read for fun on a regular basis. To be a competent reader, a child must *read*. A child should be engaged in reading books on three levels of difficulty:
1. ***Below-level reading:*** Allow him to choose books to read for pleasure that are far below his instructional reading level. This increases his enjoyment of reading, his speed and confidence, and it builds his vocabulary.
2. ***On-level reading:*** Help him choose books on his reading level that you think will interest him.
3. ***Challenge-level reading:*** For formal reading instruction, use books that gradually increase your child's ability to read harder and harder material.

Have your children read broadly. I required my children to choose one book from each of the following categories when they went to the library. Some books were kept for longer periods, some were returned the next week. My daughter Susan said to me recently, "I'm glad you had me do the different categories of reading; otherwise I wouldn't have chosen to read a lot of things that I am now glad that I read." Suggested categories are:

- Science.
- History.
- Art or music appreciation.
- Practical (craft, hobby, "how-to").
- Biography/Autobiography.
- Classic novel (or adaptation suited to age).
- Imaginative storybook.
- Book of poetry.
- Religious book (you may have to look for these books in the library of your religious community, a religious bookstore, or a homeschooling convention).

Can the "ordinary parent" teach reading?

Absolutely! Parents have been intimidated by the widespread notion that only professional educators can teach reading. Professionally-trained teachers often write about reading in technical "educationese." Phrases such as "phonological awareness," "phonemic manipulation," and "graphophonic cues" sound like a foreign language to the uninitiated. This book will enable you, the ordinary parent, to successfully teach reading in a simple, straightforward manner. You do not need special training. You do not need expensive kits.

Do I need to do a lot of reading readiness exercises or programs before I begin this book?

In the home, it is not necessary to spend lots of money and energy on commercial "reading readiness" materials. Reading readiness, simply, is immersing the child in the sounds of oral language, and then teaching him to recognize the written symbols (alphabet letters) that represent these sounds. For reading readiness instruction, see "Pre-Reading: Preparing a Young Child to be a Reader" on page 347.

How early can I start?

There is a common belief that children should start reading instruction at the age of six, because this is when reading begins in the classroom. This is reinforced by the assumption that only teachers can teach reading; parents are not equipped to do so. If you wait to let an "expert" teach your child to read, expectations may be lowered, learning can be delayed, and the early years of the ability to learn rapidly may not be utilized.

Some people even suggest that you not begin formal reading until the age of ten or eleven. They think learning to read is too difficult and too frustrating for a young child. But if you use a systematic and sequential phonics program (like the one in this book), even a young child can learn the skills necessary to become a fluent reader.

Most four and five-year-olds can learn to read. Many three-year-olds can begin. Plan to teach for ten minutes—by the clock—because in the beginning ten minutes may seem longer than it really is! Gradually extend the time until you are working about thirty minutes a day by the end of the year. Don't worry that you will harm your child's eyesight by early reading. Early work might *reveal* eye problems, but it will not *cause* them.

Why aren't there pictures in this book?

There are three reasons why pictures are not in this book:

- Pictures are often used to associate letters with sounds. The child will see the letter **a**, then a picture of an apple (which is their cue to say the short-**a** vowel sound). This is not necessary to teach letter sounds. Learning a key picture is an extra mental step; children can easily go from seeing the symbol to saying the sound for which it stands.
- Pictures distract the child from print. You want your child to focus on the letters and their sounds.
- Pictures encourage word-guessing based on the content of the picture. Later, when a child gets to a book with no pictures, he may feel that the book is too hard to read.

For very young children, seeing pictures with alphabet letters and key words may be useful as a pre-reading exercise. Saying the name of the picture may help train the child's ear to hear the alphabet sounds.

What do I need to keep in mind as I teach reading to my child?

The best teaching is done daily by direct, systematic instruction. In initial reading instruction, do not focus on speed but on the skill of figuring out and sounding out the parts that make up a whole word. When you begin to teach reading, keep these words in mind: ***patient***, ***frequent***, and ***consistent***.

Patient means you don't fuss or scold or show frustration when the child doesn't know a sound or a word after he has had time to think. On days when your child acts as if he has never heard something that you have spent days teaching him, go back and review the material, and move on. Whatever you do, do not let the child guess. (You may repeat a lesson for a number of days with no seeming success, and then one day the concept will just "click." You will see the "I get it" expression on the child's face.)

Frequent means you teach the sounds often, daily when possible. Beginning lessons should be about ten minutes in length, stretching eventually to thirty minutes as the child is able. If your child has a short attention span, start with the few minutes your child *can* pay attention, and then lengthen *one minute at a time* until he can concentrate for ten minutes. A short attention span is not necessarily a disability—attention spans can be trained.

Consistent means you continue daily. Children forget easily. If circumstances require a long period without instruction, quickly review all that you have covered before you return to your lessons.

How quickly should I move through the book?

A child does not have to perfectly master a page of phonics sounds before moving on to another page. The child may be forging ahead on new material while also reviewing a few previous lessons. If a page seems especially difficult, mark it, review some of it each day, but continue to move forward in the book. Often, the child finds the new sounds easy to master. So, you may find yourself working at three places during the lesson period: reviewing a difficult lesson you have "flagged," reviewing almost-mastered material from the previous lesson, and introducing new material. I call this "Two Review and One New," and I will remind you of this technique as you go through the lessons.

As you are going through each lesson, lightly mark with pencil the trouble words. When you review the page the next day, do the words the child can read with ease. Then review the words with the light marks. Erase the marks if he reads the words easily; this is encouraging!

Try not to hurry through lessons to the point where you rush the child. My grandson Daniel was sitting quietly, staring at a sentence. I started to tell him a word and he stopped me by saying, "I'm thinking." Give the child some time to process!

On the other hand, do not progress so slowly through the book that you give the child the opportunity to invent his own system or to become bored. Move through the phonics instruction as quickly as the child can grasp the concepts.

Occasionally the child may encounter a word that is not in his speaking vocabulary. Do not let this slow your progress. When the child encounters such a word, just tell the child the meaning of the word, use it in a sentence, and move on.

If after a couple of months the child is still having trouble making progress, and you notice that the child consistently rubs his eyes, squints, covers one eye, or turns his head sideways, have the child's eyesight examined.

Do I teach reading, writing, and spelling together?

No. Reading, writing, and spelling are three separate skills. It is overwhelming for a child to focus on the techniques of three different skills at the same time. For this reason, I advocate teaching reading first. When the child is physically able, begin a formal penmanship program. Once the child is able to form his letters, begin a sequential spelling program.

Won't I need lots of games and instructional resources to teach my child to read?

To master basic skills, young children need repetition more than variety in presentation. The simplest method of learning to recognize a letter or to say a letter sound is just to repeat it often and review it frequently. Then use it in the context of real reading.

Many companies market games and video drills initially developed for school classrooms. You don't need a large number of aids aimed at reaching a roomful of children with varying needs to successfully teach your child to read. A few fun activities will suffice. You want your child to associate learning to read with *books,* not games, videos, and computers.

If you want to reinforce or review a concept, you may use games that are uncomplicated and focus on the skill rather than on the cleverness of presentation. Do not use them as a substitute for systematically teaching phonics. Games can reinforce instruction but should not be the primary teaching method.

My child is an auditory/visual/tactile learner. Is the method of teaching in this book suitable for him?

The Ordinary Parent's Guide to Teaching Reading uses all three modes of learning. A child hears sounds and says words aloud (auditory processing). The child sees the letters in print and learns the sounds they represent (visual learning). The child also is encouraged to handle letters in a variety of exercises (tactile experience). In the teaching of reading, do not rely just on your child's strengths, whether they are auditory, visual, or tactile. You must also *teach to the child's weakness* so that he becomes a well-rounded learner.

What are the different ways of teaching reading? What is the method used in this book?

There are four basic methods of teaching reading:

- *Basal reading programs* (a series of graded reading texts) often focus on whole-word instruction enriched with activities on topics such as "The Old West" or "The Rainforest." The child must memorize words that have meaning within a story (like *cowboy* or *sloth*) rather than learning the phonetic patterns of words. If the child continues with this method, he must eventually memorize many thousands of words.
- *Sight-word programs* begin by teaching children a sight-word vocabulary of common words without reference to their phonetic elements. As with basal reading programs, the child must eventually memorize thousands of whole words to become a competent reader.
- *Incidental phonics*, as the name implies, teaches phonics incidentally—as the child encounters the word in his reading. He is taught to first look at the whole word, next to look at the parts of that word, and then to make a guess guided by context. Since the phonetic content of that word is taught in an isolated incident, it will have to be repeated many times in many stories before the child learns it. This method is often used in literature-based programs.
- *Explicit phonics* is the method used in this book. The basic sounds of letters are taught systematically and then blended into words. In this book, the words a child learns are put immediately into meaningful sentences.

Unless a child has a photographic memory so he can remember every whole word he has ever seen, there is no successful substitute for explicit phonics. The basic phonetic sounds *must* be learned!

How do I teach comprehension? Should I give comprehension tests to see if the child understands what he has read?

Do not teach comprehension at the same time you are teaching the child to sound out printed letters. It diverts the child's attention from figuring out words phonetically. When a word is new to the child, or he does not seem to understand its meaning, just tell the child the meaning, use it in a sentence, and move on.

Until the child is reading easily, formal comprehension instruction should be limited to material *you read to him*. The child will listen and respond with his own retelling of what you have read. This is called *narration*.

Teaching reading lays the groundwork for successful, independent comprehension. When a child learns to figure out words phonetically, he is able to read the words on the page accurately and automatically. This, obviously, increases the ability to comprehend what is read. Once a child is reading independently, you may start asking "who," "what," "when," or "where" questions about material he has just read. This will let you know whether the child is comprehending what he reads.

How can I teach my child to read aloud fluently?

Independent, silent reading should not replace reading aloud. Having the child read aloud increases his vocabulary, expands his general knowledge, and forces him to figure out new words. It also allows you to correct errors before they become habits.

Fluency, the ability to read aloud accurately, smoothly, and easily, takes time and practice. Reading the same passage aloud is the best way to develop fluency. Usually reading the same passage four times in a row is sufficient (this should take five to ten minutes). Have the child practice reading this same passage two to three times a week, or until the child can read it accurately and smoothly without hesitation. Then move on to the next passage. Do this periodically until about sixth grade; then check up on the ability as he matures into reading more difficult material.

Fluency should be practiced with passages that are easy for the child to read. If the child struggles to read the words, drop back to easier selections. You can choose a paragraph from what your child is currently reading for school, or you can select passages from a vintage McGuffey reader. The paragraphs in these readers are numbered and suitable for oral reading.

You can teach oral reading by:
- Modeling fluency by reading a specific passage aloud for the child.
- Reading a passage in unison with the child.
- Having the child repeatedly read the same passage as you offer guidance.
- Reading poetry to practice fluency, for variety.

How will I know if my child is dyslexic?

Letter reversals are common in young children. They are not necessarily a sign of dyslexia. It is not uncommon for young readers to say *tap* when the word before them is *pat*; or say *ten* when the word before them is *net*. If you are right there to correct errors when the child is first sounding out words, then the child won't get into a habit of reversals. You quickly and pleasantly help him by covering the word with your finger and then uncovering it letter by letter, blending the sounds from left to right. If your child persists in the habit or reversing letters, you may have to sit across from him at a small table where you can see his eyes. This will allow you to use your finger or pencil to point out and follow text *above* the line of print without getting in the way of the child's vision. You may also want to cut a window out of heavy paper that will reveal only one line at a time. Then, have the child run his finger under each word from left to right, sounding out each word as he comes to it.

With most children these reversals are a sign that the child has formed *incorrect habits* of sounding out words. When you notice a child reading words or sentences backwards, make a special effort to be with the child whenever he is reading. Use the techniques already described.

If after consistently following the suggestions above, the child still seems to reverse letters or words most of the time, you may wish to consult a professional who specializes in helping children with dyslexia.

How will I know if my child needs speech therapy?

Don't be hasty to assume your child needs speech therapy. It is very common for immature speech patterns to persist until the child is seven or eight. Many children are unable to clearly enunciate the letters r and l, or they persist in the habit of saying /f/ for /th/ (for example, *free* for *three*) or they say /th/ for /s/, (*thee* for *see*) or /sw/ for /sl/ (*swipper* for *slipper*).

Model the proper sound when you are teaching, but don't make the young child self-conscious about little lisps and immature pronunciations. When my grandson Daniel was four years old, he insisted that you pronounced the word "birthday" as "birf-day." With sensitive, gentle encouragement, he outgrew it. These early childhood speech patterns are not an issue until you begin to formally teach spelling. At that time, you may need to spend more time specifically teaching correct pronunciation.

If a school-age child is actually *unable* to form basic phonetic sounds, you may wish to consult a speech therapist.

My child has been labeled with an "auditory processing deficit." What should I do?

I get a lot of e-mail from parents whose child has been diagnosed with "auditory processing deficit." This means the child has trouble making sense of what he hears. He often doesn't pay attention, is easily distracted, and has difficulty following complicated instructions. This does not mean that the child cannot learn to read. He may just need a quieter environment with fewer distractions, step-by-step instructions, shorter teaching sessions, and extra patience. If you do not see improvement once you are using these techniques, you may wish to have the child's hearing tested.

What do I do with my toddler while I am teaching reading with an older child?

Before you begin the reading lesson, give your toddler a few minutes of your undivided attention. Read a short story to the child, and then set him up with some activities that can be done quietly without your help. Here are some suggestions:

- Play with assorted beans on a cloth on the floor. Put a big bowl of beans in the center of the cloth. Give the child measuring cups, spoons, funnels, and different-sized bowls. The child should be old enough to know not to put beans in his mouth, nose, or ears.
- Give the child tiny stickers and paper. You can draw a shape on the paper and have the child fill it completely with the tiny stickers.
- Play with magnets. Provide the child with large metal objects, metal paper clips, washers, etc....
- Cut a hole in the plastic top of a coffee can or a potato chip can to make a piggy bank. Give the child large buttons or coins to put in the piggy bank.
- Play with lacing cards. Buy these at the store, or make them yourself with cardboard, a hole punch, and shoestrings.
- Give the child a box of assorted blocks. He may build with them or sort them by size, color, or shape.
- Have a child roll a small rubber ball or toy car down a wrapping paper tube or piece of plastic pipe.
- Put Play-doh on a large cookie sheet.
- Draw with chalk on dark construction paper.
- Draw with crayons or markers on large sheets of paper or coloring books.
- Make a tunnel or a tent with blankets or furniture. Put some of the child's toys in there.

Why do you keep using the pronoun "he" for all children?

I studied advanced grammar in the 1950s as part of my training in teacher certification. I learned that the pronouns "he" and "him" were generic pronouns, used to refer to both men and women. Although I understand why some users of this book would prefer to see an alternate use of "he" and "she," I find this style of writing awkward; my early training shaped my usage! So I have used "he" and "him" to refer to the child throughout this book. If you prefer, simply change these pronouns to "she" and "her."

REMEDIAL READING WITH AN OLDER CHILD
(THE TIME TO START IS NOW)

If your child is in second grade (or beyond) and you are aware of his struggling with reading skills, don't delay proper reading instruction for another moment! The sooner he learns to sound out words systematically, the sooner he will be reading independently and enjoying increased academic success.

Some children with good visual memories teach themselves to read; they memorize the whole words they encounter in their reading. Other children have actually been taught to use this method instead of sounding out words systematically. Both groups of children face a problem between second and fourth grade when the reading vocabulary becomes increasingly more difficult. These children simply cannot memorize enough words to easily read grade-level material. This is called "the fourth-grade slump."

The remedy for this problem is to teach the child the sounds for which the letters stand and then practice blending them into the real words. The letter **a** represents the same sound in the word *cat* whether the student is four or forty! So if you have a child of any age who is having trouble with reading, start at the beginning of a systematic program and persevere to its completion. He may take longer than a beginner because he has to unlearn bad habits and replace them with a new skill.

Children who read by the whole-word method often did not learn to move their eyes from left to right through words and sentences. If you notice that your child's eyes are wandering all over the page when he is reading, he is searching for clues to guess words. If your child persists in this habit, you may have to sit across from him at a small table where you can see his eyes. This will allow you to move your pencil or finger *above* the line of print, so you will not get in the way of the child's vision. You may also want to cut a window out of heavy paper that will reveal only one line at a time. Then, have the child run his finger under each word from left to right, sounding out each word as he comes to it. If a common word is too irregular to be easily sounded out, (such as *come* or *said*) tell him that word so that the sentence makes sense.

When the child gets to the end of a line, watch his eyes and make sure they move quickly back to the left, looking for the beginning of the next line rather than searching for "words I know." Some children may even move their eyes down to the *end* of the next line. Both of these are common errors used by children who have been taught whole-language techniques. Have the child read out loud to you as long as necessary to make sure he gets into the habit of moving from one line to another.

It is a tragedy that many school-based reading programs actually encourage guessing as a learning-to-read strategy. The child is *taught* to "look at the beginning of a word, look at the end of a word, look at the pictures, and make your best guess." As I travel, speaking about reading to a nationwide audience, I hear that this technique of teaching reading is widespread.

The only cure for word guessing is to go back to basic phonics. You can explain to the child that he was not given a successful method of reading in his early schooling. For his future academic and *life* success he will have to go through a period of re-learning the proper way to read.

Meanwhile, you *read to him* the material in history and science so that he still learn the content. You may have to do this for a number of years or until the child can read independently for himself. You don't want his lack of reading skill to hinder the acquisition of knowledge.

One summer, I worked with Natalie, an eighth grader who was going to be put into special education classes. Natalie had been failing in all of her subjects because of her "inability to comprehend." Her mother came to me and said, "I know this child does not need to be in special education classes! Can you please help us?" When I heard Natalie read the first paragraph on a page, I found out she didn't know the basic sounds of her letters and she was making up words that made sense in a sentence—*but she was not reading what was on the page!* No wonder something was wrong with her comprehension! The school that had taught this girl to memorize whole words and to guess the words she didn't know was now labeling her disabled.

Many children are labeled too early and too often. Children are called "disabled" when the only special education they need is to be taught a successful method of learning how to read.

A few children do have a true learning disability and may need more intensive long-term teaching, but they do not need a different kind of instruction. *All* children need explicit, systematic instruction in phonics to learn to read efficiently. While a child is being taught to read, he should be exposed to good literature by being read to, by listening to books on tape, and by talking with someone about what is being read.

I worked with another eighth-grade girl, Christy, who was also having trouble in all of her subjects. Christy's downcast demeanor and seeming lethargy suggested discouragement with life. She told me she didn't understand what she read and was frustrated with trying. We started with learning the sounds of the letters, and then we moved on to sounding out words. After six months or so, she was finally able to read passages, working on difficult words as she encountered them. It was slow going. But she began passing her classes and eventually graduated from high school and college with a degree in nursing. Later Christy made a special visit to my home to tell me, "Thank you for helping me know that I *could* learn."

If you are helping an older student move from memorizing whole words to sounding out words phonetically, don't be discouraged at the time it will take. This is a critical life skill; it is worth all the time and effort.

INDEX TO THE LESSONS

Section 14:   Other Spellings for Short-Vowel Sounds 209

Section 15:   Silent Letters 221

Section 16:   R-Changed Vowels 242

KEY TO PHONETIC SYMBOLS

/ă/ in **a**pple

/ĕ/ in **e**lephant

/ĭ/ in **i**gloo

/ŏ/ in **o**ctopus

/ŭ/ in **u**mbrella

/ā/ in **a**corn

/ē/ in **e**qual

/ī/ in **i**ce

/ō/ in **o**pen

/ū/ in **u**se

/oō/ in **oo**ze

/ŏŏ/ in b**oo**k

/ô/ in j**aw**

/ou/ in **ou**t, c**ow**

/oi/ in b**oy**, **oi**nk

/är/ in c**ar**

/ôr/ in d**oor**

/âr/ in h**air**

/ûr/ in st**ir**,

/ə/ in **a**bout, bac**o**n, Americ**a**

/b/ in **b**at

/d/ in **d**eep

/f/ in **f**un, **ph**one

/g/ in **g**um

/h/ in **h**at

/j/ in **j**ump, **g**em

/k/ in **k**ite, **c**ut

/l/ in **l**ate

/m/ in **m**ove

/n/ in **n**et

/p/ in **p**an

/kw/ in **qu**it

/r/ in **r**ed

/s/ in **s**it

/t/ in **t**ip

/v/ in **v**an

/w/ in **w**et

/ks/ in bo**x**

/y/ in **y**es

/z/ in **z**ip, i**s**

/sh/ in **sh**ip

/th/ in **th**in

/t͟h/ in **th**at

/zh/ in vi**s**ion

/ch/ in **ch**oose

/ng/ in ha**ng**

/hw/ in **wh**ale

369

Also Available From
Well-Trained Mind Press

The Story of the World
History for the Classical Child
by Susan Wise Bauer

This read-aloud series is designed for parents to share with elementary-school children, or for older readers to enjoy alone. Introduce your child to the marvelous story of the world's civilizations!

Volume 1: Ancient Times
Volume 2: The Middle Ages
Volume 3: Early Modern Times
Volume 4: The Modern Age
Each volume is available in paperback, hardback, or digital download.

Activity Book One: Ancient Times
Activity Book Two: The Middle Ages
Activity Book Three: Early Modern Times
Activity Book Four: The Modern Age
Each activity book is available in paperback or PDF. Separate tests & additional Student Pages are also available.

First Language Lessons for the Well-Trained Mind, Levels 1 and 2
by Jessie Wise

First and second grade grammar books that are simple for the parent and fun for the child!

First Language Lessons for the Well-Trained Mind, Levels 3 and 4
by Jessie Wise and Sara Buffington

The highly anticipated follow-up books to First Language Lessons, both now available.

The Complete Writer Series
by Susan Wise Bauer
A carefully-designed curriculum that will teach every student to put words on paper with ease and grace.

The "Who in the World" Biography Series

Junior-level biographies of important, but often neglected, persons in history including Amerigo Vespucci, Ethelred the Unready King, Johannes Gutenberg, and the Empress Theodora.

To find out more about these and other products available from
Well-Trained Mind Press, visit our website:
www.welltrainedmind.com